OKA... LIBRARY

P9-EJI-643

SITUATING SADNESS

RC 451.4 .W6 S62 2003
Situating sadness : women and
depression in social context

DATE DUE

SEP 2 5 2003	
OCT 2 9 2003	
DEC 1 1 2003	

BRODART   Cat. No. 23-221

QUALITATIVE STUDIES IN PSYCHOLOGY

GENERAL EDITORS
Michelle Fine and Jeanne Marecek

Everyday Courage
The Lives and Stories of Urban Teenagers
Niobe Way

Negotiating Consent in Psychotherapy
Patrick O'Neill

Flirting with Danger
Young Women's Reflections on Sexuality and Domination
Lynn M. Phillips

Voted Out
The Psychological Consequences of Anti-Gay Politics
Glenda M. Russell

Inner City Kids
Adolescents Confront Life and Violence in an Urban Community
Alice McIntyre

From Subjects to Subjectivities
A Handbook of Interpretive and Participatory Methods
Edited by Deborah L. Tolman and Mary Brydon-Miller

Growing Up Girl
Psychosocial Explorations of Gender and Class
Valerie Walkerdine, Helen Lucey, and June Melody

Voicing Chicana Feminisms
Young Women Speak Out on Sexuality and Identity
Aída Hurtado

Situating Sadness
Women and Depression in Social Context
Edited by Janet M. Stoppard and Linda M. McMullen

OKANAGAN UNIVERSITY COLLEGE
LIBRARY
BRITISH COLUMBIA

■ ■ ■ ■ ■ ■ ■ ■ ■

SITUATING SADNESS

Women and Depression in Social Context

Edited by

JANET M. STOPPARD AND
LINDA M. MCMULLEN

■ ■ ■ ■

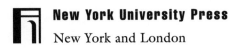

New York University Press
New York and London

NEW YORK UNIVERSITY PRESS
New York and London

© 2003 by New York University
All rights reserved

Library of Congress Cataloging-in-Publication Data
Situating sadness : women and depression in social context /
edited by Janet M. Stoppard and Linda M. McMullen
p. cm.
Includes bibliographical references and index.
ISBN 0-8147-9800-4 (cloth : alk. paper) —
ISBN 0-8147-9801-2 (pbk. : alk. paper)
1. Depression in women—Social aspects.
I. Stoppard, Janet M. (Janet Mary), 1945-
II. McMullen, Linda M.
RC451.4.W6 S62 2003
616. 85'27'0082—dc21   200151993

New York University Press books are printed on acid-free paper,
and their binding materials are chosen for strength and durability.

Manufactured in the United States of America

10 9 8 7 6 5 4 3 2 1

For the women who participated in our studies—
J. M. S., L. M. M., and contributors

Contents

■　　■　　■　　■

Acknowledgment　ix

Introduction　1
Janet M. Stoppard and Linda M. McMullen

1.　"Depressed" Women's Constructions of the Deficient Self　17
　　Linda M. McMullen

2.　Depressed Women's Treatment Experiences:
　　Exploring Themes of Medicalization and Empowerment　39
　　Janet M. Stoppard and Deanna J. Gammell

3.　The Anger of Hope and the Anger of Despair:
　　How Anger Relates to Women's Depression　62
　　Dana Crowley Jack

4.　"Imprisoned in My Own Prison":
　　A Relational Understanding of
　　Sonya's Story of Postpartum Depression　88
　　Natasha S. Mauthner

5.　Postpartum Depression:
　　Women's Accounts of Loss and Change　113
　　Paula Nicolson

6.　Legacy of Betrayal:
　　A Theory of Demoralization from the
　　Perspective of Women Who Have Been Depressed　139
　　Susan A. Hurst

7. "I Just Went On. . . . There Was No Feeling Better,
   There Was No Feeling Worse": Rural Women's Experiences
   of Living with and Managing "Depression"   162
   Yvette Scattolon

8. "Your Heart Is Never Free":
   Women in Wales and Ghana Talking about Distress   183
   Vivienne Walters, Joyce Yaa Avotri, and Nickie Charles

9. Conclusion   207
   Linda M. McMullen and Janet M. Stoppard

About the Contributors   217
Permissions   221
Index   223

■　■　■　■　■　■　■　■　■

Acknowledgments

THE IDEA FOR THIS BOOK first took shape during a conversation between Jeanne Marecek and Janet Stoppard at the 1999 Annual Conference of the Canadian Psychological Association (CPA) held in Halifax, Nova Scotia. Jeanne was invited to be a keynote speaker at the conference by the CPA Section on Women and Psychology, and before the conference she received a copy of the Section's newsletter, which she read on the flight to Halifax. Included in the newsletter was a listing of the contents of a special issue of *Canadian Psychology/Psychologie canadienne*, CPA's flagship journal, on the theme "Women and Depression: Qualitative Research Approaches," that we had guest edited. On discovering that she was chatting with one of the special issue's editors, Jeanne suggested that we submit a proposal, based on the special issue, for a book in the Qualitative Studies in Psychology series that Michelle Fine and Jeanne edit for New York University Press. The rest—as they say—is history.

We are indebted to Jeanne and Michelle for encouraging us to pursue this project and for their support during the process of manuscript preparation. Jennifer Hammer, our editor at New York University Press, was a constant source of information and advice, and we want to thank her for her guidance and support. The contributors also deserve our gratitude for their willingness to revise, and in some cases to rewrite, their original articles in accord with the style guidelines of New York University Press and editorial feedback. This book would not have been possible without the earlier publication of the special issue we edited, and we want to thank Vic Catano, past editor of *Canadian Psychology/Psychologie canadienne*, for supporting our proposal for the issue and for steering the eventual collection through the peer-review process. We are also grateful to the Canadian Psychological Association for giving us permission to use articles originally published in the special issue.

We also have some personal acknowledgments: *Janet:* I would like to thank my friend and intellectual companion, Alan Miller, for being there and for taking care of the more domestic side of my life when writing deadlines loom. *Linda:* I would like to thank my husband, John Conway, and my children, Nathan and Alix Conway, for being such an important part of my life. My work is better because of you.

Introduction

Janet M. Stoppard and Linda M. McMullen

DEPRESSION HAS BEEN IDENTIFIED worldwide as a mental health problem that occurs with alarming frequency.[1] It is the most commonly encountered mental health problem among women and ranks overall as one of the most important women's health problems.[2] One recent, large-scale study, for instance, reported that more than one out of every five American women will become depressed at some time during her lifetime.[3] The comparable figure for American men was around one in eight. Indeed, studies conducted in many countries generally have found that almost twice as many women as men become depressed.[4] This pattern occurs in research samples of people living in the community, those visiting their family doctor, and those receiving treatment in hospitals. Not surprisingly, women also predominate among those receiving antidepressant medications.[5]

Although researchers have studied depression extensively in recent decades, women's depression has rarely been the primary focus.[6] And when the topic has been addressed, the perspective represented has typically been that of researchers, rather than the views of depressed women. We know very little, therefore, about the experiences of women who have been depressed.[7] This book addresses this knowledge gap by bringing together work on women's depression from the standpoint of women, grounded in women's own stories about being depressed.

What Is Depression?

I was really depressed and . . . I did have suicidal thoughts and I had my suicide all planned out, too. . . . I did not want to get out of bed in the mornings. I just wanted to stay in bed and sleep.[8]

With depression it is total dysfunctioning. . . . I feel like there is this child inside me just crying, crying, crying, and I am the shell on the outside trying to be this different person.[9]

I had no energy, my mood swings were getting to be more frequent. . . . You feel as if you are in this black hole and there's no light. You cannot see a light at the end of that tunnel.[10]

I think it's a mental and physical breakdown . . . of everything. . . . You can't think straight, or you can't think to cook dinner for your kid, or you're going to be in bed all day. . . . You don't want to do anything.[11]

These are brief extracts from interviews with women about their experience with depression. Most people are familiar with feeling sad, down, or low, especially after experiencing a personal setback, disappointment, or loss. Although feeling sad is part of being depressed, depression involves more than a low mood. As the brief excerpts above illustrate, lack of energy, tiredness, and inability to engage in everyday activities are also aspects of depression. A depressed woman is also likely to lose interest in activities she would usually enjoy, to have difficulty thinking and concentrating, and to have low self-esteem. Her thoughts may be colored by feelings of hopelessness about her current situation and future possibilities. Such negative thoughts may lead a woman to conclude that life is not worth living and to contemplate suicide. But, being depressed does not only involve negative thoughts and feelings. A woman may also experience physical changes; in particular, she may eat less (or more) than usual and her sleep patterns may be disturbed.

In textbooks written by experts, "depression" is defined as a mental illness, a disorder caused by a biochemical imbalance in the brain. Unlike physical diseases, most mental illnesses, including depression, are identified primarily by the symptoms a person reports. There are no tests comparable to blood tests or x-rays that can determine whether or not a person is depressed. A health professional, such as a physician, asks a patient to describe her experiences, and what she reports is then evaluated against a set of symptoms, or diagnostic criteria, for depression.[12] These criteria operate as a standard template against which a particular person's experiences can be compared. For example, in the first excerpt above, a woman describes herself as having suicidal thoughts, having trouble getting out of bed, and wanting to sleep all the time. These experiences map onto several symptoms of depression—thoughts of ending one's life, reduced energy, and decreased activity, along with increased sleep. If this woman told her doctor that she had been experiencing these symptoms for two weeks or more, as well as feeling depressed and apathetic, she would probably be diagnosed as having a depressive disorder and be treated with an antidepressant medication.

When a depressed woman seeks medical attention and is diagnosed with depression, her depressive experiences are legitimized as symptoms of an illness and given a medical label. In this diagnostic process, a woman's experiences are validated—"there really is something wrong with me," "it is not just in my head," "I'm not going crazy." Her feelings of distress and ill health are not her fault, she is not to blame—she has an illness called depression, which involves a chemical imbalance in her brain. When personal blame for being depressed is removed, a woman can attribute her distress to something outside her control—her brain chemistry. This way of understanding depression implies that a depressed woman has a physical disorder, the remedy for which is a drug. However, this view of depression can also go hand-in-hand with the idea that one is flawed in some way or otherwise weak. And there is still stigma attached to being diagnosed with a mental disorder, even if it is understood to be biochemical in nature.[13]

In the diagnostic process, health professionals abstract limited aspects of a patient's experience from her ongoing life circumstances and label them as "symptoms." Shorn of their individual details, depressed people's experiences are assumed to have common symptomatic features that can be identified in anyone who is depressed. Once diagnosed as depressed and a treatment prescribed, a woman's experiences are likely to be of interest only for evaluating whether treatment is helping to alleviate her depressive symptoms. Likewise, in much research, depressed women's experiences serve primarily as a starting point for generating scores on questionnaires or surveys, which researchers transform into numerical data and statistics.

Recontextualizing Women's Depression: Qualitative Inquiry

In conventional approaches to research and diagnosis, information about a depressed person's life circumstances and everyday activities is stripped away as unnecessary detail in a process that "decontextualizes" people's experiences. When these details are retained, however, they cast new light on experiences that might be counted as instances of depression by researchers or labeled as depressive symptoms by health professionals. Recontextualizing depression enables researchers or therapists to see depression not just as an individual pathology requiring individual change, but as embedded in relationships and social settings. A qualitative approach highlights the context of people's experiences by paying special attention to the details of their lives. The advantages of this strategy can be illustrated when we add some contextual information to the first excerpt presented at the beginning of the previous section.[14] The woman whose interview was the source of this excerpt was married and had a school-aged child. She talked about becoming depressed when her husband's business failed and the family faced bankruptcy.

> Well, there was nothing we could do about it, I mean, we had no money. . . . And of course in this society, when you make debt, you want to pay it. That is the responsible thing to do and so here you owe all this money and there is nothing you can do about it.

Earlier in her interview, she had spoken about an incident that occurred when she was a student, drawing a link between this event and later becoming depressed.

> But to me the real pivotal thing was I was raped by one of the guys at university I used to have coffee with. He invited me over to his apartment . . . date rape type of thing . . . but it took me ten years to admit that I was raped.

Some contextual detail can also be added to the second excerpt in the previous section.[15] The woman interviewed was married and had a daughter. She also had a full-time job. In the following excerpt she describes what a typical day is like for her.

> I work Monday to Friday, I get up in the morning, I get ready, I get my daughter ready, we are off to work. My lunch hours are spent running around the malls to pay bills or to pick up this or whatever, I am back to work, I get home, I cook supper, I do homework, and then there is the bath, then there is quality time of playing, and she [her daughter] is off to bed, then I'm in the bedroom ironing . . . and the next thing you have to go to bed because I have to get up early again the next morning and start all over again.

This woman took care of elderly relatives in addition to looking after her own family:

> And now my husband . . . his aunt, she has got Parkinson's and she is suffering from depression herself, so she is having a hard time coping, so I am paying her bills and I am doing her laundry, and I am doing his father's laundry.

As we hope these examples show, new ways of understanding these two women's experience of being depressed begin to emerge when information about their lives is introduced. Their stories are enlivened when their own words are used, and their accounts also point to the importance of context for understanding women's depression. While conventional research seeks general patterns by stripping away social context, qualitative research attends to the details of people's lives.

The authors of the following chapters chose to use qualitative methods in their research on women's depression, approaches that seldom have been used to study depression.[16] Qualitative research contributes knowledge about the meaning of depression in women's lives and also enables a deeper understanding of the situations in which women become depressed by opening up questions about power, about ideologies and practices of gender, and about other social, structural inequities in women's lives. Understanding a woman's experience from her own point of view also has practical value because it has the potential to open up other—possibly more fruitful—avenues for intervention (in therapy and community-based programs) and change.

Situations That Increase Women's Risk of Becoming Depressed

Research using a broad-brush approach has pointed to certain types of situations that are associated with an increased risk for women of becoming depressed. These are characterized by social inequality and poverty—conditions in which women are notoriously over-represented.[17] At all stages of life, women also face an increased risk of being sexually or physically abused—forms of trauma that have been linked to women's depression.[18] Situations arising from women's reproductive capacities, particularly child-bearing and child-care, also can heighten the risk of depression for women.[19]

Some of the chapters in this book focus on women living in situations associated with an increased risk of becoming depressed. For instance, Yvette Scattolon interviewed low-income women living in rural communities in eastern Canada. Vivienne Walters, Joyce Avotri, and Nickie Charles talked to women living in low-income areas in Wales, in the United Kingdom, and to women living in the West African country of Ghana, where poverty is an endemic feature of women's lives. Women's experience of becoming a mother is the topic of Natasha Mauthner and Paula Nicolson's chapters.

Qualitative research also makes possible a more fine-grained exploration of people's experience, the way they interpret events in their lives, and the impact this understanding has on how they see themselves. Some qualitative researchers are particularly interested in the meaning embedded in people's talk. Meaning is reflected in the literal content of people's words, and also is conveyed metaphorically. Linda McMullen shows in her chapter how paying close attention to the way women talk about being depressed reveals new insights about the meaning of depression in their lives.

Talking about being depressed involves describing and making sense of subjective experience, a process in which a person draws on ideas, views, and opinions gleaned from family, friends, or professionals, and increasingly from the mass media. These understandings are likely to incorporate the prevailing stories or narratives about depression—its nature, causes, and cure—that have gained credence within a particular social context. In Western societies, the dominant narrative is one that privileges a medicalized view of depression as an illness involving a biochemical disturbance in a person's brain. Janet Stoppard and Deanna Gammell focus on depressed women's experiences of treatment—primarily antidepressant medication—to assess the implications of such treatment for a woman's sense of self and how she lives her life. In contrast, Yvette Scattolon explores the experiences of women who did not seek professional help when depressed. Women who live in rural areas where mental health services are lacking are probably over-represented among those who contend with depression on their own, with no outside help. Yvette Scattolon analyzes how rural women coped with being depressed when their experience was not validated by a medical diagnosis.

Women's feelings and actions in everyday situations and their ways of expressing emotional distress are also embedded in culturally shared meanings of what it means to be, act, and live as a woman—cultural narratives referred to as "discourses of femininity."[20] Anger, for instance, is an emotion that sits uneasily with cultural conceptions of the "good woman." In her chapter, Dana Jack charts the varied strategies women adopt to cope with angry feelings and maps the impact these strategies have on women's experience of being depressed. Other authors also draw connections between the culturally authorized narratives of what constitutes appropriate womanly behavior and the social situations in which women become depressed. For instance, Susan Hurst describes how the experience of betrayal and abandonment in an important relationship is a common theme in the accounts of women who have been depressed. These women's experiences arose from situations structured by cultural narratives that prescribe both relational and economic dependency for women.

Doing Qualitative Research

In qualitative research, people's accounts are treated as a vital source of information about their subjective experiences and the circumstances of their lives. Many qualitative researchers collect information by talking to people, either individually or in small groups, about some aspect of their experience, and most contributors to this volume used interviews as their primary data collection method. However, sometimes qualitative researchers may use material that has already been collected (e.g., archival databases) or that is publicly available, either in print (e.g., books, newspapers, magazines) or as recordings (e.g., movies, videos, CDs). Another, more "anthropological" method involves a researcher becoming a participant-observer in a social setting or organization relevant to her research question. In summary, qualitative research encompasses diverse methods for collecting data.

Analysis of qualitative data usually focuses on text—sometimes a researcher's notes or, more often, verbatim transcriptions of audiotaped conversations. Various strategies for analysis of qualitative data are represented in the chapters that follow. Several chapters—for example, those by Paula Nicolson, Janet Stoppard and Deanna Gammell, and Vivienne Walters, Joyce Avotri, and Nickie Charles—draw on thematic approaches, with the goal of identifying patterns of meaning within the content of interviewees' responses.[21] The "grounded theory" method used by Susan Hurst also involves a thematic form of analysis, in this case the aim being to reveal the social processes that best account for participants' experiences.[22] Dana Jack and Natasha Mauthner describe the analytic returns from a "voice-centered" approach, a strategy that involves reading and rereading interview transcripts from various points of view.[23] The analytic focus in Linda McMullen and Yvette Scattolon's chapters shifts to how women talk about their experience, the former from a linguistic perspective and the latter from a discursive standpoint.[24]

These various analytic approaches entail differing levels of analysis, which allow researchers to "hear" different things depending on the strategy they use.[25] In some, people's social situations are of particular interest—what is happening in their lives? The focus of others is people's subjective experience—what are they feeling and thinking? Thematic approaches are often used to shed light on the nature of people's everyday lives, as Vivienne Walters, Joyce Avotri, and Nickie Charles show in their chapter. Researchers might also use thematic analysis to study how people experience specific events or circumstances in their lives. For instance, Paula Nicolson was interested in women's experience of becoming a mother, and Janet Stoppard and Deanna Gammell explored the ways in which women experienced their treatment for depression.

Other types of qualitative analysis are "inductive"—researchers attempt to let the data "speak for themselves" without imposing a theoretical perspective. The grounded theory approach Susan Hurst employed exemplifies a form of inductive analysis in which women's accounts are used as a springboard for devising a theory that best describes their experience. Voice-centered methods, in contrast, are based on assumptions about subjectivity—people's subjective experience and how they see themselves. Researchers such as Dana Jack and Natasha Mauthner use a voice-centered approach to explore the links between a person's social location and her subjectivity, how cultural narratives shape a woman's sense of who she is, and how she attempts to resist cultural definitions and stereotypes. Voice-centered strategies trace the impact on subjectivity of power dimensions—gender, race, and social class are examples—within interpersonal relationships and through broader societal dynamics that govern access to important social resources such as money and status.

Yet other analytic strategies examine how people talk about their experience by attending to the meaning evoked by the particular words used. Linda McMullen, for instance, deploys a linguistic method of analysis to highlight how women convey their experience through use of metaphors, idioms, and figures of speech. Linguistic analysis helps us to hear more clearly the evaluative undertones in people's words—how language shapes subjectivity and channels their experience of the world. Language is also the subject of discursive modes of analysis, but at a more "macro" level than linguistic approaches. From a discursive perspective, language is not only a way to communicate experience, it is also a form of social action that embodies meaning. For instance, when a person talks about her experience, inevitably she will draw on some narratives—or stories—within her culture, rather than others. The type of narrative a person uses reveals something about the social and cultural context of her life and the dynamics of power that give authority to certain narratives but not others. The cultural narratives embedded in people's talk about their experience function discursively to circumscribe the "positions," or roles, a person can take in her own life story so that certain actions—or social practices—seem proper while others are ruled out or denied, as Yvette Scattolon shows in her chapter. Although linguistic and discursive modes of analysis differ in their analytic focus, both are designed theoretically to enable researchers to connect the personal, psychological experience of an individual—one woman's story—to broader structures and social relations. These analytic approaches help to reveal how a larger set of social forces organizes the way we experience, speak about, interpret, and live our lives.

Like all researchers, those who use qualitative methods must address ethical issues in their work.[26] Because the data in qualitative research usually consist of verbatim accounts of people's experience, often on sensitive or personally significant topics, researchers take special care to preserve the confidentiality of their sources. This is accomplished by using pseudonyms to shield the identity of participants and by masking details that might be recognized by others. Researchers also strive to disclose to participants as fully as possible why they are doing the research and how the qualitative information they collect will be used. In situations already bound by confidentiality requirements, such as conversations between a doctor and a patient or between a therapist and a client, researchers must take pains to ensure that those in less powerful positions (i.e., patients and clients) are able to consent freely to becoming research participants.

Beyond concerns for anonymity, confidentiality, and informed consent, qualitative research brings ethical dilemmas into view that may be less visible—but no less present—in conventional research approaches. These issues are embedded in the relational character of qualitative research and arise from the inherently interpretive nature of qualitative analysis. Some of the questions that researchers must grapple with include "who owns the data?" "whose interpretation of the data carries the most weight?" "who benefits from the research?" and "when do researchers' obligations to participants end?" Qualitative researchers directly confront the political dimensions of their work when deciding to pursue a particular research goal. For instance, if the goal is to better understand women's depression, should we turn to the writings of experts or should we talk to women who have been depressed? Whichever route we choose will lead to somewhat different answers because the people involved (experts versus depressed women) have different experiences and perspectives.

All of the authors included in this collection chose to ground their research in women's experience. Their essays also address questions of "difference" among women by working through intersections of gender, race, ethnicity, class, living arrangements, and geography. The new ways of understanding women's depression presented here not only challenge the views of experts—they also have implications for the kind of health and social policies needed to address the problem of women's depression. At the same time, we should acknowledge that the interpretations of depressed women's experience presented in the chapters that follow are themselves shaped by the researchers' world views. In this respect, the interpretations offered are "partial"—others might interpret the women's accounts differently—a caveat that applies equally to the findings of research using conventional approaches.

Qualitative researchers also need to consider the impact of their research on those who participate. For the women whose stories are told in this book, was their experience as a research participant helpful or harmful? From our perspective as researchers, we find that women are usually quite willing to share their stories about being depressed, often describing the process as "therapeutic." Women also express the hope that their stories will be helpful to other women who are depressed. One way for researchers to ensure that the stories research participants share with them can have an impact in the world is to make their work available to audiences beyond other researchers. This book provides a means to make accessible to a wider audience the fruits of qualitative studies on women's depression.

Aims of This Book

The central purpose of this book is to highlight the contributions of qualitative research to understanding what being depressed is like for women, the situations in which women become depressed, and what women do to overcome being depressed. Therefore, this book does not address women's depression from a medical or psychiatric perspective. Nor is it intended as a "self-help" guide for depressed women, though some of the experiences described herein may resonate with those readers who are or have been depressed. We hope that therapists and counselors will gain insight into the experiences of depressed women from reading this book, and some authors (particularly Linda McMullen and Susan Hurst) address the implications of their findings for therapy with women.

Our primary aim in collecting these studies is to show how use of qualitative approaches can open up new avenues for answering the questions "Why do women become depressed?" and "Why is depression a problem that particularly afflicts women?" Qualitative studies can also point to questions that deserve more attention, a critical one being "When do women become depressed?" The situated nature of women's depression is repeatedly documented in the following chapters. It is our hope that this collection will encourage and stimulate others to pursue studies of women's depression using qualitative approaches.

Notes

1. See World Health Organization, *The World Health Report 2001: Mental health: New understanding, new hope.*

2. See World Health Organization, *Women's mental health: An evidence-based review.*

3. R.C. Kessler, K.A. McGonagle, S. Zhao, C.B. Nelson, M. Hughes, S. Eshleman, H.U. Wittchen, and K.S. Kendler, "Lifetime and 12 month prevalence of DSM-III-R psychiatric disorders in the United States."

4. M.M. Weissman, R. Bland, G.J. Canino, et al., "Cross-national epidemiology of major depression and bipolar disorder."

5. J.A. Hamilton and M.F. Jensvold, "Sex and gender as critical variables in feminist psychopharmacology research and pharmacology"; World Health Organization, *Gender and the use of medications: A systematic review.*

6. Notable exceptions are G.W. Brown and T.O. Harris, *Social origins of depression: A study of psychiatric disorder in women*; D.C. Jack, *Silencing the self: Women and depression*; and the World Health Organization report, *Women's mental health: An evidence-based review.*

7. See J.M. Stoppard, *Understanding depression: Feminist social constructionist approaches,* for an overview of research on women's depression.

8. This quote is taken from J.M. Stoppard, A.M. Guptill, and M.N. Lafrance, "Understanding depression from the standpoint of women: Beyond medicalizing and pathologizing discourses."

9. Ibid.

10. This quote is taken from the interview with a participant in the study reported by J.M. Stoppard and D.J. Gammell; see chapter in this volume.

11. This quote is taken from the interview with a participant in the study reported by Y. Scattolon; see chapter in this volume.

12. See American Psychiatric Association, *Diagnostic and statistical manual of mental disorders,* Fourth edition, p. 327, for a listing of diagnostic criteria for depressive disorder.

13. See J.M. Stoppard, "Women's bodies, women's lives and depression: Towards a reconciliation of material and discursive accounts," pp. 17–18.

14. Contextual information is taken from J.M. Stoppard, A.M. Guptill, and M.N. Lafrance, "Understanding depression from the standpoint of women."

15. Ibid.

16. An exception is autobiographical accounts by individuals who have been depressed. Interestingly, most such memoirs have been written by men. Examples of this genre are: N.S. Endler, *Holiday of darkness: A psychologist's personal journey out of his depression*; J. Bentley Mays, *In the jaws of the black dogs*; A. Solomon, *The noonday demon: An atlas of depression*; and W. Styron, *Darkness visible: A memoir of madness*.

17. World Health Organization, *Women's mental health: An evidence-based review*, pp. 15, 20.

18. Ibid., p. 65.

19. Ibid., p. 15.

20. See S. Bordo, *Unbearable weight: Feminism, western culture and the body*; J.M. Ussher, *Women's madness: Misogyny or mental illness?*; J.M. Stoppard, *Understanding depression*.

21. Further information on thematic approaches can be found in P. Banister, E. Burman, I. Parker, M. Taylor, and C. Tindall, *Qualitative methods in psychology: A research guide*, ch. 4, "Interviewing"; and R.E. Boyatzis, *Transforming qualitative information: Thematic analysis and code development*.

22. For descriptions of the grounded theory approach, see B.G. Glaser and A.L. Strauss, *The discovery of grounded theory: Strategies for qualitative research*; R.S. Schreiber and P.N. Stern, *Using grounded theory in nursing*; and A.L. Strauss and J. Corbin, *Basics of qualitative research: Grounded theory procedures and techniques*.

23. Information on voice-centered approaches can be found in L.M. Brown, "White working-class girls, femininities, and the paradox of resistance"; L.M. Brown and C. Gilligan, *Meeting at the crossroads: Women's psychology and girls' development*; and N. Mauthner and A. Doucet, "Reflections on a voice-centred relational method: Analysing maternal and domestic voices."

24. For accounts of linguistic and discursive approaches in qualitative research, see J. Potter and M. Wetherell, *Discourse and social psychology: Beyond attitudes and behaviour*; C. Willig, *Introducing qualitative research in psychology: Adventures in theory and method*; and L.A. Wood and R.O. Kroger, *Doing discourse analysis: Methods for studying action in talk and text*.

25. For overviews of qualitative approaches used by researchers in psychology, see P. Banister, E. Burman, I. Parker, M. Taylor, and C. Tindall, *Qualitative methods in psychology: A research guide*; J.T.E. Richardson, *Handbook of qualitative research methods for psychology and the social sciences*; and D.L. Tolman and M. Brydon-Miller, *From subjects to subjectivities: A handbook of interpretive and participatory methods*.

26. See J. Marecek, M. Fine, and L. Kidder, "Working between two worlds: Qualitative methods and psychology," pp. 38–39, for a discussion of ethical issues in qualitative research.

References

American Psychiatric Association. (1994). *Diagnostic and statistical manual of mental disorders*. Fourth edition. Washington, DC: American Psychiatric Association.

Banister, P., Burman, E., Parker, I., Taylor, M., & Tindall, C. (1994). *Qualitative methods in psychology: A research guide*. Buckingham, UK: Open University Press.

Bordo, S. (1993). *Unbearable weight: Feminism, western culture and the body*. Berkeley: University of California Press.

Boyatzis, R.E. (1998). *Transforming qualitative information: Thematic analysis and code development*. Thousand Oaks, CA: Sage.

Brown, G.W., & Harris, T.O. (1978). *Social origins of depression: A study of psychiatric disorder in women*. London: Tavistock Publications.

Brown, L.M. (2001). White working-class girls, femininities, and the paradox of resistance. In D.L. Tolman & M. Brydon-Miller (Eds.), *From subjects to subjectivities: A handbook of interpretive and participatory methods* (pp. 95–110). New York: New York University Press.

Brown, L.M., & Gilligan, C. (1992). *Meeting at the crossroads: Women's psychology and girls' development*. Cambridge: Harvard University Press.

Endler, N.S. (1990). *Holiday of darkness: A psychologist's personal journey out of his depression*. Toronto: Wall and Thompson.

Glaser, B.G., & Strauss, A.L. (1967). *The discovery of grounded theory: Strategies for qualitative research*. New York: Aldine de Gruyter.

Hamilton, J.A., & Jensvold, M.F. (1995). Sex and gender as critical variables in feminist psychopharmacology research and pharmacology. *Women & Therapy, 16*, 9–30.

Jack, D.C. (1991). *Silencing the self: Women and depression*. Cambridge: Harvard University Press.

Kessler, R.C., McGonagle, K.A., Zhao, S., Nelson, C.B., Hughes, M., Eshleman, S., Wittchen, H.U., & Kendler, K.S. (1994). Lifetime and 12 month prevalence of DSM-III-R psychiatric disorders in the United States. *Archives of General Psychiatry, 51*, 8–19.

Marecek, J., Fine, M., & Kidder, L. (2001). Working between two worlds: Qualitative methods and psychology. In D.L. Tolman & M. Brydon-Miller (Eds.), *From subjects to subjectivities: A handbook of interpretive and participatory methods* (pp. 29–41). New York: New York University Press.

Mauthner, N., & Doucet, A. (1998). Reflections on a voice-centred relational method: Analysing maternal and domestic voices. In J. Ribbens & R. Edwards

(Eds.), *Feminist dilemmas in qualitative research* (pp. 119–146). London: Sage.

Mays, J.B. (1995). *In the jaws of the black dogs: A memoir of depression*. New York: Harper Collins.

Potter, J., & Wetherell, M. (1987). *Discourse and social psychology: Beyond attitudes and behaviour*. Newbury Park, CA: Sage.

Richardson, J.T.E. (Ed.). (1996). *Handbook of qualitative research methods for psychology and the social sciences*. Leicester, UK: BPS Books (The British Psychological Society).

Schreiber, R.S., & Stern, P.N. (Eds.). (2001). *Using grounded theory in nursing*. New York: Springer Publishing.

Solomon, A. (2002). *The noonday demon: An atlas of depression*. New York: Simon and Schuster.

Stoppard, J.M. (1997). Women's bodies, women's lives and depression: Towards a reconciliation of material and discursive accounts. In J.M. Ussher (Ed.), *Body talk: The material and discursive regulation of sexuality, madness and reproduction* (pp. 10–32). London: Routledge.

Stoppard, J.M. (2000). *Understanding depression: Feminist social constructionist approaches*. London: Routledge.

Stoppard, J.M., Guptill, A.M., & Lafrance, M.N. (2000, November). Understanding depression from the standpoint of women: Beyond medicalizing and pathologizing discourses. Paper presented at *Feminist Utopias: Redefining Our Projects*, Inaugural Conference of the Institute for Women's Studies and Gender Studies, University of Toronto.

Strauss, A.L., & Corbin, J. (1990). *Basics of qualitative research: Grounded theory procedures and techniques*. Newbury Park, CA: Sage.

Styron, W. (1991). *Darkness visible: A memoir of madness*. London: Vintage.

Tolman, D.L., & Brydon-Miller, M. (Eds.). (2001). *From subjects to subjectivities: A handbook of interpretive and participatory methods*. New York: New York University Press.

Ussher, J.M. (1991). *Women's madness: Misogyny or mental illness?* Hemel Hempstead, UK: Harvester Wheatsheaf.

Weissman, M.M., Bland, R., Canino, G.J., et al. (1996). Cross-national epidemiology of major depression and bipolar disorder. *Journal of the American Medical Association, 276*, 293–299.

Willig, C. (2001). *Introducing qualitative research in psychology: Adventures in theory and method*. Buckingham, UK: Open University Press.

Wood, L.A., & Kroger, R.O. (2000). *Doing discourse analysis: Methods for studying action in talk and text*. Thousand Oaks, CA: Sage.

World Health Organization. (2000). *Gender and the use of medications: A systematic review*. Geneva: World Health Organization (unpublished working document WHO/GHW).

World Health Organization. (2000). *Women's mental health: An evidence-based review*. Geneva: World Health Organization (unpublished document WHO/MSD/MHP/00.1).

World Health Organization. (2001). *The World Health Report 2001: Mental health: New understanding, new hope*. Geneva: World Health Organization.

1

■   ■   ■   ■   ■   ■   ■   ■   ■

"Depressed" Women's Constructions of the Deficient Self

Linda M. McMullen

If you're miserable and you feel weird, you think it's because you've got a flaw, there's something wrong with you.
—"Depressed" woman to her psychotherapist

FOR MANY PSYCHOTHERAPISTS, this quote will be familiar both for its content and for its speaker. It is the sort of statement often made by those who seek psychological help in Western cultures, the majority of whom are women. However, this very ordinary statement is in fact quite revealing. First, it exemplifies the dominant way in which we, in contemporary Western society, try to explain distress, particularly the distress we label "depression." Specifically, we focus on the influence of psychological factors—of the person's features, such as ability to cope, strength of character or willpower, motivation—as a way of explaining why one person experiences a debilitating psychological disorder such as depression, and another does not. Focusing on these aspects establishes "depression" and other forms of psychological distress as stemming from personal failings or inadequacies. If I am "depressed" or otherwise distressed, it must be due, at least in part, to characteristics of my person, to personal flaws or failings, to my deficiencies as a person. While in earlier times we may have believed "depression" to be the result of an excess of black bile or a reduction of nervous energy,[1] we now implicate psychological factors to a significant extent, even if we acknowledge that genetic vulnerabilities and levels of certain chemicals in the brain might be involved.

Second, the opening quote is revealing precisely because it was spoken by a woman. Although it is now well established that in Western society about twice as many women as men are diagnosed as "depressed,"[2] this was not always so. Well-documented accounts of the history of melancholia and depression[3] indicate that less severe forms of melancholia in the late medieval and Renaissance periods were thought to be afflictions of the passive, sensitive, intellectually and morally superior male. By contrast, the present-day condition we call "depression" is, as noted above, associated with weakness, deficiency, and personal failings, and with being female. As so aptly stated by Schiesari (*The gendering of melancholia: Feminism, psychoanalysis, and the symbolics of loss in Renaissance literature*), "the melancholic of the past was a 'great man'; the stereotypical depressive of today is a woman" (p. 95).

My focus in this chapter is on how the gendered, devalued condition we now call "depression" is constituted in the lives of women who have been diagnosed as "depressed." By analyzing the metaphors and other figurative expressions used by "depressed" women as they talk to their psychotherapists about themselves and their lives, we can see how the deficient self is presented by these women. I focus here on metaphors and other figurative expressions for two reasons. First, when people are asked to talk about how they view themselves and their experiences (as is the case in psychotherapy), they often have difficulty finding the words to convey their ideas and, as a result, they frequently resort to using nonliteral words and phrases. So, psychotherapy is a context that is rich in this kind of language. Second, scholars of language and culture have stressed the significance of figurative language as a window onto shared cultural understandings.[4] Figurative expressions come into being, survive, or fade away depending on the extent to which they foster communication of culturally salient conceptions. If, as I have indicated, our conception of "depression" has changed over time, then focusing on contemporary metaphors and other figurative expressions should provide a window onto how a common understanding of "depression" is constructed in a particular historical and cultural context—in the present case, early twenty-first-century America.

Historical and Contemporary Metaphors
for Depression

Dating from the time of the ancient Greek physician Hippocrates, one of the earliest (and long-lasting) metaphors for melancholia and depression is that of being in a state of darkness.[5] Originally, this metaphor was linked to the presumed cause of melancholia and depression, that is, an over-abundance of black bile in one's system, and to the experience of fear, gloom, dejection, and clouding of thought and consciousness that were typical in persons who suffered from melancholia or depression. We can see evidence of this metaphor in present-day descriptions of depression as being like a *"black cloud"* or a *"rainy day"* and in common expressions such as *"I feel blue"* or *"I feel dark."*

A second long-lasting metaphor is that of being weighed down.[6] Again, this seems to originate from the physical characteristics of melancholia and depression, specifically, the experience of a heavy head, of a body that is borne down by a weight, of a bent-over head, neck, and drooping body posture. The sense of being weighted down is clearly contained in the present-day term "depression" which actually denotes being pressed down, and in common expressions such as *"It's like I'm carrying a load around," "I feel burdened,"* and *"I feel so heavy."*

But, perhaps the most recognizable contemporary metaphor for what we now refer to almost exclusively as "depression" is that of being *"down"* or *"low."* These expressions are part of a larger metaphor theme that I call *"Depression is Descent."*[7] Central to this theme are expressions about the place that is depression (e.g., *"the dreary, dismal pit," "rock bottom," "in the gutter," "down in the dumps"*), about the ease of descent once it is started (e.g., *"spiraling down," "going through a nosedive," "sinking low"*), and about the effort and will required for ascent (e.g., *"pull myself out of it," "have to slowly work my way back up," "made efforts to climb out"*). These expressions suggest that a significant way in which we presently construct "depression" is as movement in physical space from a higher to a lower position or place.

This notion of low position or place that seems to be at the heart of our conception of "depression" is linked not only to the physical or experiential features of this state of being (i.e., drooping body posture) but to social and cultural values and moral evaluations. For example, *"down"* is correlated in Western culture with sickness and death (e.g., *"She's very low"* or *"He dropped dead"*), low status (e.g., *"being at the bottom of the heap"*), lack of power (e.g., *"low man on the totem pole"*), lack of virtue (e.g., *"low-down thing to do"*), and inferiority and inadequacy (e.g., *"being at the bottom of the trough"*).[8] In short, to be *"down"* is to be lacking in a quality that is considered essential or important in our culture (e.g., health, high status, power, or virtue). To be *"down"* is the opposite of what we value.

The Research Question and Participants

If "depression" is linked to what is not valued in our culture, then studying how "depressed" persons talk about themselves and their lives might inform us about the value of various forms of selves in our culture. To begin to address this question, I have studied how the deficient or flawed self is constructed in the language of ten women in psychotherapy. I have focused on women's talk because of the high frequency with which women are diagnosed as "depressed" and because psychotherapy is a context in which talk about one's deficiencies and flaws is often encouraged.

The women whose metaphoric talk I analyzed had volunteered to participate in a time-limited (to a maximum of twenty-five sessions) psychotherapy research project.[9] They ranged in age from twenty-eight to sixty-two years, were white, varied from having partial high school to completed university education, and presented themselves as having problems primarily with interpersonal relationships and with moods. Each of them had received a diagnosis of some form of depression.[10] They were seen by experienced psychologists or psychiatrists who were also white and who provided psychodynamically oriented psychotherapy once each week.

Because I used archival data and was not able to speak to the women themselves, the analysis of their metaphoric talk[11] must be understood as my description and interpretation of what I saw as patterns in their discourse. I brought to this analysis my personal-professional experience as a white, Western, female, clinical academic with an interest in culture and gender. What follows, then, is the product of a long period of engagement that I had with the women's metaphoric accounts of the personal deficiencies that they presented as contributing to the problems they reported.[12]

Cultural Imperatives

Implicit in the women's metaphoric accounts of their personal deficiencies were sentiments about how one should or should not "be." I organized these sentiments along two broad imperatives that I have labeled "Don't be too mothering" and "Don't be too child-like." At the heart of these imperatives are messages about cultural values and norms.

"Don't Be Too Mothering"

Three of the women presented themselves as overly involved caretakers. Two of them spoke of having embraced too completely the role of mother, particularly in relation to their husbands. One woman, Barbara (aged fifty-six years), who was having difficulty coping with her impending divorce, described herself as having gone *"to pieces"* (session 1)[13] when her husband separated from her and subsequently filed for divorce. She talked of how she had never been at the center of her husband's life despite having placed him at the center of hers. She described this perception in the following ways:

> [To the therapist in the first session] *You're going to see a lot of mothering in me, I'm sure, and maybe I have smothered him [husband] with mother love.*
>
> *I have always played at least second, third, fourth, or fifth fiddle. His [husband's] job has always been more important than [me], his mother . . . was more important than [me] . . . and I move up and down the scale but I've never played first fiddle in [husband's] life—never . . . I've been second fiddle or third fiddle or fifth fiddle or fifteenth fiddle for a long time* (session 4).

In a particularly poignant expression of the possible futility of her way of being, Barbara alluded to herself in the third person:

> *Even then you could be like the hen sitting on a nest. From all appearances, she's doing what she's supposed to be doing, you know—the mother or the earth mother or whatever. And she's doing her thing. And the community of chickens expects this and here she is—she's doing [it]—but, it occurred to me that she could be sitting on a glass egg—that even consent or even when you're doing what you feel is good and right and conscientious and what God expects you to*

do and natural—even that doesn't guarantee the reward—the ultimate re-ward (session 8).

In session 18, she summed up her views:

I tried to be his [husband's] savior and he didn't want to be saved.

and

Like the hen who sat on the nest—she was sincere but she was sitting on a glass egg, you know, maybe I'm sitting on a glass egg.

The irony in Barbara's presentation is clear: On the one hand, by mothering, she was doing what she thought she was supposed to be doing, what she thought was expected of her both in the eyes of the community and in the eyes of God. On the other hand, her mothering was not only misdirected, in vain, and ignored; but it ultimately resulted in the loss of the person to whom it was directed.

Like Barbara, Carrie (aged forty-one years) also constructed herself as "*too mothering.*" Although Carrie and her husband had been separated due, in part, to his illegal business practices, they were now living together again, and both were seeing a psychotherapist about marital concerns. Carrie reported that she "*protected and mothered*" her husband, that she "*didn't know anything different except mother, protect, shield, hide*" (session 11). Toward the end of therapy (session 21), she stated this self-construction most clearly:

So I'd pick up his load at home to relieve him to do what he enjoyed most.

I'm wondering if he thinks I'm smothering him.

It's like I'm making him check in with his mother [by having him call home].

Again, similar to Barbara, Carrie saw herself as doing for others and as having her self placed on the periphery:

To me, through all that [husband's business difficulties], I did not exist. Total energy was directed toward getting [husband] okay (session 11).

He [husband] screwed it up but yet it seems like it's up to me to fix it (session 13).

There's always some kind of stir or some kind of trauma or something that needs to be fixed, that [I] get put on the back burner to take care of whatever needs to be fixed or get involved in trying to, to fix something (session 17).

For Carrie, *mothering* was double-edged: it was necessary and expected, but also self-negating and self-ignoring.

In a variation of the construction of the self as *"too mothering,"* Susan (aged twenty-eight years), who presented with concerns about her mood swings, her weight, and her difficulty in maintaining close personal relationships, referred to herself throughout therapy as *"Aunt Susan."* She used this version of her own first name to convey her view of herself as an overly involved, self-sacrificing caregiver. Although she recognized that she had enacted this role since childhood, she was increasingly uncomfortable with it. For example, she stated:

When you need to be taken care of, it's call Aunt Susan. When you need the intellectual stimulation . . . it's call Aunt Susan . . . Aunt Susan is just not showing up this Christmas. . . . Aunt Susan is getting out; she doesn't want to be Aunt Susan. . . . Aunt Susan is sick of being Aunt Susan. . . . He [former boyfriend] knows that he could just come in my house, sweep me off my feet, have all his needs met, from being Aunt Susan to everything else, and just leave. . . . If there is something that occurs in [his] life that absolutely no one can handle for him, but Aunt Susan, Aunt Susan will be there. . . . I bred it [his sense of using the client as a nurturer] into him . . . . always being there for every need and ministering on, you know. [He] would try and pull away from some of my, you know, particularly when he got back on his feet and it was almost like a mother not letting go of a child (session 13).

[Another former boyfriend] wasn't really in love with me. [He] was in love with Aunt Susan. Aunt Susan ironed his boxer shorts, she balanced his cheque book, she hung his shirts by color in the closet. She had his car serviced, she entertained his clients. . . . Still I see [him] as my child. I still feel responsible for him (session 19).

As with both Barbara and Carrie, Susan's portrayal of herself as a caregiver and nurturer of others was coupled with a perception that she often took "*second base*" when around others. Although Susan was a very successful lawyer, she still viewed herself as consciously choosing to "*take the back seat.*" Specifically, she stated that "*I do seek people that overshadow me,*" and she asked herself, "*Why were you always standing in the shadows and trying to make him [her ex-husband] the glorious one?*" (session 9).

For all three women, excessive care-taking and self-sacrifice were clearly viewed as being central to their problems. Far from being welcomed or appreciated by others, these efforts served, in the end, to repel those to whom they were directed. Paradoxically, the more that was given, the less positive the outcome, both for the self and for others.

What are the implicit messages and consequences in the imperative "*Don't be too mothering*"? One very clear message is that one should not be too focused on others. In particular, one should not be too caring or too nurturing and should not consistently put others' needs and desires ahead of one's own. Doing so can deprive others of their freedom; it can "*smother*" them—a consequence that in an autonomy-valuing culture is considered to be a loss of a basic human right. It is also conceived of as self-sacrifice, a giving up of one's own freedom in the service of others (but not for the common good)—again, an outcome that is not especially valued in a culture in which achieving and pushing ahead of others is prized. In a similar fashion, trying to protect, save, and shield others, to prevent psychological harm from coming to them, can be viewed as stifling and restricting to them.

Another message is that one should not consistently put others "*in the limelight.*" At the heart of this sentiment is the sense that placing others ahead of oneself is often not reciprocated in kind by the other person. In other words, far from having a positive outcome for the self, promoting others can result in ensuring one's lowered position in relation to them.

Constructing one's flaws in terms of being "*too mothering*" suggests that there are strict limits in our culture on what we consider to be appropriate nurturing and care-taking. Specifically, one must be sufficiently nurturing and supportive to foster the well-being of others, but not overly so as to limit others' freedom and autonomy. The adoption of this discourse by some of the women in this sample also attests to the salience of this role as an explanatory model. It is unlikely that "depressed" men would talk of being "*too fathering*"; yet these women easily used being "*too mothering*" as a way of accounting for their difficulties. The availability of the imperative "*Don't be too mothering*" coupled with the absence of its counterpart, "*Don't be too fathering*," provides women (and men) with a handy way of simultaneously attributing responsibility to women and demeaning them. Barbara's wondering about the futility of too much "*mothering*" and Carrie's and Susan's desire to forsake their "*mothering*" role speak to the power of this imperative to invoke personal responsibility and blame.

"*Don't Be Too Child-like*"

A second broad imperative that was embedded in the women's constructions of their personal deficiencies was based on references to being like a child, including being too trusting, too submissive, too reliant on others, and needing to keep oneself in check and be responsible. Nine of the ten women drew on this discourse.

"*Don't be too trusting.*" June (aged fifty-three years), who had been severely undermined by her supervisor at work and who had come to the conclusion that she was "*a victim of [emotional] rape*" (session 5), talked of herself as having a "*child-like trust*" that people would do nothing to hurt her. In session 8 she asked herself, "*How do I learn to trust people at a realistic level as opposed to blind trust which is very child-like but not very realistic?*" and, in session 14, she continued with this theme:

> It's awfully easy to slip back [into thinking all people are good]. . . . That's kind of a dependent type thing too, this child-like trust that this person would do nothing to hurt me. That's an awfully easy mode to slip back into.

In the next session, June made the following analogy:

> It's kind of like you get mugged on a dark street, then what you learn from that is, number one, you were a victim, certainly, and you were helpless but you don't . . . walk on dark streets alone anymore. You do something. So that's what I'm reaching for—an analogy to that. So that I'm not out in the parking lot with thugs or whatever, screaming for help from the neighbors. And I think my dark street is my willingness to be so trusting because it's so easy to do—to just practice a little bit more self-care.

Toward the end of the last session (session 25), she summed up this theme as "*[Trusting people totally] may be one of those child-like things that I am simply going to have to put away.*"

Carrie (introduced previously) began talking about the history of her marital relationship by saying, "*I mean why would any fool avoid like I did all these years when I knew it—wrap up in a little cocoon-type thing and make this fantasy world, fantasy husband?*" (session 1). At the heart of the "*fantasy world*" was what she labeled "*just blind faith and trust—just blind*" (session 1). "*I believed everything that came out of his mouth on blind faith*" (session 6). As with June, this trust and faith appears to have been perceived as absolute.

"*Don't be too submissive.*" Carrie also portrayed herself as lacking in assertiveness. For example, in session 10 she said, "*Can you take advantage of people that you respect? I've heard the phrase 'If you think yourself a doormat, you will be treated as a doormat.' I've even let friends take advantage of me the way I think [husband] did.*" Later in describing her reaction to hostile, dominant responses from others, Carrie made a clear distinction between her behavior with her husband and her behavior with other family members:

> I feel like with my brother-in-law, sister-in-law, and my co-worker, I have stopped them from squishing me. . . . With the situation with [husband] being so emotional and raw, I still feel squished. I won't wiggle and get out from under it. . . . I feel, in a way, I've said to these other people, 'Hey, I'm standing up.' But with [husband], I feel like I stand up, sit down, stand up, sit down. . . . I feel like I haven't made my stand yet with him. I still feel like I allow him in certain ways to squash me or whatever (session 14).

She also said of herself, "*It's almost like I will roll over and play dead, if [husband] doesn't [respect my stand]*" (session 18).

Consistent with Carrie's construction of herself as too submissive with her husband was the view that she never really developed her own identity, and that in order to be accepted by other people, she had always tried to emulate them, to adopt their characteristics and opinions—a position that caused her considerable discomfort:

It's like to be friends, I have to sell my soul. . . . It's like I'm selling my soul to be a carbon copy of somebody else. And I'm kicking and screaming and I don't want that anymore. . . . I don't want to be a carbon copy anymore. . . . I can't sell my blood. I can't sell my soul. I can't be a carbon copy anymore (session 5).

Another woman, Caroline, who focused to a significant extent on her feelings of anger toward both her deceased husband and her family of origin, spoke of herself as "*Momma's little girl*" (session 11). Despite being in her early sixties, Caroline saw herself as being "*treated . . . as a kid*" by her mother and, in turn, as wanting not "*to accidentally slip back that I act like her little girl again*" (session 11). Specifically, she was concerned about perpetuating a pattern of hostile submissiveness in which she would do everything her mother demanded of her and then feel extremely hostile and resentful.

"*Don't be too reliant on others.*" Three women talked explicitly about how they conceived of themselves as relying too much on others, either for help with specific tasks or for emotional well-being. Barbara (introduced previously) said that she was someone who did not "*go on the attack*" (session 3) and who would be unlikely to "*fight*" for herself during divorce proceedings. Rather than "*fighting*" for herself, she often "*let others do battle for her*" (session 4). She wondered aloud: "[*Having other people fight for me] makes me look like a kid, doesn't it?* (session 3) and "*Maybe I haven't even grown up yet and I'm fifty-six years old*" (session 6).

Cathy (aged forty-nine years), who had come to therapy because of her difficulty with getting over a divorce that had occurred seven years previously, acknowledged that, although she had provided stability and encouragement for her husband for many years, she was also deeply dependent on him. Having been described by her husband as "*his rock*" (session 2) and viewing herself as "*his chief enabler*" (session 11), she said:

I put him [ex-husband] on such a pedestal (session 2).

I made [ex-husband] the whole object of my existence which was stifling and smothering to him (session 6).

I was hooked on him. And I still feel that dependency . . . I think I was also addicted to him. . . . I'm dependent. I'm addicted (session 11).

Cathy's construction of herself as dependent was not limited to her relationship with her husband. She also viewed herself as highly reliant on the approval of other people in her life, a position that she considered to be "*a weakness*" (session 11):

> *So I want to be patted on the head and told, "That's good. You did really well"* (session 11).

> *I'm still acting like a child.... I always—like everything I do, and did, and do now, and will do in the future, I always wanted applause for. People saying, "Yeah, you're doing well. I approve and I applaud"* (session 18).

> *I think I still way down deep in my heart, I really want to be patted on the head [like a child]* (session 24).

Another woman, Elizabeth (aged fifty-four years), who expressed significant concerns about both her work and family life, and who saw herself as being overly sensitive to criticisms and slights from co-workers, expressed dismay over her reaction to the loss of one of her customers. She stated:

> *I should really be hardened to it. What I should say to myself [is] "You should turn around and walk off."... Be above something like that.... You'd think that I could just shake something like that off, but I can't.... That means my emotional well-being is tied to what other people say and do.... I would like to be able to stand on my own two feet* (session 9).

"*Don't upset others; keep yourself in check.*" Just as children are often told to "Control your emotions!" Elizabeth portrayed herself as having learned to control herself around her husband. Although she admitted to "*lashing out*" (session 3) at her daughter on occasion, the climate with her husband was presented quite differently:

> *Over the period of twenty years, we just kind of came to, I had come to the place where I know that I can't criticize him or lash out at him.... As long as I don't rock the boat and as long as I don't do anything like that, then everything's fine. ... It isn't a platonic relationship at all—it's, it's not that exactly, but the idea is there that as long as the waters aren't ruffled on the surface, everything's fine.*

... I don't strike out at him [husband] verbally because I know he doesn't like it. ... As far as he's concerned, I have learned to bridle my tongue (session 3).

The imperative to keep oneself in check was also part of the self-construction of Lynne, a thirty-nine-year-old woman who was divorced from her husband and especially concerned about her relationships with others, including her children. She described herself as "*[finding] it difficult to keep a tight rein on myself in order to channel myself in a direction where it's to my benefit*" (session 5). Her relationships with men were presented as particularly difficult and as ones in which she perceived herself as coming on "*too strong to suit most [of them]*" (session 8). Her relationships with co-workers were also difficult and she often found herself being "*rebellious and stand[ing] up for myself because I hurt*" (session 23).

A particularly salient implicit injunction that Caroline (previously introduced) had lived by for a number of years, and which seemed to be brought into relief with the death of her husband, was "*Stop acting like a three-year-old.*" Using this imperative was a way for Caroline to chastise herself for crying and for being angry. For example, she stated: "*So I put myself down a lot by saying to myself, 'There you go again—acting like a three-year-old'*" [because of her crying] (session 3) and "*Here I am such a baby, crying because my mother doesn't like me*" (session 8).

By session 9, Caroline began to talk extensively about how the therapist was beginning to see her "*angry, scared little girl.*" On the one hand, she seemed to experience considerable relief that the therapist had been able to acknowledge this construction of herself: "*You [therapist] said, 'I see your scared little girl and, God knows, she had reason to be scared and there was nobody there to love her and keep her safe.' You were the first one to say, 'Yeah, she's there'*" (session 14). On the other hand, Caroline wanted to rid herself of this position:

The week before I had bared my soul and showed you my little girl. You'd been seeing edges of her, but that time you really saw her and saw how scared she was and all that and you told me you saw her ... you validated her. You said she had reason for being. ... I said, in effect, now if I can just ... kill her off ... stop being such a little girl. I've been a little girl all these years and I couldn't grow up because I couldn't get past that (session 21).

Be responsible; do something in life. While some of the women placed child-like characteristics at the center of their difficulties, others extended the imperative to *not* be child-like to what might be considered its corollary, in other words, be more adult-like. The injunction to be more adult-like took a couple of different forms. For example, Louise (aged forty-one years), whose major concerns were her difficult relationships with her husband and children and her perception that she was "*in a rut*" (session 18), described herself in the following way:

> *I feel like I'm starting to be stronger and yet weaker at the same time. You know—like there's two people in me fighting and I don't know who's going to come out ahead because part of me wants to just, you know, be weak, and the other part says . . . "Do something," not just be a child without responsibility* (session 2).

Louise elaborated this construction of herself at various points over the course of therapy, often oscillating between feeling pressure to do something in life and being content, in part, with "*not making a mark*" (session 11):

> *I let my life drift a lot* (session 4).

> *I'm still not good about pushing myself in a direction. That's my biggest problem. . . . I'm floating again* (session 7).

> *[A male friend] told me that I was afraid of making skid marks on the earth. . . . I thought that was like etched in stone or something. It just seemed like the answer to everything . . . like I didn't want to make an impression on anything. I wanted to keep everything clean and no marks. . . . In other words, I don't make a mark. I want to just kind of slice through life and not let anybody notice that I'm there* (session 11).

This injunction to "do something" in one's life was also central in the talk of Julia, aged thirty-four years. Julia voiced concerns about her marital relationship, about her role as a housewife, and about being "*stuck*" in life (session 3), and these concerns were clearly related to her sense of herself as not having matured and not having embraced achievement:

And I came to the realization that I didn't want to do anything for fear that I wouldn't do it right. It was kind of the road that I chose to take and I—I feel like I'm still stuck on that road to a great degree (session 11).

And he [husband] seems to be maturing and . . . I feel like I'm just wallowing. And I got scared that he's going to leave me behind. . . . I see him growing in ways that I'm not growing (session 14).

And he [brother] used the word "mediocrity," which is real interesting, because that's pretty much the hole that I'd put myself in . . . anything that I do is only half-assed, "C-minus." . . . I get a "C" in life instead of an "A" (session 18).

Constructing oneself as having child-like characteristics or as failing to acquire adult-like characteristics was clearly a common way in which the women in this sample presented their personal deficiencies. Nine out of the ten women used some variation of this broad imperative. For some, the conclusions they reached about their future actions contained directions for change. June was going to "*put away*" her "*child-like trust*" and Carrie was not going to "*be a carbon copy anymore.*" But, for most of the women, the constructions of their personal flaws as child-like were embedded in implicit judgments about the difficulty of change (Cathy was "*addicted*"), in self-admonishments (Elizabeth "*should be hardened to it*"), in self-criticisms (Julia got a "*C*" *in life instead of an* "*A*"), and in self-loathing (Caroline wanted to "*kill off*" her "*little girl*"). On the whole, there was little that was positive about being child-like or failing to be adult-like.

Just as the injunction to not be "*too mothering*" carries implicit messages about what is considered to be appropriate nurturing and care-taking, the imperative to not be "*too child-like*" carries equally clear messages about what is considered to be culturally appropriate adult behavior. Specifically, do not naively believe in the goodness of others and permit others to take advantage of you. In addition, you should be your "own person," should not need approval from others or otherwise be emotionally needy, and should be a responsible person who, in some fashion, "*makes a mark*" or "*stands out*" from others. As with the injunction to not be "*too mothering,*" there is also a strong message about the importance of not being too tied to others. At the core of the imperative to not be "*child-like*" is, of course, the equating of maturity with autonomy.

Cultural Context

By analyzing the metaphors of depression we can see that depression is linked to what is not valued in our culture. In addition, because of the pervasive presence of psychological factors (or features of the person) as an explanatory model for depression, the analysis of how "depressed" persons construct and present their "selves" tells us about the value we place on various forms of "self." The women in this sample either directly or indirectly constructed their personal deficiencies as being "*too mothering*" or "*too child-like,*" indicating both the availability of these discourses as ways of accounting for "depression" and the presence of a devaluing of mothers and children in our culture. By recognizing the presence of this devaluing, I am not denying that there is much that is valued in mothers and children in our culture. For example, there is evidence that most women continue to long for motherhood,[14] and that a dominant, contemporary view of children is that they are priceless, "sacred gifts."[15] However, there is also ample evidence that mothers and children are often relegated to a low position and devalued for their inability to participate significantly in the important (public) tasks of our culture. For example, if a woman who is asked "What do you do for a living?" replies "I'm a stay-at-home mom," her answer is often met with a minimal acknowledgment ("Oh"), an awkward silence, or a quick attempt to change the topic of conversation. Each of these responses is typically interpreted as indicating social discomfort on the part of the other: If this woman is *only* a mother, what place does she have in our society's public hierarchy? If she does not occupy a significant public place, what is there to talk about? In addition to being relegated to a low (or invisible) position, mothers are a target of blame in our culture.[16] Mothers are blamed for whatever goes wrong with their children, either because they did too much or did not do enough. The category of "mother" is, then, a convenient space in which a woman who is "down" can both locate and implicate herself.

Just as being "*too mothering*" is a discourse that is predicated on a devaluing of mothers, being "*too child-like*" is a culturally available way for adults to locate themselves in a low or devalued position. Although we prize children for what we believe are their innocent, trusting, carefree, unreserved natures, we are disdainful of these features in adults. One of the most common ways in which we insult older children and adults is to call them "babies" or "little kids" or to tell them to "grow up." We easily invoke the discourse of being "*too child-like*" as a way of criticizing, belittling, or demeaning older children and adults. It should not be surprising, then, that the "depressed" women in this sample used this discourse both as a way of locating themselves in a low position and of blaming themselves for their present circumstances.

What kind of a society makes it possible for these ways of talking to develop and thrive? Perhaps the most obvious link between the discourses of being "*too mothering*" and "*being too child-like*" is their message about the value of autonomy and personal control. This message is a central feature of many Western cultures that are characterized by free markets, private ownership, and increasing wealth, but it is particularly characteristic of U.S. society. As a product of a capitalist system, the American individual is seen as a relatively autonomous, unique, self-contained person who is motivated by a desire to push ahead and to gain control of his or her surroundings.[17] This societal stance of self-contained individualism helps to sustain certain cultural values, namely, freedom, responsibility, and achievement, each of which figured prominently in the ways in which the women in this study accounted for their role in their "depression." These women took responsibility for their "depression" by condemning themselves for curtailing others' (and, indirectly, their own) freedom and for failing to display the markers of adult achievement.

Embedded within this larger cultural context is the particular subculture of psychotherapy. In North America, psychotherapy is a setting in which talk of the deficient self is especially encouraged. Individuals who choose to participate in psychotherapy most frequently do so in an effort to *understand* themselves, to try to make sense of why they are feeling a particular way or experiencing certain difficulties in their lives. Typically, the task of psychotherapy is for clients to talk about themselves, and the goal is to work toward a satisfying account of how they came upon their current difficulties and how these difficulties can be prevented in the future. Considerable effort is spent on the part of both the client and the therapist in trying to understand the role of the individual in these difficulties. In this effort, the individual is often given full (or nearly full) responsibility both for creating and for correcting these problems. This type of therapy clearly flourishes in a cultural context in which individual autonomy and personal responsibility are paramount. It is not surprising, then, that the women in this study used culturally encouraged forms of talk that centered around themes of self-sufficiency, independence, freedom, and individual influence and control.

If being "*too mothering*" and "*too child-like*" are readily available ways in which "depressed" women in our culture can construct themselves and if psychotherapy is a context that is chosen by some "depressed" women as a means of help,[18] what practical suggestions might be provided for these women and their psychotherapists? First, it is important that both parties be keenly attuned to the forms of talk that are being used. Although conventional, everyday metaphors and other figures of speech can reveal our culturally embedded concepts and practices, they are often not heard, precisely because they are so commonplace. We need to be aware of our taken-for-granted forms of talk, and we need to make them unfamiliar to us. We need to stop in mid-sentence, view our discourse from a distance, and query it. What does it mean to "*smother with mother love*"? Why do we not speak so readily of "*smothering with father love or with brother love*"? What are the effects of constructing oneself as "*a three-year-old*"? Why is this particular age a readily available space in which we can locate ourselves? Why do we not so easily condemn ourselves and others for "*acting like a six-year-old or a seven-year-old*"? How do these conceptions structure our relationships with others, and what do they say about the social, political, and cultural contexts in which "depressed" women are embedded?

Second, both the personal particularities and the social, political, and cultural generalities in what "depressed" women are saying should be attended to. It is important to understand all of what, for example, being "*Aunt Susan*" entails, and to connect this understanding with what it means to be an aunt in our culture. Although individual women will resonate with different balancings of personal and social-political-cultural understandings, the words of the women in this study suggest that both kinds of understandings are prevalent and readily available for therapeutic work. The task of a client and her therapist is to find a way of talking in these terms that is beneficial to her in particular.

Third, recognizing the context of most North American psychotherapy as a venue conducive to the use of discourses of individualism, personal responsibility, and control might enable clients and therapists to reflect on how this context contributes to certain ways of understanding women's "depression." Although a variety of kinds of psychotherapy are available to women who are "depressed," including therapies based on different theoretical orientations (e.g., psychoanalytic, interpersonal, cognitive-behavioral, experiential, feminist, etc.) and on different formats (e.g., individual, group, couples, marital, etc.), the very act of identifying oneself as having problems and of seeking help for these problems tends to invoke a focus, albeit in varying degrees, on the deficiencies or flaws of the individual. Being aware of and examining this pull as part of the context of psychotherapy might sensitize "depressed" women to its presence in the wider culture and enable them to see that blaming themselves for being "*too mothering*" or "*too child-like*" says a great deal about the contexts in which they are located.

If blaming oneself for being "*too mothering*" or "*too child-like*" is understood as a culturally available means for women to understand "depression," then the way is opened for the development of alternative constructions. "Being miserable" and "feeling weird" could be understood as a signal that a woman is not being sufficiently valued and recognized by others, that the critical and controlling behavior of others (usually a woman's partner, family members, or co-workers) is causing harm, or that societal expectations of women are too demanding. "Depression," then, could be understood not as a personal flaw or deficiency, but as a form of isolation or disconnection,[19] a relational event, or an embodiment of social responsibilities.

The Research Process

Exploring the culturally embedded discourses of the flawed or deficient self used by the "depressed" women in this study required that I both immerse myself in the words of the women and attempt to make them unfamiliar or foreign to me. Being a resident of the culture in which the women lived had advantages and disadvantages. While I was able to use my own experience in the culture as a basis from which to reflect upon and interpret what the women were saying, I was able to achieve only a limited amount of distance from their words. I was able to make their words and phrases unfamiliar in only a very conscious and deliberate way. I was not able to be "struck" by them as one is when viewing the practices of persons from another culture, as a visitor or new arrival might be. I heard statements about "*mothering*" and "*being child-like*" and I interpreted them with words like "autonomy," "responsibility," and "personal control" because my own experiences and values both constrained and enabled me.

I was also constrained and enabled by having access only to archival data. Working only from audiotapes and not having the opportunity to speak directly with the women at any point in the research process meant that I could not find out more about what it was like to be "*Aunt Susan*" or "*Momma's little girl*" and that I did not have the benefit of the women's responses to my analysis. However, it also meant that my focus was exclusively on the words in front of me. As such, my attention was concentrated on my own subjectivity as a Canadian, a woman, an academic, a psychotherapist, a feminist, and a mother, and on an imagined audience. I continually asked myself what I was hearing and what I thought various members of an audience might hear in what the women were saying. Having an audience in mind (myself or others) constantly reminded me of the importance of context. In the end, the extent to which I have been successful in managing these constraints and opportunities will be judged by the responses of readers.

Notes

1. S.W. Jackson, *Melancholia and depression*.
2. S. Nolen-Hoeksema, *Sex differences in depression*.
3. See S.W. Jackson, *Melancholia and depression,* as one example.
4. N. Quinn, "The cultural basis for metaphor."
5. S.W. Jackson, 396–397.
6. Ibid., 397–398.
7. In an analysis of conventional metaphors for depression used by clients in psychotherapy, we (L.M. McMullen and J.B. Conway, "Conventional metaphors for depression") found that over 90% of the instances in our corpus were subsumed under this particular metaphor theme.
8. G. Lakoff and M. Johnson, *Metaphors we live by*.
9. See W.P. Henry, T.E. Schacht, and H.H. Strupp, "Patient and therapist introject, interpersonal process, and differential psychotherapy outcome" for a fuller account of this project.
10. Eight of the women had received a DSM-III (APA, *Diagnostic and Statistical Manual of Mental Disorders*) diagnosis of Major Depressive Disorder or Dysthymic Disorder, one of Cyclothymic Disorder, and one of Atypical Bipolar Disorder.

11. See L.M. McMullen, "Metaphors in the talk of 'depressed' women in psychotherapy," 104, for details on the selection of metaphors and on how these metaphors were analyzed.

12. I want to emphasize that the production of metaphoric constructions of the deficient or inadequate self is only one type of cultural activity that is assumed to constitute "depression" in Western culture.

13. Session numbers refer to the particular psychotherapy session from which the quoted material was derived.

14. M. McMahon, *Engendering motherhood.*

15. V.A. Zelizer, *Pricing the priceless child.*

16. P.J. Caplan and I. Hall-McCorquodale, "Mother-blaming in major clinical journals"; Paula J. Caplan, *Don't blame mother.*

17. See E.E. Sampson, "The debate on individualism: Indigenous psychologies of the individual and their role in personal and societal functioning," and H.R. Markus and S. Kitayama, "Culture and the self: Implications for cognition, emotion, and motivation."

18. By focusing on the implications of my analysis for "depressed" women and their psychotherapists, I am not intending to privilege psychotherapy as a way of responding to women's "depression." I recognize that "depressed" women can benefit from many kinds of professional and nonprofessional interventions (as outlined in J.M. Stoppard, *Understanding depression: Feminist social constructionist approaches*). I have chosen to focus on the implications for psychotherapy because it was the context from which data for the present study were drawn.

19. D.A. Karp, *Speaking of sadness: Depression, disconnection, and the meaning of illness.*

References

American Psychiatric Association (APA). (1980). *Diagnostic and statistical manual of mental disorders* (3rd ed.). Washington, DC: Author.

Caplan, P.J. (1989). *Don't blame mother: Mending the mother-daughter relationship.* New York: Harper and Row.

Caplan, P.J., & Hall-McCorquodale, I. (1987). Mother-blaming in major clinical journals. *American Journal of Orthopsychiatry, 55,* 345–353.

Henry, W.P., Schacht, T.E., & Strupp, H.H. (1990). Patient and therapist introject, interpersonal process, and differential psychotherapy outcome. *Journal of Consulting and Clinical Psychology, 58,* 768–774.

Jackson, S.W. (1986). *Melancholia and depression: From Hippocratic times to modern times.* New Haven: Yale University Press.

Karp, D.A. (1996). *Speaking of sadness: Depression, disconnection, and the meaning of illness.* New York: Oxford University Press.

Lakoff, G., & Johnson, M. (1980). *Metaphors we live by.* Chicago: University of Chicago Press.

Markus, H.R., & Kitayama, S. (1991). Culture and the self: Implications for cognition, emotion, and motivation. *Psychological Review, 98,* 224–253.

McMahon, M. (1995). *Engendering motherhood: Identity and self-transformation in women's lives.* New York: Guilford.

McMullen, L.M. (1999). Metaphors in the talk of "depressed" women in psychotherapy. *Canadian Psychology, 40,* 102–111.

McMullen, L.M., & Conway, J.B. (2002). Conventional metaphors for depression. In S.R. Fussell (Ed.), *The verbal communication of emotions: Interdisciplinary perspectives,* (pp. 167–181). Mahwah, NJ: Lawrence Erlbaum.

Nolen-Hoeksema, S. (1990). *Sex differences in depression.* Stanford: Stanford University Press.

Quinn, N. (1991). The cultural basis for metaphor. In J.W. Fernandez (Ed.), *Beyond metaphor: The theory of tropes in anthropology.* Stanford: Stanford University Press.

Sampson, E.E. (1988). The debate on individualism: Indigenous psychologies of the individual and their role in personal and societal functioning. *American Psychologist, 43,* 15–22.

Schiesari, J. (1992). *The gendering of melancholia: Feminism, psychoanalysis, and the symbolics of loss in Renaissance literature.* Ithaca: Cornell University Press.

Stoppard, J.M. (2000). *Understanding depression: Feminist social constructionist approaches.* London: Routledge.

Zelizer, V.A. (1985). *Pricing the priceless child: The changing social welfare of children.* New York: Basic.

2

■   ■   ■   ■   ■   ■   ■   ■   ■

Depressed Women's Treatment Experiences

Exploring Themes of Medicalization and Empowerment

Janet M. Stoppard and Deanna J. Gammell

WHAT HAPPENS WHEN A WOMAN is diagnosed as depressed by her doctor and she is given a prescription for an antidepressant drug? How does her diagnosis and treatment for depression influence a woman's understanding of being depressed? To answer these questions, we interviewed nine women[1] who had been diagnosed as depressed and treated by a physician (e.g., family doctor or psychiatrist). All of the women had been prescribed antidepressants by their doctor; only one woman chose not to use these drugs.

Feminists who work in mental health fields have been critical of conventional, medical approaches to treatment of depressed women, especially when antidepressant drugs are used, because such treatment potentially fosters a medicalized understanding of women's experiences.[2] Instead, they have argued that women's depression is better understood as arising in the context of their everyday lives rather than as an illness caused by disturbances within the body's biochemistry.[3] We wanted to know whether women's understanding of being depressed became more medicalized as a result of their treatment.[4]

We were also interested in whether personal empowerment was possible when women received medical treatment for depression. Medical approaches to treatment of women's depression can be contrasted with feminist therapy,[5] an approach that has empowerment as its guiding principle.[6] Empowerment informs both the goals of therapy and how the therapist conducts therapy with a woman client. A feminist therapist attempts to reduce the power imbalance inherent in the therapist-client relationship, validates a woman's experiences, and acknowledges her right to make decisions affecting her own life.[7] Thus, an important goal of feminist therapy is that of empowering women to make choices that lead to more control over their lives. Increased awareness by women of their power to make changes in their lives is also expected to have a positive impact on their well-being.[8]

Some feminists believe that use of antidepressant drugs to treat depressed women contradicts the goal of personal empowerment, because treatment in a medicalized context is inherently disempowering for women.[9] Others have argued that the goal of women's empowerment is best served when women are free to make their own choices about the treatment they receive when depressed.[10] According to this alternative feminist position, a depressed woman has the right to choose to take antidepressant drugs if she believes that this will help her to feel and function better in her everyday life. In actuality, however, the treatment options available to many depressed women, at least in the context of the current inquiry,[11] are limited to medical and psychiatric services. Feminist therapy is largely unavailable to women who live in rural areas and, in any case, many women (perhaps especially those who are depressed) are unable to pay for such services. Thus, our study investigated the experiences of women who had sought help from a medical doctor when depressed and antidepressant drugs were part of their treatment. Our aim was to assess the validity of feminist claims that such treatment fosters a medicalized understanding of women's depression and, in the process, disempowers women.

We chose to study women's experiences of treatment for depression because of our background in clinical psychology,[12] our shared commitment to feminist approaches to women's mental health, and our interest in using qualitative methods to explore issues that have been relatively neglected in research on women's depression. Although the majority of those treated for depression are women, gender issues have tended to be overlooked in research on depression.[13] Not only have few studies focused on depressed women's experiences, but the concerns raised by feminists about the potential for medicalizing and disempowering consequences when depressed women receive conventional, medical forms of treatment have not been investigated directly.

Studies of women's understanding of their health and mental health problems have shown that women tend to "normalize" experiences that physicians and other health and mental health professionals might label as "symptoms of depression."[14] That is, women tend to discount experiences such as feelings of distress and fatigue as understandable consequences of their everyday lives as women and as not, therefore, a cause for concern. A woman may decide to consult a physician only when her capacity to perform everyday activities, either inside or outside the home, is compromised.[15] Although women may attempt to normalize their depressed feelings, there are limits to the effectiveness of this coping strategy, and persistent difficulty in carrying on with her life as usual (e.g., being unable to handle family or job responsibilities to her own satisfaction) is likely to be interpreted by a woman as a sign that "something is really wrong with me." At this point a woman may decide to seek professional help or be encouraged by others to do so. If a woman is then diagnosed as suffering from depression, a condition for which treatment consists of being prescribed an antidepressant drug, how does this treatment influence her understanding of the experiences that first prompted her to seek professional help? Does being offered an antidepressant drug medicalize a woman's understanding of her experiences and is this form of treatment as disempowering as feminists have claimed?[16] In an attempt to answer these questions, we interviewed women who had been treated for depression about their experiences of being diagnosed as depressed, their views on what caused them to become depressed, and their treatment experiences. Because of our interest in feminist concerns about medicalization and disempowerment as consequences of women's treatment for depression, we paid particular attention to these two themes in our analysis of the interviews.

Participants, Interviews, and Analysis

The nine women who volunteered to be interviewed were between nineteen and sixty-six years of age.[17] All of the women were white and Canadian-born, and their first language was English. We contacted four women through the counseling services at the university in the town (population approximately 50,000) where we work. The other five women were contacted through local mental health services. Background information on the women we interviewed is summarized in Table 1. The interviews lasted between one and two hours and took the form of guided conversations focused on the women's experiences of being depressed, including their diagnosis and treatment. We analyzed the interview transcripts for material relevant to the following topics: women's reactions to their diagnosis; their understanding of why they had become depressed; their treatment experiences; and how being diagnosed as depressed had affected their view of themselves and their lives in the future. As mentioned already, the themes of medicalization and empowerment were also of interest to us as researchers, although these terms were not used during the interviews.

Being Diagnosed as Depressed

The women described having both positive and negative reactions to being diagnosed by a physician as depressed. Being given a diagnosis was accompanied by feelings of relief, as a first step toward getting treatment for their symptoms. Having this diagnosis enabled women to reinterpret the experiences that had led them to seek professional help and, for some, it was an opportunity to make changes in their lives. After their diagnosis, the women were more likely to attribute difficulties in their lives to being depressed rather than to personality flaws. As Kelly, a twenty-three-year-old student, said in describing how she felt after being diagnosed:

> I'm not crazy, I'm not just a spoiled brat, I'm not being selfish. . . . In that
> respect it was really really good . . . and so I mean from there I managed to
> solve a lot of things with myself and I stopped hating my family. You know,
> that sort of thing because you can sort of put things in perspective and from
> there you can re-evaluate things.

Table 1
Background Information on Participants

Name	Age	Number of children	Relationship status	Employment status	Approx. time since diagnosis
Amy	19	0	Single	Employed part-time/ Full-time student	2 months
Tracy	19	0	Boyfriend	Full-time student	3 years[a]
Susan	20	0	Single	Employed part-time[b]	3 months
Kelly	23	0	Boyfriend	Full-time student	7 years
Debbie	Early 30s	2	Married	Homemaker	1 year
Jane	47	2	Married	Long-term disability	5 years
Ann	Early 50s	2	Married	Homemaker	15 years
Sarah	52	2	Married	Employed part-time	7 years
Gloria	66	2	Married	Homemaker	11 years

The names of the women and key details of the circumstances of their lives have been changed to ensure confidentiality.
[a]Tracy has been offered antidepressant medication by general practitioners a number of times over the past few years; however, she believes that being asked to participate in this study was the first time a health professional confirmed that she was depressed.
[b]Although Susan indicated part-time employment status, she held three part-time jobs and tutored young children.

Although being diagnosed allowed some women to re-evaluate their experiences, others had difficulty coming to terms with their diagnosis because of the stigma they associated with having a "mental illness." Several women had been reluctant to tell family and friends about their diagnosis. Being mentally ill was seen as weak and shameful, and it did not fit with how the women viewed themselves. Gloria, a married woman in her mid-sixties, said the following about being diagnosed with depression.

> I'm not ashamed of it anymore. . . . When I was first this way, I was ashamed to think that I was depressed. All my friends were fine. But I shouldn't say that, two close friends, they have a lot of physical things wrong. . . . I would rather have a physical ailment, than this.

When talking about their diagnosis, women were likely to use such terms as "disease" or "illness" to refer to depression, comparing it with physical health problems as a way of making their diagnosis more acceptable. As Gloria said:

It isn't something to be ashamed of, I mean it's the same as any other illness. You're depressed, well you've got a bad heart so what's the difference?

Some of the women identified family members' responses, or lack of response, to their diagnosis as difficult to deal with. Ann, a married woman in her fifties, recounted the reactions of family members after she was first diagnosed with depression: "When I was having my mental breakdown back in the '80s, my family didn't talk about it. . . . They didn't acknowledge it at all." Following her diagnosis, Sarah (a married woman in her early fifties) attempted to hide her ill feelings while at home, a pattern that she linked to her husband's reaction.

My husband had a difficult time relating to my illness and he would not talk about it and so there was no talk. And so you just put on a mask and you go about life and you try to do the best you can.

Debbie, a married woman in her early thirties, talked about hiding her depressed feelings from others by playing a role in order to live up to what she believed others expected of her. For Debbie, being depressed did not fit with her own sense of herself.

I play this role that I thought was expected of me, in order to survive. And depression . . . that wasn't the role, that wasn't part of the role, that's for sure. . . . You're not really yourself.

Other women talked about having two "sides," one depressed and the other not depressed. The nondepressed, strong, confident side was the one they showed their friends and co-workers. The depressed side was seen as weak and was hidden from others. As Susan, a twenty-year-old single woman, said:

You're just being someone else. . . . I've got to be that other person, otherwise I'm only the other one. Like if I'm not the strong one, then I'm only the weak one. . . . Who I want to be is the person that people think that I am. That's who I want to be, because she comes across as this strong, confident person.

In describing their experiences, the women attempted to separate their "true" self from their depressed self, which was seen as weak and shameful. Yet, while women tried to hide their depressed feelings from others, they also wanted others to acknowledge their experiences.

Causes of Being Depressed

When asked about why they had become depressed, all nine of the women said that it was because of a chemical imbalance in the brain, an explanation usually given to them by a physician. The older women were also likely to identify bodily changes associated with menopause as a reason they became depressed. As Jane, a married woman in her late forties, said: "Plus I went through, started, menopause when I was forty so I'm on hormone replacement therapy." In contrast, none of the younger women mentioned female biology as a cause of their depression. When Tracy (a nineteen-year-old student) was told by her family physician that her depressed feelings were due to premenstrual syndrome (PMS), she had dismissed this explanation as being "ridiculous."

Although brain chemistry, genetics, and female biology were mentioned as playing a role in why they had become depressed, the women did not focus solely on medical explanations. They also considered their everyday lives. Poor interpersonal relationships, difficulty coping with job- or school-related stress, and the heavy workload involved in combining family and employment responsibilities were believed by some women to have contributed to their becoming depressed. The following excerpts illustrate how women drew on these varied reasons to explain why they had become depressed.

[A]n accumulation of stressful things. My husband was transferred to [city]. . . . I stayed behind in [town] for quite a few months, before our house was sold . . . and I came down here and got a job right away, unexpectedly. . . . And of course [this] involved working evenings. My kids weren't very happy that I was working, I'd never really worked out of the home. . . . And then sort of the final crunch was that very close friends of ours marriage broke up. And I couldn't do anything for them, couldn't fix it. (Ann)

> I don't think it's purely like a physiological thing, I mean there are the psychological triggers. . . . I'm learning now that if I can see those signs and I can figure out, okay, I am so stressed because of school, okay, this is going to make me collapse, I have to stop now. (Kelly)

Treatment Experiences

Each woman was diagnosed as depressed by her family physician who prescribed antidepressant medication and then referred her to a psychiatrist. Some women had also seen another mental health professional, such as a counselor, psychologist, or social worker. The eight women who had used antidepressants all felt that this had been an important part of their treatment, although the views of older and younger women differed somewhat. The four older women (Ann, Gloria, Jane, and Sarah) did not want to stop taking drugs because they believed that antidepressants were crucial to alleviating their depressed feelings. They believed they would become more depressed if they did not take the drugs. As Ann said,

> I was afraid that she [her physician] was going to say that I didn't need an antidepressant drug. . . . I think I would fight tooth and nail if anybody refused to prescribe it for me.

Among the younger women, four (Amy, Debbie, Kelly, and Susan) had used antidepressants but they were much less comfortable than the older women with the idea of taking drugs. The younger women wanted to be able to cope with being depressed without relying on medication. Although antidepressants might help to alleviate "physical" symptoms, these women also wanted help in learning to cope with stress in their lives. The following excerpt from Susan's interview reflects the younger women's views about medication:

> It made me feel weak . . . to have to take a chemical. . . . Then I got thinking about the medication. . . . So what does this mean if I have to take this medication in order to be normal? It just felt so weird. . . . I haven't told my doctors but I have stopped taking my medication.

Tracy, a twenty-three-year-old student, was the only woman who had decided not to take antidepressants, and instead chose to discuss her depressive experiences with counselors. Lack of knowledge about the drugs and their effects influenced her decision and like the other younger women, Tracy did not want to take a chemical in order to feel "normal."

> [A]t this point I'm still deciding. . . . I think partly it's fear of the drugs themselves. I'm not really sure what, in terms of side effects and in terms of addiction. And, I guess the idea of needing, whatever drug to feel okay. . . . It's kind of a nasty idea.

Although the women who used antidepressants found them helpful in alleviating some of their symptoms, most felt that drugs alone were not enough. They had also wanted to talk to someone about being depressed and to learn new ways of coping. These women reached a point where they identified a need for something beyond drugs and then either asked their physician for a referral or sought out treatment alternatives on their own. Sarah, for instance, asked her psychiatrist to refer her to a psychologist. She said that her sessions with the psychologist were helpful, because she was able to talk to someone about her feelings, something she was unable to do with family or friends, or even her psychiatrist.

> I felt I couldn't talk to my psychiatrist. You're in five minutes and okay we'll try you on this pill. We'll try you on that pill and there was no counseling. And I'd come home and there was no counseling, like there was nowhere to go. And so Dr. [psychiatrist] said I'll put you in touch with a clinical psychologist . . . and that was the best thing that ever happened.

Debbie attributed her recovery from being depressed to individual and group therapy to deal with past sexual abuse. She said that talking to others who had similar experiences to her own was helpful in dealing with being depressed.

> I think counseling has helped probably the most though. Yeah, taking time to look back and go over, you know, things that should have been dealt with.

. . . When I started going through all the healing for my sexual abuse, the depression started lifting.

Jane and Sarah became involved in a support group after receiving treatment at a hospital-based day therapy program. Five of the women had been treated as inpatients in a psychiatric unit and most felt that their time in the hospital had been beneficial. They described the psychiatric unit as providing a safe environment where they could take a break from everyday activities, think about their lives, and meet other people with similar experiences.

> It was good to be there [the psychiatric unit]. It was a safe place, a good time to get away and think. . . . You get to know people, I got to know some really good people in there. (Debbie)

Life after Diagnosis

At the time of their interview for our study, most of the women had come to accept their diagnosis. Only two women were reluctant to think of themselves as being depressed, because they associated having this diagnosis with being weak and abnormal. Being depressed made them feel different from others, something they did not like. As Susan said,

> I mean even after all this, I really don't consider myself to be depressed, just because I hate that classification. . . . I don't think about myself as depressed because I don't want to be. . . . Right now, I don't consider myself to be depressed. . . . But I know I am. If that makes sense. They tell me I am.

Following their diagnosis, most of the women had made changes in their lives with the aim of reducing stress. The changes they made typically involved setting limits on the scope of their everyday activities in areas they thought were contributing to their depressed feelings. The women who were married and had children usually reduced their employment or volunteer activities outside the home. For instance, Sarah took a disability leave from her full-time employment, although she still continued her activities within the home.

I still did my daily activities . . . had supper ready, had dinner ready, had their lunches ready. Did the wash. But none of that had ceased.

Jane, a married woman in her forties, was the only one to curtail her work at home.

But I just let go and went with the illness. I thought to hell with other people, I'm not going to. If I want to lay on this couch, I'm going to lay on this couch.

For Jane, this was the first time she had made changes in her life without worrying about how they would affect those around her.

The women who were students took time off from their studies, although these breaks from studying usually were intended to be temporary. Some women had also decided to modify their career plans in less ambitious directions as a result of being depressed. For instance, Kelly no longer believed she could handle medical school and Susan was reconsidering her decision to go to law school.

I want to go to law school and that's another seven years and I just think, if I can't handle second year Arts, how am I supposed to be able to deal with this?

Most women felt that, after their treatment, they were able to cope better with being depressed than they had been before. At the same time, they expressed some uncertainty about whether they would recover entirely. They hoped that they would not become depressed again, but also thought of depression as something they had to live with.

I'm hoping I won't have any recurrence. . . . I'll never say that it'll never happen again, but I'm hoping that with each time and with my experience, I'm hoping that I can minimize [it]. . . . I hate this feeling, but you know that you can overcome it and you know that it's going to get better. (Sarah)

I don't think it's something that can ever be permanently fixed. I think it's something that you can deal with better, I think it's something you can learn how to live with. But I don't think it's something you can ever cure. (Kelly)

Medicalization and Women's Experience
of Being Depressed

Our analysis for the medicalization theme focused on the language women used during the interviews. We paid particular attention to the terms women used when talking about being depressed and about what had caused them to become depressed. We also considered the role women's diagnosis and treatment experiences had played in shaping their understanding of being depressed.

All of the women drew upon a medical vocabulary, using words like "illness," "disease," "sick," and "cure" to describe their experiences of being depressed. Women's use of this medicalized language may have been prompted in part by the way we presented the purpose of our study. Before a woman agreed to be interviewed, she was told that the purpose of the study was to investigate depressed women's experiences of diagnosis and treatment, and this may have signaled that we expected them to use medical terms when talking about their experiences. Nevertheless, the pattern of medical language within the interviews suggested a somewhat different possibility. During the course of the women's interviews, the content tended to become more "medicalized" when they talked about being diagnosed as depressed. After this point, women were more likely to use medical terms. Kelly, for example, describes in the following excerpt how she felt before being diagnosed as depressed.

> There was always something wrong, a lot of physical . . . couldn't sleep, always tired, didn't want to eat and things like that. The big one was the insomnia. I just couldn't sleep.

Later in the interview, after talking about her diagnosis, there was a shift in the way Kelly described her experiences.

> I've got a small group of friends who are all suffering from various mental illnesses and we all joke about it. . . . We use the term "crazy" but we don't use it in a derogatory sense you know. But I mean there's still that, when someone tells you your brain chemistry's all messed up you're sort of like ooh.

In an attempt to distance themselves from the negative implications of being diagnosed with a mental illness, several women compared being depressed to having a physical health problem, such as diabetes or heart disease. When women drew this analogy between depression and a physical illness, they emphasized the medical nature of being depressed.

> I'm not ashamed of it [depression], I mean it was . . . something that's natural, it was a natural occurrence. . . . People aren't ashamed to walk around with diabetes or a heart attack. . . . People get cancer, it's not something you're going to hide. It's the same thing. (Debbie)

The women also drew upon various medical explanations in discussing why they had become depressed. Several women believed that family genetics played a role in their depression, pointing to relatives who had had similar experiences. As discussed already, all of the women explained being depressed in terms of an imbalance in the chemicals of the brain, and the older women also attributed being depressed to menopause.

> It's a chemical imbalance and, to me it just happened, it may have had something to do with my menopause. (Gloria)

The treatment most women had received when they were first diagnosed was medically oriented, which also probably influenced the explanations they gave for being depressed. In each case, the physician they consulted had prescribed an antidepressant drug. Like the other women who had used antidepressants, Sarah found the drugs helpful: "You do need your medication, or I felt I needed my medication, to alter [the] thought process." Most of the women who used antidepressants had also sought additional treatment, usually some type of counseling. As the following quote from Debbie indicates, benefits were gained from both treatment approaches.

> I think counseling probably was the best thing . . . more so than the Paxil [antidepressant drug]. . . . I don't know, I shouldn't say that. But I think I probably could have healed without the Paxil too, but the Paxil's like an aid

. . . giving you your ability to calm down. It takes awhile for it to work, though I think it helped initially.

Medicalization was also reflected in a more subtle way in the interviews when the women talked about being depressed as something different from how they usually experienced themselves, as a condition over which they had little control. This view of being depressed is illustrated in the following quotes, when the women talked about their lives in the future.

[Y]ou're going to have to acknowledge that sometimes you know it [depression] is going to invade your life . . . and at times like that you have to ride it out. (Kelly)

[I]f I had something that brought it [depression] on or something to keep it here, but like I said there's nothing. I have a really good life with my family. And I have my car to drive and no problems. If I want to go shopping and buy something I can go shopping and buy something so there's nothing, not a thing. (Gloria)

Empowerment and Women's Experience of Being Depressed

Our analysis for the empowerment theme focused on women's views about themselves after their diagnosis and treatment experiences. We were particularly interested in the changes women made in their lives in conjunction with their diagnosis and treatment. To what extent could the changes women made be considered empowering? Was a woman's ability to determine the direction of her life increased as a result of the changes she made? Were the changes a woman made likely to have a positive, rather than a negative, impact on her well-being and life circumstances?

For most of the women, being diagnosed as depressed had validated their feelings of ill health. Being prescribed an antidepressant drug by a physician provided confirmation that their depressed feelings warranted treatment. In addition to medical explanations (e.g., brain chemistry, genetics, etc.) for being depressed, the women had also considered other influences, particularly sources of stress in their lives.

But it may have a bearing, the stress of work, on the genetic. . . . But I was
always one to strive, like I've always had many irons in the pot. And whether
I just let myself get overwhelmed by too many things going on at the same
time. (Sarah)

After their diagnosis, several women had made changes in their lives that
involved setting limits on the scope of their daily activities so that they had
more time for themselves. For Jane, this meant having more time to relax.

I still have to limit myself and that's the hardest thing . . . trying to limit.
And, take time for Jane, take that bubble bath.

As discussed earlier, the changes women made more typically focused on
reducing their involvement in activities outside the home. For instance,
when Sarah was depressed, she took a leave from her full-time employment, but did not change her work at home.

So, therefore, they [family members] did not see a whole lot of change in me
except that I couldn't work [outside the home], because I worked around
here [at home].

Although a woman might cut back on her responsibilities outside the
home as a way of coping with stress, her work within the home was likely
to continue as usual. From our perspective, a change of this kind would appear to contradict feminist notions of women's empowerment, especially
if it increased a woman's financial dependence on her husband. Nevertheless, for women like Sarah, reducing the amount of time spent in paid employment helped to relieve the distress experienced in balancing the demands of home and work responsibilities. However, reducing their involvement in family caregiving activities (e.g., by having partners and
children take on a more equal share) was not an option these women considered. Even Jane, who took a break from household chores when she was
depressed, expected to resume these family responsibilities when she felt
better.

As discussed, the changes made by the women who were students
after they were diagnosed as depressed involved either withdrawing
from courses, taking time off from their studies, or dropping out of

school altogether. Although these women reduced their work as students, they continued or even increased their involvement in part-time employment. In the following excerpt, Amy, a full-time student when diagnosed as depressed, talks about the way her life has changed.

> When I go to work I feel very comfortable there, very safe. I'd rather just work there forever. I just work part-time as a sales person and as far as school, surprisingly it hasn't affected [it] as much as I thought it would. I figured I'd just fall behind really bad. I dropped a course immediately and just said forget this.

From our feminist perspective, although empowering in the short term, the longer-term consequences of these changes in educational goals seem disempowering, because they set limits on these young women's career plans and employment prospects.

Another aspect of empowerment we considered was the impact of women's diagnosis and treatment on how they viewed themselves and their lives. If a woman reported having a more positive outlook on life, then it is reasonable to conclude that her diagnosis and treatment experiences were empowering. Several women did tell us that they felt more positive about their lives after their treatment. Kelly, in particular, had experienced a marked positive change in her level of well-being.

> I've been off medication for a year or so, I have managed to straighten out a lot of things in my life. . . . I mean I'm doing much better in school now and I'm enjoying it a lot more and so I mean for the most part I'm pretty happy. . . . I didn't know like happiness, how cool it could be, how great it could be.

Debbie also said that her treatment had helped her to become a stronger, more confident person.

> I feel so totally healed and so positive about myself and, oh gosh, it's just like on top of the world. Really I just feel like I have a total grip on life and a lot stronger than I used to be. . . . Having to go through depression just to get where I am is worth it for sure.

Other women expressed more ambivalent views. Susan, for instance, wondered about the implications of her diagnosis for involvement in a long-term relationship.

> Let's say I have a long-term relationship with somebody and it never comes up. Is that something that I should tell them, like is it going to affect our future? If I get pregnant am I going to get depressed? I just don't know.

When women understood being depressed from a medical perspective, they tended to see themselves as having an illness over which they had little control and believed that they could become depressed again in the future.

Discussion

We contacted the women who participated in this study through mental health services that are fairly typical of those available outside major urban centers. The women interviewed had been diagnosed as depressed by a physician and then prescribed an antidepressant drug. Most of the women had also seen a counselor or another mental health professional. Thus, the women we talked to had received fairly conventional treatment when depressed, including being prescribed antidepressants (which all but one had used).

From a feminist perspective, treatment of women with antidepressant drugs has been criticized as promoting a medical understanding of women's depression. In Canada and the United States, drug prescription is restricted to physicians, so that medication is inherently a medicalized form of treatment.[18] Being prescribed an antidepressant drug implies that a woman's depression is an illness with root causes within her body's biology. Thus, when a woman's experiences of being depressed are conceptualized within a medical framework as symptoms of an illness, her experiences become medicalized. Conventional approaches to treatment of depressed women have been criticized as intrinsically disempowering, because the focus is on a woman's symptoms, and the social context and circumstances of her everyday life are taken for granted or ignored entirely.[19] We explored two main issues in this study. The first was whether a medicalized understanding of depressed women's experiences is promoted when they receive medical treatment. The second was the extent to which women's empowerment is compatible with treatment for depression.

During the women's interviews, a medicalized understanding was reflected in their use of medical terms to describe their depressed experiences and in their acceptance of medical explanations for being depressed. All nine women said that they had become depressed because of a chemical imbalance in the brain, an explanation given to them by a physician. Older women were also likely to attribute being depressed to menopause and to view antidepressants as a central part of their treatment. As Sarah said, "I know I do need medication. . . . We've tried three, well four different drugs now and this is the one that seems to be working the best."

Thus, a consistent theme in the women's interviews was a medicalized understanding of being depressed. The extent to which women drew on medical accounts of depression did not particularly surprise us, given the widespread promulgation of medical perspectives in the popular media (e.g., women's magazines, TV programs, the Internet). Moreover, a medicalized understanding of being depressed probably made sense to the women who had used antidepressants, because of the beneficial effects they attributed to these drugs.

As feminist scholars have pointed out, medicalization of women's distress offers certain advantages to depressed women.[20] When depressed women's experiences are medicalized, their distress is validated as a medical problem, as something for which they can legitimately seek a physician's help. Defining women's depression as a medical concern also shifts the responsibility for treatment from women to their doctors.[21] But medicalization also has some disadvantages for women, a key one being the potential for disempowerment. When depressed women's experiences are defined as symptoms of an illness, best treated by medical means, less attention is paid to their everyday lives and social circumstances in understanding their distress. Through the medicalization process, women become patients, expected to comply with their physicians' advice.

Nevertheless, between appointments with physicians and other professionals, depressed women must go on with their lives. Most of the women we talked to had made changes to cope with being depressed. However, the women tended to make changes in their lives that, to us, seemed to contradict feminist notions of empowerment, in which increasing, rather than limiting, women's options is emphasized. For instance, women with family responsibilities reduced their involvement in paid employment (or in some cases volunteer work), but generally continued their caregiving work for family members within the home. The women who were students when they became depressed had scaled down their educational endeavors and career plans, while maintaining or even increasing their involvement in part-time (and typically low-paid) jobs. Although the goal of these changes was to reduce stress, another effect was to limit the women's opportunities for personal empowerment. Being diagnosed as depressed may have provided women with an acceptable reason for disengaging from activities which they found burdensome. Rather than continuing to struggle with the dual demands of work and family, being diagnosed as depressed legitimized a woman's decision to reduce the scope of her work outside the home. For the younger women, being diagnosed as depressed enabled them to cut back their educational commitments, while avoiding academic failure. But diagnosis and treatment also had less positive implications, especially when women adopted a medicalized conception of being depressed.

When a woman understands her experiences of being depressed as symptoms of an illness, she is also likely to think of herself as someone who has "depression," a condition that may be controlled by taking antidepressant drugs but also is liable to re-occur. Thus, even though they may no longer be feeling depressed, the women who participated in our study tended to see themselves as vulnerable to becoming depressed again in the future. Having a medicalized understanding of being depressed also helped the women to avoid the stigma associated with having a "mental illness." They used various strategies to counteract the negative connotations of their diagnosis, such as drawing a parallel between being depressed and having a physical illness.

Adoption by women of a medicalized understanding of being depressed was also facilitated by the beneficial effects attributed to antidepressant drugs by those who used them. In other studies, women have identified use of antidepressant drugs as an important resource for coping when depressed.[22] An issue that emerges from our findings, therefore, is whether depressed women can benefit from conventional, medical treatment without other aspects of their experience also being medicalized. To put this another way, can medicalization co-exist with women's empowerment?

Our analysis of the women's interviews suggests that medicalized treatment may tend to work against empowerment in the lives of women who have been depressed. At the same time, if a woman rejects medicalized treatment approaches, she also forecloses on one avenue for validating her distress, as well as a potential source of symptom relief.

Although feminists have been critical of conventional, medical treatment for depressed women, especially reliance on drugs, we are not advocating that women's choice to use antidepressant medication should be preempted; but neither should treatment options be restricted to drugs. In our study, women were prescribed antidepressants when they consulted a physician but rarely were made aware of other sources of help. Women had to request such help or seek it out themselves. This latter finding suggests the need for better communication among mental health professionals, so that physicians become more aware of the contributions that other professionals can make to treatment for depressed women. Among the women who had used drugs, most reached a point when they decided that antidepressants alone were not enough. They also wanted to talk to someone about their experiences, and the women who had visited counselors or other professionals generally found their sessions helpful.

An element missing from the women's interviews was an understanding of being depressed from a feminist perspective. Certainly, none of the women indicated that they had seen a feminist therapist. Although there is some evidence that a combination of treatment approaches (e.g., antidepressant drugs and cognitive therapy) can be helpful with depressed women, little attention has been given to ways of combining feminist therapy with other treatment approaches.[23] Integration of feminist perspectives with medical and nonmedical approaches would offer depressed women more options, without precluding the possibility of women's empowerment.

Notes

The research described in this chapter was supported by grants awarded to J.M. Stoppard from the Social Sciences and Humanities Research Council of Canada and the University of New Brunswick Research Fund.

1. Deanna Gammell was the interviewer.

2. See B. Ehrenreich and D. English, *For her own good: 150 years of the experts' advice to women*; M. Greenspan, *A new approach to women and therapy*, P.S. Penfold and G.A. Walker, *Women and the psychiatric paradox*; D. Russell, *Women, madness and medicine.*

3. See P.J. Caplan, *They say you're crazy: How the world's most powerful psychiatrists decide who's normal;* Greenspan, *A new approach*; Penfold and Walker, *Women and the psychiatric paradox.*

4. Medicalization refers to the process through which a depressed woman's experiences become defined as a medical problem best treated by a physician (often using drugs). Within a medicalized context, the power to define a woman's problems rests largely with her doctor and the causes of her problems are presumed to lie primarily within her body and/or her psychology.

5. See Greenspan, *A new approach*; T.A. Laidlaw and C. Malmo, *Healing voices: Feminist approaches to therapy with women.*

6. See L.S. Brown and A.M. Brodsky, "The future of feminist therapy," and S. Sturdivant, *Therapy for women: A feminist philosophy of treatment*, for discussion of empowerment as a central principle of feminist therapy.

7. See J. Marecek, "Bringing feminist issues to therapy."

8. See Brown and Brodsky, "The future of feminist therapy"; Greenspan, *A new approach*, for discussion of personal empowerment as a goal of feminist therapy.

9. See Greenspan, *A new approach*; Penfold and Walker, *Women and the psychiatric paradox*; J. Worell and P. Remer, *Feminist perspectives in therapy: An empowerment guide for women.*

10. For a somewhat different feminist position on treatment for depressed women, see R. Perkins, "Choosing ECT"; J.M. Ussher, *Women's madness: Misogyny or mental illness?*

11. Our study was carried out in a town located in central New Brunswick, a province in Eastern Canada. In this largely rural province, treatment options for depressed women are restricted to those provided through the publicly funded health system. Such services include those provided by family physicians, psychiatrists, hospital inpatient units, and community mental health centers. Women who are students also have access to counseling services at their university. Other treatment services, such as counseling, psychotherapy, etc., are available on a limited basis from private practitioners, and must be paid for directly by users or through third-party (insurance) coverage.

12. Janet is a professor of psychology at a medium-size university in Eastern Canada, where she teaches clinical psychology and does research in the area of women's mental health. In her mid-fifties and never married, Janet has always worked at a full-time job. When this chapter was written, Deanna was a full-time student in her late twenties, completing doctoral training in clinical psychology at the university where Janet teaches.

13. See J.M. Stoppard, *Understanding depression: Feminist social constructionist approaches.*

14. See M. Blaxter, "Why do the victims blame themselves?"; J. Popay, "'My health is all right, but I'm just tired all the time': Women's experiences of ill health"; V. Walters, "Stress, anxiety and depression: Women's accounts of their health problems."

15. Blaxter, "Why do victims blame themselves"; Walters, "Stress, anxiety and depression."

16. Greenspan, *A new approach*; Penfold and Walker, *Women and the psychiatric paradox.*

17. See D.J. Gammell and J.M. Stoppard, "Women's experiences of treatment of depression: Medicalization or empowerment?" for a detailed description of the procedures we used in this study.

18. In the United States, clinical psychologists are currently seeking drug prescription privileges.

19. See reference sources listed in note 2.

20. See D.A. Findlay and L.J. Miller, "Through medical eyes: The medicalization of women's bodies and women's lives."

21. Ibid.

22. See J. Brandt, "The balancing act: Being faithful to a theoretical position while maintaining the voice of participants"; H. Graham, *Hardships and health in women's lives.*

23. See E. McGrath, G.P. Keita, B.R. Strickland, and N.F. Russo, *Women and depression: Risk factors and treatment issues,* for a discussion of treatment approaches that involve combining antidepressant drugs and psychotherapy. See S.A. Hurst and M. Genest, "Cognitive-behavioural therapy with a feminist orientation: A perspective for therapy with depressed women," for suggestions on how a feminist perspective could be integrated with one type of therapy.

References

Blaxter, M. (1993). Why do the victims blame themselves? In A. Radley (Ed.), *Worlds of illness: Biographical and cultural perspectives on health and illness* (pp. 125–142). London: Routledge.

Brandt, J. (1998, May). *The balancing act: Being faithful to a theoretical position while maintaining the voice of participants.* Paper presented at the Fifteenth Annual Qualitative Analysis Conference, Toronto, Canada.

Brown, L.S., & Brodsky, A.M. (1992). The future of feminist therapy. *Psychotherapy, 29,* 51–57.

Caplan, P.J. (1995). *They say you're crazy: How the world's most powerful psychiatrists decide who's normal.* Reading, MA: Addison-Wesley.

Ehrenreich, B., & English, D. (1979). *For her own good: 150 years of the experts' advice to women*. Garden City, NY: Anchor.

Findlay, D.A., & Miller, L.J. (1994). Through medical eyes: The medicalization of women's bodies and women's lives. In B.S. Bolaria & H.D. Dickinson (Eds.), *Health, illness and health care in Canada* (2nd ed.) (pp. 276–306). Toronto: Harcourt Brace.

Gammell, D.J., & Stoppard, J.M. (1999). Women's experiences of treatment of depression: Medicalization or empowerment? *Canadian Psychology, 40,* 112–128.

Graham, H. (1993). *Hardships and health in women's lives*. Hemel Hempstead, UK: Harvester Wheatsheaf.

Greenspan, M. (1993). *A new approach to women and therapy* (2nd ed.). Blue Ridge Summit, PA: McGraw-Hill.

Hurst, S.A., & Genest, M. (1995). Cognitive-behavioural therapy with a feminist orientation: A perspective for therapy with depressed women. *Canadian Psychology, 36,* 236–257.

Laidlaw, T.A., & Malmo, C. (1990). *Healing voices: Feminist approaches to therapy with women*. San Francisco: Jossey Bass.

Marecek, J. (2001). Bringing feminist issues to therapy. In B.D. Slife, R.N. Williams, & S.H. Barlow (Eds.), *Critical issues in psychotherapy: Translating new ideas into practice* (pp. 305–324). Thousand Oaks, CA: Sage.

McGrath, E., Keita, G.P., Strickland, B.R., & Russo, N.F. (1990). *Women and depression: Risk factors and treatment issues*. Washington, DC: American Psychological Association.

Penfold, P.S., & Walker, G.A. (1983). *Women and the psychiatric paradox*. Montreal, Quebec: Eden Press.

Perkins, R. (1994). Choosing ECT. *Feminism and Psychology, 4,* 623–627.

Popay, J. (1992). 'My health is all right, but I'm just tired all the time': Women's experiences of ill health. In H. Roberts (Ed.), *Women's health matters* (pp. 99–120). London: Routledge.

Russell, D. (1995). *Women, madness and medicine*. Cambridge, UK: Polity Press.

Stoppard, J.M. (2000). *Understanding depression: Feminist social constructionist approaches*. London: Routledge.

Sturdivant, S. (1980). *Therapy for women: A feminist philosophy of treatment*. New York: Springer.

Ussher, J.M. (1991). *Women's madness: Misogyny or mental illness?* Hemel Hempstead, UK: Harvester Wheatsheaf.

Walters, V. (1993). Stress, anxiety and depression: Women's accounts of their health problems. *Social Science and Medicine, 4,* 393–402.

Worell, J., & Remer, P. (1992). *Feminist perspectives in therapy: An empowerment model for women*. Chichester, UK: Wiley.

3

■   ■   ■   ■   ■   ■   ■   ■   ■

The Anger of Hope and the Anger of Despair[1]
How Anger Relates to Women's Depression

Dana Crowley Jack

Like with Jerry, I just, if I have a certain feeling or something I don't express it if I know it's going to piss him off. Sometimes I don't express certain feelings that I need to and it causes a lot of stress and pressure on me. And I don't know how to release them later. And I—it just bugs me. I get really down, really depressed. [*Are there certain kinds of feelings that have to be kept to yourself more than others?*][2] Yeah, what pisses me off.

> —Donna, age eighteen, white, unemployed

I just don't talk. But then when I don't throw out things, I don't feel well, you know, because I swallow—I don't know how else to say it—I swallow all my anger and then I feel like crying, I feel depressed, I feel very uncomfortable.

> —Chilean, age fifty-one, white, architect,
> originally from Germany

I have a hard time being angry immediately in the face of injustice in my relationships. And so what happens is I take it inside and I'm willing to hurt and really process what about this situation isn't right? And that's where the depression starts kicking in.

> —Michelle, age thirty-eight, white, writer

THESE THREE WOMEN hail from vastly different backgrounds, yet each describes how she keeps her anger to herself, and how silenced anger transforms into depression. The language women use to depict keeping their anger out of dialogue—swallowing it, taking it inside, not expressing it—reveals that they consciously and deliberately *choose* to silence anger, seeing it as problematic to their relationships in some way. Yet they also know the certain outcome of their choice: depression.

Since Freud's description of "melancholia," the psychological literature has considered that harsh self-criticism and the fall in self-esteem reflect anger turned against the self. Popular belief also holds that anger turned inward leads to depression. Yet, interestingly, depressed people often report feeling angry and hostile. In fact, increased irritability is one of the symptoms of depression. From the 1970s on, studies report depressed women's unexpressed anger as a possible factor in the onset and maintenance of their depression. For example, in 1974, a study of depressed women observed that depressed mothers' interactions with their children are characterized by friction and lack of warmth, a hostile style of interaction, and lack of responsiveness to the children's expressed needs for affection. In their words, depressed women "*tempered direct expression toward the spouse out of fear of the consequences. She was less fearful of the immediate consequences with the children, and they became the misdirected targets of her unexpressed rage toward her spouse*" (emphasis added, p. 74).[3]

Though women's unexpressed anger may link to their vulnerability to depression, a startling lack of basic inquiry surrounds this critical issue. I decided to look more intensively at women's patterns of anger expression in relation to their depression. Do women think that their anger relates to their depression? What patterns of expressing anger, or not expressing anger, do women link to their self-reported depression? Do women identify certain ways of expressing anger as fostering their well-being, and not their depression? Finally, if there is no clear threat of retaliation, why would women fear expressing their anger in positive ways?

To explore the relation of women's anger expression to depression, I interviewed sixty women at length in semi-structured interviews about their experiences of their anger, aggression, and depression.[4] In this chapter, I offer a picture of how women silence their anger, what patterns of anger expression they describe as keeping them free from depression, and how specific patterns of anger expression relate to women's self-reported depression. Women's narratives offer compelling evidence of anger's central role in the onset and maintenance of their depression. They also clarify anger's role in helping a woman move out of depression.

Self-Silencing, Anger, and Depression

What does it mean to "silence" anger? Why and how do women do this? In 1991, I described how depressed women "silence the self," a pattern of keeping feelings out of relationships in an effort to attain intimacy and security. Following the moral language in depressed women's narratives, I found that women tried to live up to cultural images of feminine goodness that promised social approval, love, and security. These images contained, most often, standards of the "good wife," "good mother," and/or "good woman."[5] Women from varying social contexts and differing ethnicities may hold different definitions of what makes a woman "good," but consistently, depressed women describe the anger that comes from trying to live up to impossible standards, and say that their anger must remain hidden. Jenny, age thirty-four, a white physician in part-time practice, married with two young children, talks about the origins of her sense of inadequacy and failure:

> That made me fall off the cliff, into a real depression. I think these issues of feelings of inadequacy as a person—I'm not doing enough, I'm not doing my jobs well, kind of thing. Feeling of guilt around my feelings about my husband. Feeling of guilt that I'm not a good enough parent. I was raised not to be angry and to be selfless and sort of that stereotypical female New England particular female role. And so my success as a parent is to sit quietly with my kids and do fun kid things and it just doesn't happen, and I get angry but can't say so. I felt like a failure all the time and each day I'd say, "I'm going to be more patient, I'm going to do this better." And it never happened.

As Jenny tries to force herself into the outlines of a "good enough" wife and parent, she feels a pervasive sense of inadequacy. She does not fit. The requirement "to be selfless" arouses anger as she tries to place her needs second to those of her husband and children; yet her anger continually proves to her that she is *not* selfless, nor a "good" mother. Instead, anger reminds Jenny of her separateness, of her self-full desires and needs other than "to sit quietly" with her children. She tries anew each day to make herself do "better," but her anger, that outlawed emotion, remains unruly.

Jenny does not speak about resentment from trying to fulfill the incessant demands of being a physician, mother, and wife. Instead of viewing the anger as a signal to take action to renegotiate roles or reveal her feelings, she tries to eliminate the signal itself. True to her socialization, she tries to be selfless, feeling her anger is unjustified since her needs "should" come second, feeling her anger can't be communicated because it shouldn't exist. Her pervasive sense of guilt reflects the unexpressed depth of her anger and feelings of resentment toward those she loves.

Jenny's Over-Eye, which views the self from the perspective of the culture's internalized eye, steps in to condemn her as a "failure." I have called this condemning voice of the self the Over-Eye because of its surveillant, vigilant, definitively moral quality.[6] It exerts pressure, through moral self-judgment, to conform to her subculture's consensus about feminine goodness and value. Jenny's Over-Eye harshly judges not only her failed attempts to behave as a good enough parent, but also her resentful anger. Among depressed women, anger ranks as the central emotion that they try to mute, transform, or eliminate from expression in their relationships.

Self-silencing contributes to feelings of a loss of self, to a decline in self-esteem, and to the experience of a divided self, all central to depression. Trying to keep relationships by pleasing others, Jenny experiences a hidden self that is bitter, angry, and increasingly hopeless about how to bring this secret self into relationship. Jenny has been diagnosed by her treating therapist as depressed, and has been taking Prozac for six months.

The factors that restrain Jenny from expressing her anger are both personal and social. Society views women's anger as "unnatural," aggressive, and leading to harmful consequences. Cultural rules and norms tell us when and how we can express anger and who has the privilege to display their angry feelings openly and directly. Women's struggle with expressing anger arises, in large part, from "a situation of subordination that continually produces anger, along with the culture's intolerance of women's direct expression of anger in any form."[7] At odds with a lifetime of socialization to attend to relationships and to the needs of others, expressing anger often feels unacceptable and dangerous to women, both inwardly and externally in terms of how others might judge and respond. As Elizabeth Spelman argues, while women and other members of subordinate groups "are expected to be emotional, indeed to have their emotions run their lives, their anger will not be tolerated." Such anger is likely to be called irrational, "redescribed as hysteria or rage." This is so because the expression of anger is intimately tied to self-respect, to the capacity to direct one's life. For this reason, women's anger is often considered not only inappropriate but threatening, an act of insubordination. To express my anger means that I take myself seriously, that I believe I have the capacity, as well as the right, to judge those who treat me unfairly, who might exclude me, silence me, misname, stereotype, or betray me.[8]

In general, research shows that women have higher levels of anger than men do.[9] And clinical studies confirm that women perceive less freedom for the direct expression of anger than do men. The double bind that many women experience—anger's arousal by social inequality, yet anger's ban from expression by social norms—creates confusion and denial among many women regarding their anger.

Depression, Anger, and Disconnection

Both depression and anger share disconnection at their core. The experience of depression is one of profound separation, from others and from oneself. Likewise, situations that arouse anger and aggression—injustice, inequality, and violation—create harmful rifts within relationship.

Both anger and depression are also *interpersonal*, arising out of relationships and profoundly affecting relationships. Though biochemical explanations dominate current formulations of depression, most theorists agree that society and an individual's psychology also play critical roles in precipitating depression. From an interpersonal perspective, depression occurs when a person feels hopeless about the possibility of emotional closeness with others. In fact, theorist John Bowlby, who investigated attachment behaviors in humans and other animals, believes that "In most forms of depressive disorder . . . the principal issue about which a person feels helpless is his [*sic*] ability to make and to maintain affectional relationships."[10] Bowlby also describes anger as a response to disconnection or obstacles to relationship, as a protest over a disrupted bond. Anger functions to restore relationship and discourage the loved person from going away.

Studies find that women's anger is more likely to be triggered by another's actions within a close relationship, whereas men are more likely to become angered by the actions of strangers.[11] Women describe their anger primarily in relational terms, placing it squarely in stories about relationships and focusing on the interpersonal effects of their anger, while men's stories are more impersonal and self-focused.[12] Researchers surmise that women's greater tendency to be angered in interpersonal contexts may reflect their higher sensitivity to the quality of their close relationships and their stronger motivation to achieve intimacy in these relationships.[13] As feminist theorists have described, women's sense of self is organized around connection, mutuality, and relationships. Self-esteem is tied to the quality of attachments; feelings of guilt, shame, and depression are associated with the failure of intimate ties.[14]

Anger occupies a healthy yet problematic place in a woman's emotions. Healthy, because anger reminds a woman of her own self within relationship; problematic if a woman fears anger's negative effects on relationships or stays in a situation where its expression is punished. The longstanding focus on the *individual as the container of anger* who internalizes, externalizes, or controls it misleads inquiry. To understand women's anger and its relation to depression, we must shift our attention to examine anger's origins and expression within relationships.

Transforming an Anger of Hope into the Anger of Despair

Donna, whose quote opens this chapter, describes herself as depressed. Through her example, we see how anger moves from hope to despair, and how this shift relates to depression. Donna came from a working-class family and used drugs heavily in adolescence to act out her rebellion and anger against her family. Now drug free and trying to be a responsible mother and a "good" woman, she makes explicit how subordination in relationship instigates anger. Listening to her, we hear how healthy, protesting anger goes awry, leading to the hopeless resignation central to depression.

> I can't say what pisses me off. Because sometimes he'll be like in a really bad mood and I won't even be looking at him, I give dirty looks off to the sides or whenever, when he says something and I get mad and I'll look off like that

and he'll say, "Don't fucking look at me you bitch!" kind of stuff. It's like, I didn't do anything! Sometimes I feel like it's just me and maybe it's my fault that he's like that. [*How could that be?*] By something I've done, maybe I've ticked him off or I did something that made him mad and instead of him just telling me, he's using something else to get back at me for it. I feel like that a lot. [*And what do you do when you feel like that?*] I try to make him nice dinners, I try to keep the house clean, try to make the beds, try to keep everything just perfect for him. It doesn't work. He doesn't ever say anything. . . . He'll come in and start throwing things on the floor. Doesn't even care. And sometimes when he's got a day off and I'm cleaning the house he'll just sit there and watch me. And I get so mad and can't do anything about it. I just give up and get depressed.

Anger acts as an emotional compass, pointing to violations in relationship and locating sources of emotional pain. Donna's protesting, healthy anger signals that she has been violated. Anger calls us to action; it *activates* a person to respond to a perceived threat, including to self-esteem. Anger is essential to survival; it can trigger the physiological changes that lead to fight or flight, such as acceleration in heart rate, elevations in blood pressure, adrenaline, and noradrenaline. These changes energize a person to respond to the situation that caused anger. But the action a person chooses to take is an altogether separate issue. It may be an aggressive act that is destructive and hurtful, or it may be a constructive act that fosters self-definition, increased communication, and even social change.

Positive anger, "the anger of hope," requires a belief that one can communicate and be heard, and that anger and conflict can have positive benefits to relationships. In contrast, an "anger of despair" often arises from feeling powerless to restore relationship, or when hostility over separation has replaced the bonds of attachment.[15] Women's anger of despair most often finds expression through hostile aggression directed toward the self or toward others.[16]

Donna's anger offers hope because it could provide a catalyst for positive change. Anger's clarity could pull her beyond her fears to see what effect this devaluing relationship has on her. Anger could strengthen her backbone; expressing anger could provide space for her needs and feelings. Or anger could propel her to leave if nothing changes.

But Donna doesn't speak her anger. Instead, she sends it into "dirty looks off to the side." Because she wants this relationship and fears expressing her anger, Donna disconnects her anger from the interaction that caused it. Loosened from its moorings, her anger floats free to seize on the possibility that *she* created his bad behavior: "Maybe it's my fault that he's like that." She gets confused even about where the mistreatment in the relationship occurs: "Maybe I ticked him off, or I did something to make him mad." As she mystifies the origin of her anger, she turns it against herself as the one who is creating the problems by displeasing her partner. This explanation offers her a way to affect this man's behavior other than by confronting him, even positively, with her anger. She could, instead, try to please him through selfless giving. Trying to create closeness, she resorts to traditional subordinate housewife behaviors, locating the cause for his behavior to some fault in herself, trying to keep "everything just perfect for him," giving and giving until she gives up. Donna also accepts abusive, humiliating treatment because of reasons common to women who stay in devaluing relationships: fears of violence, abandonment, economic loss, single parenting, and low self-esteem.

Donna's unspoken anger contributes to her depression. Her hopelessness arises because the most important dilemma of her life seems to have no solution: She wants intimacy but cannot love her partner if he treats her so badly. Fearing that expressing anger will only lead to more problems, she tries to create closeness by eliminating her anger. Her hopelessness also stems from an anger that can serve no purpose: "And I get so mad and can't do anything about it. I just give up and get depressed."

Without anger's positive expression, problems in relationship cannot be improved; intimacy requires that partners struggle around their differences. Feeling that her anger cannot be expressed, Donna becomes hopeless about how to improve the relationship. This move from hopeful anger—the outrage over violation and the belief that disconnections can be overcome—to despairing anger ushers in the hopelessness of depression. Since the quality of relationships is the strongest predictor of women's depression, and since despairing anger has given up on removing barriers to closeness, silencing one's anger becomes a pathway to depression. After anger has been ineffective or goes unexpressed, after it has become an anger of despair, it is easy to feel more hopeless about having any effect on one's relationships and control over one's life. As with Donna, when women perceive that anger is dangerous to relationship or to themselves, their children, or jobs, they will mystify the source of their anger, and easily misattribute its cause to some flaw in the self.

Women's Anger-Expression and Depression: An Overview

Silencing the self is one pattern of anger expression known to associate with women's depression across a number of studies.[17] Even though many women are socialized to hide their anger from their partners/friends, clearly women deal with anger in many more ways than just keeping it hidden. They also become destructively aggressive, use their anger to make positive changes, use anger for self-protection, and engage in a full range of actions to convey anger indirectly. For this chapter, I examined how sixty women's patterns of anger expression relate to their self-reported depression. Since the sample and method of analysis have been detailed elsewhere,[18] I will only briefly describe them now. I interviewed the sixty women an average of two hours each about their attitudes, experiences, and past histories regarding anger and aggression with other adults in everyday life.[19] The forty-one white women and nineteen women of color ranged in age from seventeen to seventy-five (mean = 36), and included eight lesbians.[20]

In what follows, I describe patterns of anger expression other than self-silencing and how they relate to women's self-reported depression. Women's narratives reveal that the most important factor shaping how they express anger is the anticipated reactions of others. In general, women who do not express their anger directly and positively to others report being depressed. They tie their hesitance to express anger to a fear that negative consequences will swiftly follow if they communicate anger. For example, Mary (age forty-three, white, therapist) said, "In my communication with people, it [anger] usually kind of fizzles out because I'm afraid of them getting mad at me. I mean I'm really afraid of that. . . . They might leave, they might hit me, they might hate me, they might punish me in some other way down the road where I'm not expecting it. That something negative will come." Though specific contexts, such as work, friends, and intimates, affect fears around anger expression, women in this study talked primarily about their relationships as most important for their well-being. Ninety-eight percent of their narrative segments about anger discussed the interpersonal aspects of their anger, with the focus of discussion on the anticipated or actual reactions of others.[21]

As we consider patterns of anger expression, two caveats must be kept in mind. First, the patterns are not pure types. Most women utilized all types, except physical aggression, at some time. What appears to matter in regard to depression is how the habitual or usual mode of dealing with anger relates to a woman's sense of ability to affect her relationships, the ongoing arousal of her anger, and her experience of self within relationships. Second, a woman may utilize more than one type of anger expression habitually. Silencing anger, for example, often pairs with aggressive outbursts, with anger explosions outside relationship, and with indirect anger expression.

Freedom from Depression: When Anger Expression Increases Connection

Women describe two patterns of anger expression that keep them free from depression, or that have helped them move out of depression.

Positively and Directly Bringing Anger into Dialogue

Women who describe a sense of freedom to bring their anger into relationships directly, and who say others recognize and respond reasonably to their anger, report being free of depression. Thirteen women described the consistent use of this anger pattern within intimate relationships. The women link their positive anger expression to moving out of depression, and not to the onset or experience of depression. In fact, they detailed how learning to express anger positively stood as a marker of their personal development.

Women engaging in positive anger expression regard their *anger as a call for action to overcome the disconnection in relationship*. They thoughtfully respond, knowing they will be able to deal with whatever situation caused the feeling. Carrie (age thirty, African American, social worker), for example, says: "So if something's making me angry, if it's a slow onset, then I sit back and I calculate and I get mental notes. I write mental notes and I put it two and two together and I work it out and then I go and I address the issue, whatever it may be. I address it and when I'm addressing it, I know that I'm going to deal with it."

Women who are not afraid of expressing anger have confidence that they can handle its interpersonal consequences. They are convinced that positive anger expression benefits others and themselves. Rhonda (age thirty-two, African American, social worker) says:

> So anger is good. It is. It can be positive. It stimulates people. If you always say things trying to be nice and passive and be so worried about hurting their feelings, you know, then I think—I don't know, they just kind of—I don't know if they respect you. I think they respect you more when you be more firm and you make them mad a little bit. . . . I don't really worry so much about people getting mad at me and I'm not scared of people getting mad at me. I'm not. I don't always like when people get mad at me but I don't have a fear of it, you know.

Rhonda tells the story of her supervisor at work who was "always controlling" and demeaning her. "We clashed big time. I wrote letters to his supervisor and everything and they would get on him. . . . I could have lost my job but I didn't care if I did lose it. I feel good about myself. I'm not fearful about nothing. I ain't scared of nothing."

Like Rhonda, women who use anger constructively regard it as a signal that they need to take positive action. They believe that they have the right and the capacity to defend themselves against those who treat them unfairly. Using anger in this way builds self-esteem as others are moved to respond. Such anger brings clarity to problems in relationship and helps a woman stand up for herself.

Each woman who expressed her anger positively saw it as a turning point in movement out of depression. Rhonda, for instance, was in a brutally abusive marriage, and Carrie learned the necessity of expressing anger as she confronted racism in her high school. Anger propelled each to remove herself from relationships that retaliated against her anger expression to find ones that respond positively. Though these women still face the possibility of negative consequences from expressing anger in their work and friendships, they are willing to take the risk. They have learned through experiences of depression that they must regard anger as a call to action and dialogue. As Toni (age forty-four, white, librarian) said, "I'm willing to take on the consequences of expressing my anger much more than not expressing it, because I know what happens if I suppress it. I get more and more angry and uncomfortable and get close to doing very harmful things to myself."

Keeping Anger Out of Relationship Consciously and Constructively

In some instances women perceive that bringing anger directly into the offending relationship will result in harmful consequences to themselves, their children, or their jobs. Rather than doing nothing, they heed anger's call to action by responding in a positive, constructive way outside of the relationship that created it. Anger spurs them to set useful goals and take effective action. They report that doing so made them feel empowered and, in most cases, served as a means of moving out of depression. None of the women who described consciously choosing to express or enact anger outside relationship tied such anger expression to their depression.

For example, Maria (age thirty-two, Latina/Native American, attorney) used the anger she felt from racial discrimination to fuel her resolve:

> I think for a lot of people of color, and specifically for me, there's a component of anger, you know. It's a motivator; it's been part of what's fueled me to move on. I think the anger was from, you know, you don't belong here, you can't do it, you're not smart enough, that kind of stuff. I mean, anger's a great emotion. . . . It just gets you going. . . . It's definitely a motivator.

Using her anger as a stimulant to action helped Maria fight against internalizing damaging messages and spurred her high achievement. In another situation, Karen (age forty-one, white, police officer) described a situation in which she was sexually harassed at work. She says,

> It's almost like my anger emotions and stuff are what made me survive, because I was so angry at the system. I was angry at everything. And I thought, you know, if I give up, then that little small change that maybe I could make wouldn't occur if I was gone. . . . I just knew that if I gave up, nothing was going to get different. Nothing was going to be different if I gave up.

Karen's anger moved her to fight for change within the system. As Elizabeth Spelman has observed, anger is a political emotion: A woman's systematic denial of her anger becomes a means of subordination, and the recognition and expression of anger an expression of equality and freedom.[22]

Ways of Bringing Anger into Relationship That Women Tie with Depression

Women link two patterns of bringing anger into relationship to their depression: expressing anger aggressively and expressing it indirectly.

Bringing Anger into Relationship Aggressively

When using anger aggressively, women state that their goal is to hurt someone, to retaliate, or strike back for emotional pain they are feeling. Aggressive anger does not seek to overcome a problem in relationship; rather, it often furthers the relational disconnection that caused anger. We must remember that not all aggression is fueled by anger; here I focus only on women's angry aggression and how it relates to their depression.

Though many women occasionally resort to aggressive uses of anger, those women who used aggression habitually often experience chronic, free-floating anger whose causes they cannot always pinpoint or articulate. They feel incapable of talking about their feelings of anger, and instead act them out. While aggression is usually overt, women also describe secretive, indirect aggression such as manipulations and covert actions to hurt others. Though aggression defends against the dread and anger of deep disconnection, women feel trapped and further isolated by their aggressive acts. Their anger is despairing and leads to hopelessness and depression.[23] Six women utilized a pattern of physical anger expression regularly, and all six had been physically abused as children. All six were depressed, and two of the six were substance addicted.

Women's aggressive anger expression ranged from verbal to physical assaults. Cassondra (age thirty-four, white, artist) used verbal and physical aggression from childhood, modeling abusive parents who used drugs. Though her family situation continually incited anger, she had no models for positive ways to bring anger into relationship in order to resolve disagreements or restore closeness. As Cassondra's partner of two years left her, he told her that he loved someone else. Her anger at this man is mixed with shame at her own inadequacy that, she thinks, drove him away: "I just felt deficient, I felt violent. I wanted to be this really loving person, this loving, giving woman. And I was made to feel that I was anything but that." Her anger quickly became rage at herself and at him as she realized he was leaving. Her despairing anger lept into aggression:

> I wanted to hurt him. I really wanted to hurt him. I didn't care whether he thought I was crazy anymore, I didn't care anymore. I said, "I'm gonna go and I'm going to be absolutely insane and I don't give a shit anymore. . . ." I said, "Fuck you, and if she shows up on this island, I'll fucking kill her." I told him that. I've never said anything like that to anybody in my life. But I did say all, I, and then I grabbed his wallet and I tried to take money, because I had just loaned him money. And he was getting ready to go out, on this date where he was going to bring her onto the island and do knows, do who knows what, but the only money he had was money I gave him. So I was going to take money from him, so we got into this wrestling match, where he was trying to take the wallet away from me, and, and I just told— I left. I said, "I hope you burn in hell."

To affirm her existence and her power in a situation where she felt none, Cassondra became aggressive. She easily experiences the loss of this relationship as a loss of self; she combats the loss of self by acting out the kind of destruction she feels is occurring to her. Trying to harm the other person externalizes the psychological experience of being destroyed; it offers some brief sense of control over self and other. Cassondra told how this incident caused her deep shame and depression.

Women also describe resorting to aggression when they have no models for positive anger expression. Angela (age twenty-eight, first-generation Mexican American, social worker) feels no ability to communicate her anger through words. Angela explains,

> I couldn't fight back with words because in the first place as we were growing up we weren't even allowed to say any bad words at home or we would get slapped for it or you know spanked for it. . . . And so he [husband] just made me very angry and I just turned around and slapped him because I

didn't have any words. I kept thinking, what do I tell him so that he will stop? . . . All I wanted to do is hurt him back so I just turned around and slapped him really hard and I ran out the door. At that time I felt really bad and I felt really, I don't know, like ashamed of myself . . . but I wanted to defend myself and I didn't know how. I didn't know what to tell him so that he would shut up. . . . I do say bad words I say them but I can't come out and say them *to him*.

Angela's example illustrates a common pattern of anger's expression swinging from one extreme (silencing anger) to another (aggressive anger expression), followed by intense self-recrimination, guilt, and depression. An additional five women described, like Angela, a pattern of silencing their anger most of the time but, at times of extreme provocation, resorting to aggressive responses. Such aggressive outbursts only reinforce their determination to hide their anger. The aggressive incidents make them feel "really bad," and "ashamed." These five women, like Angela, self-reported depression.

Bringing Anger into Relationship Indirectly

In this form of anger expression, women say their goal is to keep anger disguised and out of dialogue as a strategy of safety. All women in the sample relied on disguising their anger as a strategy of safety at times. But fourteen women presented indirect anger expression as their dominant pattern. Eleven of these women self-reported depression; three did not.

Expressing anger indirectly allows a woman to deny her anger when confronted, and thus attempt to avoid retaliation or other negative consequences. Women recount feeling badly about expressing anger indirectly, and describe guilt, diminished self-esteem, and continuing anger over the relational difficulties that arouse the anger. Though ways of masking anger are as varied as the human imagination, three patterns, or strategies, for expressing anger indirectly were associated with women's depression.

Hostile Distance

Women frequently use hostile silence to convey anger but at the same time, to cut off communication. Behaviors such as withdrawal, pouting or sulking, or "shorten[ing] my sentences," as well as numerous others, are used to bring anger into a relationship but keep it out of direct dialogue. The distance is intended to convey angry displeasure while it allows the woman, if confronted, to deny her anger and thus avoid its consequences. This strategy keeps conflict covert, and fosters more disconnection rather than resolution and reconnection.

For example, Angie (age twenty-five, Native American/Latina, unemployed), in an abusive relationship, says, "I think I should start opening up to him but I don't really do anything to him. I don't talk to him for awhile. And then he'll start saying, 'What's this, the silent treatment?' And I'll say, 'No.' I just don't talk to him for awhile." Hostile distance is safer for Angie than honest dialogue about her feelings.

Brenda (age thirty, African American, unemployed), who was in treatment for major depression, said that she didn't talk to others about her feelings. She immediately corrected herself to say, "I do talk. Talk to myself, talk to people. Be walking around here talking to myself, I know somebody be hearing me, because I make sure they hear me. I don't know exactly what I be saying to me. Probably cussing, calling people crazy and, why is people bothering me, I don't bother them and all stuff like that."

Angry silence often carries a confusing controlling aspect: It provides nothing specific to engage with. It allows a hasty retreat if one is confronted: "I wasn't angry," or, "I wasn't angry with *you*." Angry silence that leaks anger into relationship often reinforces women's feelings of powerlessness and continues situations that aroused anger in the first place. At times, however, leaking anger into the relationship indirectly allows women to maintain some sense of active resistance when outward expression seems too dangerous, such as in abusive relationships. The relational context powerfully affects anger's meaning for a woman's self-experience for this and all patterns of women's anger expression.

Loss of Control as a Way to Attempt to Control the Other

Women describe being "out of control" through statements such as, "I had PMS," "I lost it," "I didn't mean to," while the expression of their anger affects the relationship. Explosive anger displays such as slamming doors, throwing objects, and yelling, not *at* another person, but *in the presence of another*, fall under this strategy of indirect anger expression. Though women demonstrate their anger, they do not openly discuss what problems in the relationship aroused it. They disavow responsibility for the anger, describing that they feel *taken over* by anger beyond their control; they report feeling unable to address the relationship issues that cause the anger even while they appear so outwardly angry.

For example, Mary (age forty-three, white, therapist) reported that she was furious with her partner. She entered the apartment, slammed doors, turned up the stereo as loud as possible, and attributed her actions to PMS. In this way, she could communicate anger, affect her partner, and deny responsibility for her behavior, all without directly addressing problems in relationship and all with the attempt to avoid interpersonal consequences.

Women also describe their angry tears as a form of "losing it," that is, of losing self-control. Tears are a socialized, behavioral display of women's anger that offers a solution to the puzzle of how to express anger in ways that do not threaten others. Tears may or may not be associated with depression. When they are, women describe tears as linked to their inability to directly express anger. Arliss (age twenty-seven, white, student): "If it is something deeply personal, I'm one of those people that get so angry I can't talk and tears just come pouring out of my face. So I'm crying but I'm not crying because I'm upset or—I'm crying because I can't verbalize what I need to say."

Quiet Sabotage

Women report that, when angry, they create the appearance of not being angry to conform to gender expectations regarding women's behavior, or to remain safe in a dangerous relationship. Yet, on another level, they resist these restrictions on their anger, using sabotaging behaviors such as "forgetting" to do what is requested, acquiescing to requests then refusing to enact them, or using a variety of behaviors that sabotage the other person's expectations. This way of communicating anger indirectly creates relational impasses, as the anger remains invisible and disavowed. It includes behaviors women often label "passive-aggressive" and "manipulative" in their own descriptions of their behavior. For example, Tillie (age twenty-four, white, social worker) was angered by her husband's habit of giving her lists of things to do as they left for work. Instead of confronting the problem directly, she reported that her practice was to acquiesce, take the list, and either "forget" it, get the wrong things, or basically subvert her outward compliance. She described feeling "lousy" about her way of dealing with her anger, and described negative interpersonal consequences resulting from her inability to deal directly with her anger over unfair demands.

Ways of Keeping Anger out of Relationship that Women Tie with Depression

Women tie their self-reported depression to three patterns of trying to keep anger to themselves and out of the relationship in which it arose.

Explosively But Alone

Women describe how they release anger through various ways—yelling, pounding objects, slamming doors, crying—but *out of anyone's presence.* Arliss (age twenty-seven, white, student) describes such an incident: "Just the other night at work I got so mad. The chef was snippy with me and all I wanted to do was find out where something was, and we were busy, so I went back in the store room and I kicked this box about twenty times. . . . Then I went, 'God I wonder if I broke anything.' Oh well. I didn't go check."

In other cases, women habitually explode with anger out of others' presence as a way to deal with anger in intimate relationships. For example, Anna (age forty, white, student) says, "I've never been angry in anyone's presence. . . . In the past, when I've been really, really angry, I'll go out and get a stick and beat the weeds, or I'd pound something or I'd do something . . . *but never around anyone else, not ever around anyone else.*" Angela (age twenty-eight, first-generation Mexican American, teacher) says, "Sometimes if I get angry with my husband if he tells me something or sometimes if he does something . . . sometimes he'll like tell me things and I take it and take it and take it and finally I just can't take it anymore. I'll just go to my room and just bang on the wall or whatever, you know, just smack my pillow. . . . *But not talk to him about it.*"

Explosive anger release outside of relationship appears to be unrelated to depression unless the woman feels a requirement never to voice anger in her intimate relationships. Angela, for example, says that she cannot talk to her husband about anger. Earlier, we saw that Angela swings from self-silencing to aggression because she feels prohibited from expressing anger to her husband. In this example, she erupts explosively outside the relationship. Like Angela, women who vent their anger on objects away from others' presence, most often, within their relationships, communicate anger indirectly or silence it altogether. Only two women in the sample reported a pattern of self-silencing accompanied by venting anger outside relationships. Both these women were depressed. Other women, who were not depressed, reported venting anger outside relationships as well as expressing it directly to others. Whether or not the ability to express anger explosively but outside relationship serves as a positive coping measure that offsets the negative effects of anger suppression needs to be investigated more fully.

Switching Targets

Women report a well-known pattern of displacing their anger into a relationship different from the one that instigated it. Women who displace anger are affected by anger and fear, and report themselves as being depressed.[24] For example, when a woman fears the consequences of becoming angry at her partner she may redirect it to safer targets, such as her children. Jessie (age thirty-four, white, single mother on welfare), who is depressed, talks about where she directs her anger: "But usually it snowballs. I'll let it build in me. Angry, aggression, bitterness, whatever. It usually snowballs in me. . . . If I've gotten really mad at something that's, whatever the situation is, and keep it in, I tend to take it out on my kids later. I tend to get agitated real easy."

When women cannot identify specific sources of their anger, as when anger has been habitually silenced, they more easily displace it on to others. For example, Kim (age thirty-four, Filipina/Danish American, social worker) says,

> It took a long time to pinpoint my anger. For a while I was just placing anger here or there and they're [kids] like looking at me like "what's wrong?" I go "I'm sorry, I'm so sorry I'm taking this out on you. You didn't do anything to me." . . . So I start talking to myself going "Why are you taking this out on your kids? They didn't do anything. Okay you've got to focus on what you're mad at. What are you mad at?" It took me a long time to start focusing. It's hard.

After a lifetime of learning to ignore anger's signal, women must learn to uncover what specific incidents instigate their anger. Then they must take the difficult steps of learning to express anger appropriately, and gain confidence that they can deal with the consequences.

Turning Anger against the Self as Part of Self-Silencing

Turning anger against the self is characteristic of depression. In women's narratives, anger turned against the self appears to be both cause and symptom of their self-reported depression. Each woman who habitually turned anger against herself also described a pattern of blocking her anger from positive, direct expression. Nine women presented clear patterns of self-silencing that include anger turned against the self; all these women reported being diagnosed with major depression by treating professionals.

Women describe turning anger against themselves aggressively, through physical self-harm, or through nonphysical but constant negative self-talk. Physical self-harm serves to express unbearable feelings symbolically and thereby to provide some emotional release. Latisha (age thirty-two, African American, single parent on welfare) says of her anger, "If I do anything to anybody, it's going to be me. I'm so used to cutting on myself or either punching the wall. Because I turn it all in on me." Or Cassondra (age thirty-four, white, artist), angry after her partner decided to leave her, said that she "emptied all the bottles out and made little piles and then I took a couple of muscle relaxers. I thought I'm just going to get fucked up instead of hurting myself . . . and I just got fucked up and then I didn't feel much of anything at that point." Women also abuse substances to numb the anger they feel against their perceived failures.

More commonly, women turn their anger against themselves with harsh self-criticism than with physical self-harming behaviors. If a woman perceives some aspect of her *self* as the barrier to what she desires—positive relationships, inclusion, success—then she may direct her hostile anger against herself for not being "pretty" enough, smart enough, or lovable enough. Culture plays a vital role in women's tendency to self-blame and self-attack, providing images of how they "should" be and look, and holding them responsible when relationships fail. In self-attacks, social factors contributing to women's feelings of powerlessness become converted into hated personal deficits as a woman perceives that she has created the problem. Both Jenny, the physician, and Donna, the young mother, whose examples appeared earlier in this chapter, illustrate how they turn their anger against themselves, and how society has prepared them to do so.

While women silence anger through keeping it out of dialogue, some women try to keep anger even out of their conscious recognition.[25] They condemn anger's presence in their feelings; having learned that anger is "bad," they have taken the step to think, "I am bad for having angry feelings." They stop awareness of anger even before it has a chance to signal that a wrong has been done, which leads them to confusion over what they feel and the sources of psychological pain or distress. For example, Fern (age fifty-eight, white, in therapy for major depression) said, "I've never told anyone else that I was angry with them. *I don't allow myself to feel angry.*" Fern suffered from high blood pressure and had suffered from one serious heart attack. Disconnecting from one's own recognition and experience of anger robs the self of authenticity, of an energizing force, and keeps one feeling acted upon rather than an actor. Only two women described silencing their anger from conscious awareness, both professing they "never feel angry." These two women were both in treatment for major depression.

The Ties between Anger Expression and Depression

In summary, two patterns of expressing anger help protect women from depression: Bringing anger into relationship positively and constructively, and keeping anger out of relationship by choice. Using anger aggressively, exploding in front of others but not saying why, deflecting anger onto safer targets, silencing anger through keeping it out of direct expression— women tie all these forms of anger expression to their depression. The most critical issue regarding anger's linkage with depression appears to be whether anger's expression fosters a closer, more authentic relationship or increases disconnection. Thus, other people's responses to a woman's anger matter, as do her ways of communicating it. Are those who instigated her anger open to listening and responding constructively? If not, those women who move out of depression have learned that they must take steps to find new relationships that allow open dialogue. Interestingly, fourteen women detailed silencing their anger to keep it out of relationship earlier in their lives. Thirteen of these women described how changes in self-silencing behaviors corresponded with leaving relationships and with moving out of depression.

Why might anger expression play a critical role in women's vulnerability to depression? Anger works in the service of relationship, furthering intimacy by removing barriers, fostering honest conflict that reveals more about oneself and others through engagement around difference. Anger also works in the service of equality by acting as a call to address unfairness and violations in relationship and society. When women fear to express anger because they anticipate negative responses from others, they work hard to divert it, mute it, disguise it, and often learn to turn it against themselves, the safest target.

Why is it so difficult for women directly and positively to voice their anger? The same social realities that affect women's vulnerability to depression also stop them from directly expressing their anger. These social realities include poverty, violence against women, and women's general social inequality as well as their inequality in intimate relationships with men.[26] Women's fear about the negative consequences of communicating their anger, which many equate with aggression, appears to be related to the inhibited behaviors and styles of thinking that researchers find associated with female depression. Research suggests that directing angry hostility inward creates depressed feelings; when anger cannot be expressed, it often finds an outlet in negative self-talk and self-deprecation. Whether a woman's anger expression relates to her depression in any given instance depends on a number of factors: the social situation that caused her anger and depression, the woman's understanding of the situation, the social supports she has available, and her perception of the choices she has in response to the situation.

Why might anger, when kept out of positive dialogue, create a vulnerability to depression? Anger is an adaptive emotion that arouses a person physically and mentally to take action in response to perceived social threats, violations, or frustrations. Anger also floods the mind with feeling, and people search for explanations for what caused the anger. When anger remains unexpressed, unable to fulfill its function to overcome rifts in relationship, the physiological changes that accompany anger can have serious physical health consequences. Anger suppression and self-silencing have been linked not only to depression, but also to eating disorders, irritable bowel syndrome, hypertension and cardiovascular disease, and suicide. Research also suggests a relationship between racial discrimination and higher blood pressure in African American women due to anger's arousal and its suppression.[27] Clearly, racial and gender contexts affect whether or not people choose to reveal their anger.

Often, though, women experience their anger as presenting a bind. Suppressing anger can affect depression when the stressful situation continues; expressing anger can affect depression when it results in worsening the interpersonal situation. Currently, the physiological relationship of chronic anger arousal and suppression to the biochemistry of depression is not well known. But it is easy to speculate that raised levels of cortisol (occurring during anger), which affect neurotransmitter activity, could be one of the pathways linking anger to depression.

Anger demands positive expression; its function is to regulate relationships, to restore connection, to have an interpersonal effect. Silencing anger eliminates the possibility that ongoing conditions that create the anger will change. With anger gone awry, a vital, energizing force for change is lost. Women feel less sense of confidence and force to affect their relationships, leading to feelings of hopelessness and helplessness at the heart of depression. When the anger of hope—the belief that barriers to connection can be overcome—changes into an anger of despair—the feeling that anger cannot address continuing violations—depression seems inevitable. We can learn from these women's narratives that their positive uses of anger are associated with freedom from depression. Women must have the courage to use anger positively, including leaving damaging relationships, in order to break the link between anger and depression.

Notes

1. John Bowlby uses these phrases in *Separation: Anxiety and anger.*
2. Italicized text refers to the words of the interviewer.
3. M.M. Weissman and E.S. Paykel, *The depressed woman.*
4. Specifics of the study have been reported in D.C. Jack, *Behind the mask* and "Understanding women's anger."
5. Described in D.C. Jack, *Silencing the self,* and D.C. Jack and D. Dill, "The Silencing the self scale."
6. See D.C. Jack, *Silencing the self,* 94–95, 103–107.
7. J.B. Miller, "The construction of anger in women and men," 193.
8. E. Spelman, "Anger and insubordination," 264, 267.

9. See C.E. Ross and M. Van Willigen, "Gender, parenthood, and anger."

10. J. Bowlby, *Loss, sadness and depression*, 247.

11. See J.M. Lohr, L.K. Hamberger, and D. Bonge, "The relationship of factorially validated measures of anger-proneness and irrational beliefs," and B. Fehr, M. Baldwin, L. Collins, S. Patterson, and R. Benditt, "Anger in close relationships: An interpersonal script analysis"; also S.P. Thomas, *Women and anger.*

12. See S.P. Thomas, "Narratives of power and powerlessness: Anger of African American and Caucasian American Women."

13. See B. Fehr et al., "Anger in close relationships."

14. See G.W. Brown, B. Andrews, T. Harris, Z. Adler, and L. Bridge, "Social support, self-esteem and depression"; C. Gilligan, *In a different voice*; D.C. Jack, *Silencing the self*; and J.B. Miller, "The development of women's sense of self."

15. J. Bowlby, *Separation: Anxiety and anger.* The phrases "anger of hope" and "anger of despair" are his.

16. See a fuller explanation in D.C. Jack, *Behind the mask.*

17. See studies by A. Ali and B. Toner, "Symptoms of depression among Caribbean women Caribbean-Canadian women"; L.M. Duarte and J.M. Thompson, "Sex differences in self-silencing"; L.V. Gratch, M. E. Bassett, and S.L. Attra, "The relationship of gender and ethnicity to self-silencing"; J.R. Page, H.B. Stevens, and S.L. Galvin, "Relationships between depression, self-esteem, and self-silencing behavior"; and by J.M. Thompson, "Silencing the self: Depressive symptomatology and close relationships."

18. See D.C. Jack, *Behind the mask*; "Ways of listening to depressed women"; "Understanding women's anger."

19. In order to include a range of social expectations regarding aggression and anger expression, I chose women from a variety of contexts: politicians, administrators, attorneys, police officers, social workers, teachers, college students, homeless women, legal secretaries, and substance abusers.

20. Using Ethnograph software, each interview was first coded for anger segments by two coders working independently. Segments coded "anger" were then printed out across all the interviews without any identifying subject information. Two additional student coders were assigned the task of coding the anger segments according to categories described in detail in D.C. Jack, "Ways of listening to depressed women." I then examined patterns of anger expression in relation to previously coded women's talk about their depression for the description that follows. Women's patterns of anger expression have been detailed in D.C. Jack, "Understanding women's anger." Here I have examined those anger patterns in relation to women's self-reported depression.

21. See D.C. Jack, "Understanding women's anger" for a fuller analysis.

22. See E. Spelman, "Anger and insubordination."

23. For more on women's angry aggression, see D.C. Jack, *Behind the mask.*

24. See M.M. Weissman and E.S. Paykel, *The depressed woman.*

25. Self-silencing, as described in the first section, includes more than simply silencing anger. Self-silencing refers also to specific images of self in relationship that guide a woman's behaviors and her self-assessment. These images include an understanding of care as self-sacrifice, externalized self-perception (or seeing and judging the self through others' eyes), and the experience of a divided self which comes from presenting a self that feels false in relationship because specific feelings are kept hidden, including anger.

26. See E. McGrath, G.P. Keita, B.R. Strickland, and N.F. Russo, *Women and depression*, for more detail on social conditions as risk factors for women's depression.

27. Nancy Krieger conducted a study with fifty-one African American women and fifty white women, ages twenty–eighty years, who described how they dealt with unfair treatment from others. Among black women, those who stated they usually accepted and kept quiet about unfair treatment were 4.4 times more likely to report hypertension than those who said they took action and talked to others. No clear association between anger expression and hypertension was found among white respondents.

References

Ali, A., & Toner, B.B. (2001). Symptoms of depression among Caribbean women and Caribbean-Canadian women: An investigation of self-silencing and domains of meaning. *Psychology of Women Quarterly, 25*, 175–180.

Bowlby, J. (1973). *Attachment and loss, vol. 2: Separation: Anxiety and anger*. New York: Basic.

Bowlby, J. (1980). *Attachment and loss, vol. 3: Loss, sadness and depression*. New York: Basic.

Brown, G.W., Andrews, B., Harris, T., Adler, Z., & Bridge, L. (1986). Social support, self-esteem and depression. *Psychological Medicine, 16*, 813–831.

Duarte, L.M., & Thompson J.M. (1999). Sex differences in self-silencing. *Psychological Reports, 85*, 145–161.

Fehr, B., Baldwin, M., Collins, L., Patterson, S., & Benditt, R. (1999). Anger in close relationships: An interpersonal script analysis. *Personality and Social Psychology Bulletin, 25*, 299–312.

Gilligan, C. (1982). *In a different voice*. Cambridge: Harvard University Press.

Gratch, L.V., Bassett, M.E., & Attra, S.L. (1995). The relationship of gender and ethnicity to self-silencing and depression among college students. *Psychology of Women Quarterly, 19*, 509–515.

Jack, D.C. (1991). *Silencing the self: Women and depression*. Cambridge: Harvard University Press.

Jack, D.C. (1999a) *Behind the mask: Destruction and creativity in women's aggression*. Cambridge: Harvard University Press.

Jack, D.C. (1999b). Silencing the self: Inner dialogues and outer realities. In T.E. Joiner & J.C. Coyne (Eds.), *The interactional nature of depression: Advances in interpersonal approaches* (pp. 221–240). Washington, DC: American Psychological Association.

Jack, D.C. (1999c). Ways of listening to depressed women in qualitative research: Interview techniques and analysis. *Canadian Psychology, 40,* 91–101.

Jack, D.C. (2000, January). *Reconsidering internalization/externalization as categories for understanding anger: A new phenomenology of women's anger.* Paper presented at the Eleventh International Congress on Women's Health Issues. San Francisco.

Jack, D.C. (2001). Understanding women's anger: A description of relational patterns. *Health Care for Women International, 22,* 385–400.

Jack, D.C., & Dill, D. (1992). The silencing the self scale: Schemas of intimacy associated with depression in women. *Psychology of Women Quarterly, 16,* 97–106.

Krieger, N. (1990). Racial and gender discrimination: Risk factors for high blood pressure? *Social Science and Medicine, 30,* 1273–1281.

Lohr, J.M., Hamberger, L.K., & Bonge, D. (1988). The relationship of factorially validated measures of anger-proneness and irrational beliefs. *Motivation and Emotion, 12,* 171–183.

McGrath, E., Keita, G.P., Strickland, B.R., & Russo, N.F. (1990). *Women and depression: Risk factors and treatment issues.* Washington, DC: American Psychological Association.

Miller, J.B. (1984). The development of women's sense of self. Wellesley, MA: Stone Center Working Paper Series, Paper #12.

Miller, J.B. (1991). The construction of anger in women and men. In J.V. Jordan, A.G. Kaplan, J.B. Miller, I.P. Stiver, & J.L. Surrey (Eds.), *Women's growth in connection: Writings from the Stone Center* (pp. 181–196). New York: Guilford.

Page, J.R., Stevens, H.B., & Galvin, S.L. (1996). Relationships between depression, self-esteem, and self-silencing behavior. *Journal of Social and Clinical Psychology, 15,* 381–396.

Ross, C.E., & Van Willigen, M. (1996). Gender, parenthood, and anger. *Journal of Marriage and the Family, 58,* 572–584.

Spelman, E. (1989). Anger and insubordination. In A. Garry & M. Pearsall (Eds.), *Women, knowledge and reality: Explorations in feminist philosophy* (pp. 263–273). Boston: Unwin Hyman.

Thomas, S.P. (Ed.). (1993). *Women and anger.* New York: Springer.

Thomas, S.P. (2000, January). *Narratives of power and powerlessness: Anger of African American and Caucasian American women.* Paper presented at the Eleventh International Congress on Women's Health Issues. San Francisco.

Thompson, J.M. (1995). Silencing the self: Depressive symptomatology and close relationships. *Psychology of Women Quarterly, 19,* 337–353.

Weissman, M.M., & Paykel, E.S. (1974). *The depressed woman: A study of social relationships.* Chicago: University of Chicago Press.

4

■　　■　　■　　■　　■　　■　　■　　■　　■

"Imprisoned in My Own Prison"

*A Relational Understanding of Sonya's
Story of Postpartum Depression*

Natasha S. Mauthner

When you're in the worst part of this thing you're almost paralyzed. . . .
It's like in one of the books I read recently it says when you have a baby
it's like a bag of sand has been deposited outside your front door . . .
and the ones that have settled down with their babies then burrow out
through this sand. . . . I thought that described very well the postnatal
depression. It was like, you know, there were sandbags on each door
and even though I knew I could open them and walk out I didn't.

IT WAS EARLY IN MARCH when I visited Sonya in her home in a
rural village in England.[1] My interview with her lasted six hours and was
spread over two meetings, a week apart. She described the year-long depression she had been experiencing since her daughter was six months old.
Her sense of paralysis, of being locked into a lonely and isolated world, was
a recurring theme. Depression, she said, was like being "imprisoned in my
own prison." Even though she wanted to confide her feelings, her sense of
shame and fear of moral condemnation prevented her from reaching out.
Instead, Sonya told me, she put on a "mask" and "played the role" of the

coping mother. "I can act if you like," she said, "I can appear okay to the rest of the world even though I feel terrible inside."

Sonya's silence echoes a much more pervasive cultural silence surrounding the difficulties of motherhood and postpartum depression.[2] Her efforts to conceal her feelings of depression are not surprising given that society idealizes and romanticizes motherhood and readily condemns women who fall short of the ideals. Motherhood is still overwhelmingly depicted in images of joy, serenity, and contentment. As Sonya explained, the message within pregnancy and childcare advice books is "Having a baby is wonderful *but* as a footnote you might get postnatal depression." Postpartum depression is a taboo topic and there is a reluctance, among many health professionals, relatives, and friends, to discuss this form of depression which affects one mother in ten in Western societies.[3]

This individual and collective silence that Sonya described dominates women's stories of postpartum depression. Sonya is one of many women I have interviewed in Britain and North America about their experiences of motherhood and postpartum depression.[4] Being depressed, these women told me, was like being stuck in a dark space, a "tunnel," a "cage," a "box," a "great big hole" they could not climb out of. Not only did they feel that society was hostile to their difficulties, but mothers themselves could be very protective of the ideal of motherhood, preferring not to admit their own vulnerabilities to one another. According to these women, the lived reality of motherhood was a far cry from cultural representations; and this gulf between their expectations and experiences of motherhood left them with a deep sense of personal failure and shame.

Although I explore in greater detail the particularities of Sonya's story of postpartum depression here, this chapter is not simply about one individual woman. Each woman's experience of motherhood and postpartum depression is unique, but taken together women's stories reveal many common themes. By focusing on Sonya as a case study, I wish to illustrate both her individual circumstances as well as broader issues that recur across women's stories of postpartum depression.

Choosing Sonya as a Case Study

I have chosen Sonya as a case study for several reasons. Sonya was a talkative person who had thought and read a lot about postpartum depression and had much to say about it. She was analytical and insightful about her depression, and I learned a great deal from her about postpartum depression, not only by hearing about her experience but perhaps more importantly by benefiting from her own analysis of what she was going through.

My interview with Sonya was among the longest I conducted. This was partly because she had few relatives or friends she felt comfortable confiding in. It was also because, as many women explained, I was the first person to express an interest in, and explicitly ask them about, an aspect of their lives they felt was silenced and condemned by society and the people around them. I was prepared to listen to them and give them time, space, and permission to tell their stories. The relatively unstructured nature of the interview also provided an opportunity for women to talk at length about their experiences. I began each interview with an open question: "Perhaps you would like to begin by telling me a bit about what motherhood has been like for you." This question created an open space for women and usually prompted a lengthy monologue in which I was a responsive listener. I then used an interview guide to encourage women to further elaborate on certain issues, or to address new questions.[5]

My status as a twenty-something woman without children may also have given women greater freedom in recounting their experiences in that I was not another mother to whom they would be tempted to compare themselves. While my lack of experience as a mother may have left them feeling that my understanding of their lives was partial and remained at an intellectual rather than experiential level, it may also have freed them to speak more openly about their thoughts and feelings in the knowledge that I would not be able to evaluate and judge them against my own experiences and practices as a mother.

Developing a Relational Understanding of Postpartum Depression

Although this chapter focuses on Sonya's story, it is my telling of her story. In reducing and making sense of six hours of interview material, I have made decisions about which elements of her story to highlight and which to edit out. In my interpretation I have attempted as much as possible to stay close to her words, sentiments, and analyses, but I have also drawn on a particular body of theory to guide my interpretations, namely "relational psychology."[6]

Relational psychology has been described as "one of the most influential strands of feminist social psychology today."[7] It grows out of over two decades of research and clinical work predominantly with girls and women, but increasingly with boys and men, in the United States. Relational theorists question traditional theories of human development, in which separation, individuation, and independence are seen as the hallmarks of adult development, maturity, and health.[8] Instead, they argue that women experience themselves fundamentally as relational, connected, and embedded in a web of intimate social relations. Identity is defined in a context of intimacy, care, and relationship.[9] Jean Baker Miller notes that "women's sense of self becomes very much organized around being able to make, and then to maintain, affiliations and relationships."[10] Other aspects of subjectivity such as creativity, autonomy, and assertion are seen to develop within this primary context in which relationships are the central, organizing feature of women's development.[11]

Theories of "normal" development implicitly or explicitly contain within them theories of "psychopathology." Within classical theories, psychological problems are generally seen to arise when a person fails to separate from others and become an independent and autonomous human being. Women with psychological problems have tended to be seen as too "dependent" and insufficiently individuated and autonomous.[12] From a relational perspective, psychological problems result from a sense of "disconnection" from oneself, other people, and the surrounding world.[13] The experience of disconnection occurs when, for different reasons, a person cannot participate in a responsive relationship, the surrounding relational context is unresponsive, or a person feels her or his experience does not resonate with cultural norms and expectations.[14] For example, a recurring theme within relational writings concerns the sense of disconnection girls and women experience when they come under pressure to conform to cultural standards and norms of femininity and womanhood.[15]

A relational approach opened up a space for me to theorize postnatal depression as a relational problem involving interpersonal and cultural "disconnections." Depressed women feel their experiences of motherhood are not reflected in other mothers' experiences or cultural representations of motherhood.[16] Their sense of difference and deviance leaves them feeling cut off from the world and unable to confide their emotions in other people. This dual emphasis on the cultural context and interpersonal relationships constitutes the core of this "relational" understanding of postpartum depression. Women's depression, I suggest, is intimately linked to cultural ideas about what it means to be a "good" woman and mother; to gendered expectations of mothers and fathers; and to broader societal conditions which support and reinforce this gendered division of roles and responsibilities (for example, poor provision of public and private daycare facilities; limited family-friendly, parental and paternity leave policies). I also argue that it is within the context of women's interpersonal relationships that these cultural and gendered norms and expectations take on meaning and define women's understanding of motherhood.

Listening to Sonya's Story

"I Was Trying to Be the Perfect Mother"

Sonya had worked for fifteen years before she and her husband decided to have a child. She became pregnant at the age of thirty-seven. The birth was complicated, eventually leading to an emergency caesarean, but she did not experience it as traumatic. She thoroughly enjoyed the time she spent in hospital and the first six months of Suzie's life. When Suzie was six months old, Sonya's state of mind and emotions suddenly changed. The catalyst for this change was Suzie's growing independence. Suzie was an easy baby. As she got older, she became more willful, active, and mobile. Although Suzie's behavior was typical for her age, Sonya blamed her daughter for behaving badly because she did not conform to her expectations of her:

> I could feel panic rising up in my stomach if she wouldn't put her coat on to go out, if she cried a bit. . . . It was all these exaggerated feelings of not being in control and panic . . . as soon as she did anything that was not what I expected. I expected her to be like a robot, you know, I'd dress her, she'd put her arms up and I mean that's not reality. If she wants to run around a bit before she puts her nappy [diaper] back on then that's normal. But to me, I was thinking "She shouldn't be doing this, she should have her nappy on now" and it was almost like when a housewife is obsessionally tidy. It was like

an obsession about "She will always look clean, she will always eat her dinner without a spot going on the you know." It was almost that sort of, I'm imposing standards on her that are much much too high and I was trying to fulfill them and making myself feel ill.

When I met her, Sonya was still depressed and on antidepressant medication. Despite her striking insights into her depression—and her apparent awareness that her image of the serene and calm mother and baby was "part of the fantasy that made me ill"—she struggled to let go of her high standards and expectations. As she tried desperately to live up to her ideals, but continued in her mind to fall short of them, she condemned herself more and more for failing not only as a mother, but as a human being:

> It's like if someone comes for a cup of coffee . . . when you're ill you think "Well I have to clean the house from top to bottom so they can sit and have a cup of coffee." Do you understand? And this obsession drives you. . . . I'd be almost looking in the corners of the room and thinking "God, it's dirty down there, I feel really depressed because there's a piece of fluff down there." Can you imagine feeling like that? And it's *stupid* but it's what you feel. I used to think "The kitchen floor is dirty therefore I'm a terrible person, which goes to prove that, you know, I'm even worse than I thought I was." You know, you're *crucifying* yourself all the time. . . . When you're in the illness everything is the end of the world. It's black and white, good and bad. "You were bad, you didn't do the cooking right, you didn't socialize enough, you didn't make enough witty sparkling conversation," you know, as soon as someone's gone you're saying to yourself, "You're bad, you're bad, you didn't do this, you didn't do that."

This relentless self-criticism is commonly expressed by women experiencing postpartum depression. Other scholars have similarly noted the moral and condemnatory dimension of depression. Most notably, in an article on depression or what he termed "melancholia" first published in 1917, Sigmund Freud notes that "In the clinical picture of melancholia, dissatisfaction with the self on moral grounds is far the most outstanding feature."[17] More recently, in her North American study of depression in women, Dana Jack detected the presence of an internalized moral voice within women's accounts. She termed this voice the "Over-Eye" because of its surveillant, vigilant, and moral quality. The Over-Eye, she notes, carries a patriarchal flavor both in its collective viewpoint about what is "good" and "right" for a woman and in its willingness to condemn women's feelings when they depart from expected "shoulds," and from cultural standards, norms, expectations, and imperatives. Jack also describes an inner division and two-voice dialogue in women's narratives of depression between this moral voice and what she terms the voice of the "I," the voice that speaks from experience and knows from observation. Depression, she notes, is associated with an inability to believe and legitimate the voice of the "I," and act on its values.[18]

Jack's analysis echoes the inner dialogue and struggle I heard depressed women speak about. Sonya described her depression as a state of constant "*mental* strife and fighting with yourself." During the depression, she said, "there's too much dialogue going on with yourself and you believe what you're saying because you only know you." She felt torn between two voices, and two parts of herself, which offered competing perspectives on her life. One voice told her what she should be doing—"I must put on a good face. I must always be marvelously dressed. Suzie must always behave well"—while another voice questioned these imperatives. For example, she felt a constant pressure to provide intellectual stimulation and emotional reassurance for Suzie even though another part of her realized it was unrealistic to impose such expectations on herself:

> In the past I've thought you know "God I should be sitting down reading a book with her, cuddling her, holding her." But they need space, you know. I'm trying to be *easier* on myself and say "Well so what? She's playing in the corner on her own. My main job is to make sure that she doesn't fall off her chair and crack her skull open. . . . I'm here to keep her safe." . . . I keep putting this pressure on myself to be "The Intellectual Mother," to hothouse her . . . and I think well I don't particularly have all those skills anyway. . . . I always have this thing, "Am I giving her enough," but I mean they don't need bombarding twenty-four hours a day, do they?

Sonya simultaneously questioned, and felt pressure to conform to, a cultural ideal of motherhood that Sharon Hays calls "the ideology of intensive mothering." This is a gendered, child- rather than parent-centered model of child rearing in which women are encouraged to devote their time, energy, and resources to raising their children.[19] Sonya's aspirations to be "a perfect mother" also stemmed from experiences earlier in her life. She came from a working-class background and was among the first in her family to go to university. However, she did not complete her studies and left university with a deep sense of failure. Sonya also expressed shame about her background. She had spent much of her life in the shadow of her working-class roots, trying to escape them by excelling at being middle-class. Striving for recognition was tied to her class and gender. She had spent her life "trying to please everybody," trying to be a "good" woman:

> I'm constantly striving for recognition for things that I do without getting the peace, that's the problem. I'm *driven, driven* by wanting people to say "Isn't she successful, doesn't she do this well," but I don't internalize the praise. . . . I'm insatiable for praise and recognition and . . . I'm on a treadmill of constantly trying to please everybody for them to think "I'm a jolly good person" you know all the bad things a woman does 'cos of conditioning.

Sonya's preoccupation with trying to be "the best mother of all time" was another manifestation of her need for approval and validation as a human being. Her strivings as a mother, however, appeared more extreme partly because she felt devalued in this role. At some level, she felt that "just" being a mother did not justify her existence. In order to feel a sense of moral worth, she felt she had to be an "exceptional mother" and have an "exceptional child." Sonya was struggling to give value and meaning to what is devalued by society.

"I Wasn't Being True to Myself"

Sonya's thoughts and feelings about combining motherhood with paid work provide a stark illustration of how women's internalization of the idealization and devaluation of motherhood can negatively affect their experiences of motherhood. When Suzie was six months old, Sonya's friends with babies the same age started to return to their jobs and careers, and she started to question her identity and role as mother. It was around this time that she began to feel depressed. The return to work by other mothers led her to question many of her assumptions about motherhood and expectations of herself, including her ideas about having to be the sole caregiver for Suzie. She felt that trying to live up to her ideal of "the stay-at-home mother" was beginning to "damage" her, but she could not let go of it. Devoting her identity and time to the care of her child represented, for Sonya, the epitome of motherhood; it was what she grew up with and what she came to expect of herself:

> I suppose if you look back to my mother I was thinking that, you know, once I have a baby then I'm no longer the business woman I'm you know the person who should always be there with the hugs and does the ironing. And I was almost pushing the rest of me out of the way saying "Okay, I had those skills but those are not useful in what I'm doing now," you know. I wanted to revel in being at home and doing the housework and this, that and the other but I wasn't really being true to myself.

Sonya recognized that she may be happier combining motherhood with paid work, but she also felt pressure to look after Suzie herself. In the following passage we hear how she alternated between competing voices and positions on this issue:

> Sometimes I think if I hadn't been ill, would I have gone to work quicker possibly and maybe felt happier? Because it's more my natural personality to have part work, part Suzie but I kept thinking, "No, if I'm going to do this mother thing properly, I'm going to be at home, I'm going to watch *Neighbors* [soap opera], I'm going to make jam and I'm going to go to the local play-groups." What I did was again sort of sweep the business woman under the carpet and say, "Ah, but I'm this now" but by denying the skills there, right, I was harming myself. . . . I think I damage myself by trying to shut that off. . . . I was intent on this is my big sacrifice, this is me changing my life style for the good of Suzie and pushing my own needs completely down to the bottom of the bag . . . which is a stupid thing to do but that's what I did because I thought . . . "I will be the best mother of all time," you know, like people do and then they start putting pressure on themselves because of unrealistic expectations.

In trying to live up to a certain ideal of motherhood, Sonya was denying the person that *she* was. Although she wanted to regain her identity as a business woman, she found it difficult to authorize these feelings because she was caught between a confusing array of internal and external voices. Her childhood images of motherhood, her culturally derived beliefs about what "good" mothers should do, and the cultural idealization of motherhood compelled her to devote herself exclusively to Suzie's care. On the other hand, the "business woman" in her, the return to work by other mothers, the cultural devaluation of motherhood, her husband's apparent devaluation of what she does as a mother (see below), and her need for recognition led her to question the value and sufficiency of her life as a mother. What was striking about Sonya's story was how difficult it was for her to know what she wanted and who she was amidst these competing pressures. She was so concerned about what other people would think of her that she no longer had a clear sense of what was good for her.

"I Was Left on My Own Too Much by My Husband"

Sonya's struggle to value herself was made worse by the fact that her husband Johnie valued neither her job as a mother nor her voluntary work because neither were financially remunerated. Inevitably, Johnie's attitude began to affect how she felt about herself:

> Occasionally I think "Well, he doesn't ask me what I do during the day therefore it's no surprise that I don't value it," do you see what I mean? As soon as he comes in I am ready to give *him* comfort because he has a bad time . . . I wish he would say to me "Well what have you done today?" . . . I mean he's aware that I do go out . . . but he doesn't know if I'm going to lunch with Janet or whether I go to a play group or you know. So I suppose to me that time has no value, it's starting to have no value to me because it has no meaning to him.

Sonya's relationship with her husband was difficult partly because his words and behavior reinforced the cultural ideals and expectations of motherhood she was striving both to fulfill and resist.

Sonya had known Johnie for fifteen years and been married to him for twelve. Until they had Suzie both had worked hard and long hours. Johnie ran his own company where Sonya used to work. For years, they shared a similar lifestyle that was dominated by work. After having Suzie, Sonya felt conflicting emotions about Johnie. She wanted to accept him as he was but she was disappointed by his lack of domestic involvement: "He's not the textbook . . . father who becomes totally involved and as soon as he comes home from work you know picks up the baby." Sonya hoped that Johnie would turn into a "new father," even though she questioned and resisted this ideal. For example, she wanted him to be an attentive, caring birth partner while also challenging the notion that the husband is necessarily the support figure women want when they are in labor. Sonya felt let down more generally by Johnie's apparent lack of interest and involvement in their daughter. However, she also tried to deny her disappointment, and her depression seemed connected to the way she kept fighting her feelings. For example, she said she was not upset by Johnie's failure to take any time off work after his daughter was born, but her words suggest otherwise. When I asked her whether she would have liked Johnie to take some time off, she says:

> Yes, yes so that he could have hands on caring for Suzie and get to know her if you like. But I mean the day I had Suzie he went back to work with champagne. . . . I didn't mind him going back to work. I didn't feel "Oh this is great, I've just had a baby and you're leaving me now" because, you know, I was devoting time to Suzie, and he'd done his bit. But he never thought, you know, "Shall I take three or four days off." He might have taken the odd day but it wasn't a chunk of time, you know, "This is the time I'm taking to get to know Suzie." But he got to know Suzie well, I mean there's no question that I look after her and he just passes through okay? I don't want to give that impression. I mean you know he'd do anything for her and if you like he's translating the effort of his work into care for her, do you see what I mean?

Sonya explained that having Suzie had hardly affected Johnie's lifestyle or daily routine. He left for work at seven o'clock, came home at nine in the evening, and often spent the weekend playing golf. Sonya, however, had radically altered her life since becoming a mother. She felt she had to obliterate the person she once was, deny her own needs and identity, and become a selfless, self-sacrificing mother. Their different and gendered responses to parenthood became a critical point of tension within their relationship:

After having Suzie I think my lifestyle changed a lot more than his. And I think that was one of the main things, that I was accepting a complete obliteration of what I was doing before, you know, to care for Suzie. And Johnie was changing his behavior slightly . . . but still I mean on a Saturday morning if he wants to watch his favorite TV program he'll watch it and he still reads the paper even if we're in bed, me and Johnie and Suzie together, he still *tries* to read the paper. Whereas a mother gives up reading the paper, doesn't she? She gives up watching the TV program she wants to watch you know. And he'll say "Well I want to go off and play a round of golf" and I'll think "Well he hasn't been with us all week. Why does he want to go and play golf?" you know, that sort of thing. He still does what he's always done.

Sonya's feelings about Johnie's behavior as a father were mixed and confused. She knew he was a "workaholic" and expected he would not be a very involved father, and this was partly why she put off having children for many years. She nevertheless struggled to accept his lifestyle, particularly his long working hours which she linked to her depression:

When I was first ill part of the thing going on in my mind is that if you like, he let down his part of the bargain slightly . . . and I believed I was working in an impossible environment. . . . My job seemed to be an endurance test if you like because this baby was relying on me. And . . . I started thinking "Well I'm filling in the day because I know Johnie isn't going to be back till a certain time." . . . It'd be six o'clock and then I'd think "Okay isn't this the bit where the father comes in now and picks up Suzie and plays with her for an hour and bathes her and you know generally gets to know her and I'm looking on as the proud mother" . . . and she's getting a balanced caring whereas me, you know, I'd been ground down a bit. . . . Yeah I feel I was left on my own too much by my husband.

By working long hours Sonya felt that Johnie failed to appreciate the physical and emotional exhaustion of looking after a young child all day, and her need for a break and time to herself. Johnie's behavior also reinforced the cultural pressure Sonya felt to devote herself exclusively to looking after her daughter:

I mean we love Suzie dearly but like me and Johnie we don't want to be with each other all day do we? And even with a baby there's got to be that sort of "Right you're separate to me." . . . I've always longed for that time when I can say to Johnie "Here's Suzie," I hate the expression "I've had the baby all day" 'cos it sounds as if you can't wait to get rid of them but you've got to be realistic and think well, what if the baby's been crying or grizzly and you've been giving them a lot of support and tenderness and you're a bit sort of worn out now and it's your turn to give them this support and tenderness. But I could never say "Here is Suzie," you know, "I'm *me*, I'm *me* for an hour. I'm going to sit in the bath, here she is." I've never done that with him and I think that did put pressure on me to get obsessional about "I'm the only one that looks after her" you know I think that did make it hard. . . . It just loaded the dice a bit more you know on me feeling run down, utterly depended on. . . . I'd wake up at seven in the morning and think "Well Johnie will be home at eight tonight so I'm filling the time for thirteen hours, just me and Suzie."

Sonya struggled to define motherhood in her own terms and to convince herself that being a loving mother did not entail a twenty-four-hour presence and mother-child fusion. In her account, Johnie's attitude and his unchanging daily habits and rituals made it difficult for her to validate this point of view. His prolonged absences from home during the day and at weekends left her confused about what she could realistically and legitimately expect of herself and him.

"Imprisoned in My Own Prison"

A recurring theme within Sonya's interview was her desire to talk to people about her feelings of depression and her knowledge that this would help her recovery. However, she felt the individuals around her were not prepared to listen. When she tried talking to Johnie at the end of the working day his response was: "I don't want to hear all this." Gradually, Sonya withdrew and found it increasingly difficult to confide in people, even in those whom she suspected might have been supportive and sympathetic. For example, although she wanted to confide in her best friend Clare, her fear of rejection prevented her from doing so:

I'd love to sit [Clare] down here and tell her the whole lot, and then, if you like, in my book, I'd expect her to walk out and say "You're a terrible person, I never want to see you again." But she won't do that, but that's what my brain is telling me people will do, that they'll say, "My God, we thought you were okay, but you know you're telling us all this now." But people are not like that, are they, they don't say, "You are dysfunctional therefore we don't want to know you," but that's how I feel inside. . . . If you like, if I open up and show them that core in the middle, are they going to stab it and say "Ugh." . . . They're not going to say "Well fine, you're still you, this is part of you, this is an experience you're going through"—yes, it's the fear of rejection when they know the full story.

Sonya changed her public persona in order to fit in with what she believed others wanted and expected of her. She wore a mask and disguised her feelings. She talked about "being able to convince friends that I was alright"— "To 97 percent of the world I was a very strong, confident person." This outward presentation of herself was driven by her fear that if other people found out she was depressed, they would judge, criticize, and ultimately reject her. She feared that by being herself she would lose the friendship and respect of others. Paradoxically then, Sonya concealed her thoughts and feelings to gain approval and maintain a semblance of relationships with other people. Yet this also left her feeling alone and depressed.

Sonya hid her depression from other people in order to protect herself but also as a way of denying that this depression was happening to her. She realized that revealing her feelings and having them accepted by others would in turn help her to accept herself for who she was, despite what she saw as her imperfections. But although she knew that reaching out to others, and trusting that they would listen to her and be there for her, was a critical initial step in the journey out of depression, she felt she could not make this leap of faith:

My psychotherapist says, "What would it hurt if you were yourself, if you slumped in the corner and said 'Look, I'm ill, this is how I am, take me or leave me.'" I can't do that. Would that be so terrible? And in my mind, yes. I'd think—well none of those people will want to know me when I'm well because they've seen me so bad, you see? . . . Which makes the illness go on longer. . . . I'm accepting points now from . . . the psychotherapist. She is saying, "If you pretend it didn't happen, or just hide from it or whatever, it's not going to go away, because if you don't walk into it and accept that this is an experience that I have to face . . . then it's gonna linger on." . . . And like now, when I said to her I was feeling so much better and I want to put this under the carpet a bit, I'm already trying to do that. . . . As soon as I'm well for five minutes I'm thinking, "Right, it was bad but we don't want to talk about that now." But that's denying it, d'you see? But I find it painful to say, "I've been through it, it wasn't a nice experience, but it's made me stronger." I know all those things logically, but in my heart of hearts, in a way, I wanna say, "No, that wasn't me. . . . This is me," which is not positive for recovery, is it?

"I Wanted Somewhere I Could Sit Down and Say 'This Is How I Am'"

Sonya had taken antidepressants for a year when I met her. Like many women, she felt unhappy about taking medication. She felt she should have the moral strength to manage without antidepressants. She feared addiction and felt debilitated by the side effects. The antidepressants dulled her feelings. They kept her deep feelings of despair and hopelessness at bay, for which she was grateful, but she felt they were not helping her toward recovery. Sonya really wanted to talk about her feelings but struggled to find a conducive and receptive environment in which she felt she could open up and freely discuss what she was going through. As we saw above, she gave up talking to her husband and feared confiding in her friends. She tried talking to her doctor, but felt constrained by the short ten-minute appointments:

> The doctor's job is to give you the medication, to keep an eye on you, to listen to you every two weeks and then decide whether you're ready to . . . decrease the medication. I'm not saying she's just a pill-pusher but I appreciate it's not the medium to talk for a long time.

Sonya was also unhappy about the lack of support from her health visitor (nurse).[20] During the summer, when her depression was at its worst, she felt very withdrawn and isolated. She wanted to see her health visitor on a regular basis, and she needed her help to find appropriate sources of support:

> In that isolation in the summer I wasn't reaching out and that's why the health visitor was the one who'd have to come in and say "I'll reach out for you." Do you understand? "Either I'll come myself or someone will come round and talk to you." But because you're so numbed you can't take the initiative, therefore you can't reach out yourself.

The health visitor, however, hardly visited her. Four months before I met her, Sonya started seeing a psychotherapist privately. She went once a week and felt this was one of the few places she could be herself and talk openly:

> I wanted somewhere I could sit down and say, "This is how I am," and for someone to say "Okay," you know they wouldn't judge it, they wouldn't criticize me for maybe not trying hard enough. They would just say "Okay, you're in it but one day it will end." . . . At the end of the day I mean I went to the psychotherapist simply because I wasn't getting any help anywhere else. I go there every Tuesday morning without Suzie. I sit and have a cup of coffee. I talk for fifty minutes, I pay £25 for that privilege and come away and feel better every time.

While the psychotherapy was helping her, Sonya wanted to go to a postpartum depression support group. She felt she had reached a point where she needed to hear other women's stories, and share her feelings with a wider group of women:

> The ultimate reason for going is not that we're all sitting there in tears but it's like any group where everybody's got something in common—you feel that there's no holds barred. You can say "I did this. Isn't it terrible?" and somebody else will say "But I did *that*," you know. And it reaffirms the fact that you're not isolated and you're not alone and that's the main point of why I want to go and at this point I feel strong enough to talk. I'm still a bit scared of breaking down, you know this thing about well it'll be weakness, but at least you'll be in a warm, sympathetic response.

For several months Sonya looked for a group but could not find one. The week before I met her, she saw the health visitor from a neighboring village who informed her about a group running there. She described her sense of relief when she found out about the group, and in doing so pointed to the important role health professionals can play in referring women to appropriate support services:[21]

> She said there's a meeting of people over at Milton tonight for postnatal depression and I said to her, "Well I should be in that, you know, I should be there." She said, "Well okay go to the next one" . . . and in three minutes she'd given me more help than the other health visitor had given me in six months. . . . The moment the health visitor said the group *existed*, then I felt a hundred times better you know it lifted, it lifted off me because there was a solution and all these months I've thought, well you know what I want, isn't there, you know, like a self-help group?

Like Sonya, most of the women I interviewed stressed the importance of postpartum depression support groups, which they saw as offering receptive, validating, and accepting environments in which they could safely disclose their feelings. They wanted to talk to other women who would listen and understand because they were going, or had been, through similar experiences. Women valued these support groups because they made them feel less alone and isolated in their feelings. Realizing that other mothers experienced similar feelings also enabled them to re-evaluate their own competence and moral worth, and question normative constructions of motherhood. In this sense, these relationships with other mothers enabled them to resist and redefine cultural prescriptions and representations of motherhood.[22]

At the time I met her, Sonya was beginning to realize that her ability to look at other mothers in nonidealized terms would help her overcome her feelings of depression. "Instead of being hard on myself," she said, "I should think 'Well look at her. She looks fine but you know maybe she's got problems.' And I think this is part of the recovery process, being able to do that." The mothers who had recovered spoke about moving beyond their projected and idealized images of motherhood and being able to build more realistic expectations of themselves and their children, and more realistic ideas about how other mothers cope.

An intriguing question here is whether talking to other mothers with similar feelings earlier on may have prevented women like Sonya from becoming depressed in the first place. Research studies and anecdotal accounts suggest that support groups that enable women to talk to one another, and give them "permission" to express negative or ambivalent feelings, can prevent postpartum depression.[23] This kind of evidence points to the role of prenatal classes in providing a forum in which mothers can talk to each other, learn from each other, and form friendships that might continue into the postnatal period. Prenatal classes can also inform women that sharing their feelings with another mother could reassure them. Extending prenatal classes into the postpartum period may also be valuable. Providing continuity in the women's relationships with other mothers, and with the health professionals running the groups, can provide a "safe" environment within which women may find it easier to discuss their negative or ambivalent feelings. Discussion of their feelings as they experience them may help them accept and come to terms with their emotions, which in turn may prevent these feelings from becoming worse and turning into more severe forms of depression.[24]

Learning from Sonya's Story

Sonya's story reveals the lucid and articulate quality of mothers' accounts and how much we can learn about postpartum depression by eliciting and attending closely to their words. One of the themes to emerge from Sonya's story, which was a common thread across other mothers' accounts, was a striving for perfection. Women who had always set high standards for themselves said they continued to do so when they became mothers. They expected perfection from themselves and their children. Their compulsion to be "perfect mothers" must be understood within the context of the cultural devaluation of motherhood. Despite the fact that Western cultures idealize motherhood, the high value placed on paid work in societies such as Britain and the United States compelled these women to justify devoting time to the unpaid work of motherhood. Just being a mother was not enough—they had to be perfect and exceptional mothers. The conflict women like Sonya experienced between the perfect mother they wanted to be and the mother they perceived themselves to be was at the heart of their depression. This discord occurred in relation to various aspects of their mothering experiences, such as childbirth, breast-feeding, whether to combine motherhood with paid work, their feelings about their child and about motherhood, and their ability to cope with motherhood and their children. Each mother experienced a different set of conflicts reflecting her own notion of what it means to be a "good" or "ideal" mother. For example, Sonya's ideal mother was one who stayed at home to look after the children; devoted herself almost exclusively to the physical, emotional, social, and intellectual care and development of her child; had a "perfect" and immaculate home and baby; and felt totally fulfilled in her life and role as mother. For Vera, another mother I interviewed, being a good mother entailed bonding and loving your child from birth, breast-feeding, not using a pacifier, and keeping a spotless home. Both Sonya and Vera struggled to live up to their individually constructed but culturally derived ideals. Although they questioned these ideals, they nevertheless interpreted their inability to fulfill them as a deep and personal failure.

The moral standards Sonya and other mothers used to judge their behavior and their feelings came from at least two sources: the surrounding culture and their interpersonal relationships. The cultural context is one in which strong normative prescriptions about "the right way" to be a "good" mother still prevail, while at the same time mothers are told that there is no *one* right way to mother a child.[25] Sonya and other mothers, however, picked up on the idea that there was only one "right" way to be a "good" mother, and constructed notions of "good" mothering in highly rigid ways. They attempted to conform to these norms in part because they were also picking up on the idea that mothers who fail to do so are seen as lacking and inadequate. Within such a context the mothers feared expressing their difficulties and their negative or ambivalent emotions. They feared being judged "bad" mothers, having their children taken away, and possibly being institutionalized.

The ways in which individual mothers interpreted, negotiated, and experienced social and moral norms of motherhood depended in part on their interpersonal relationships, for these were sites where cultural prescriptions could be reinforced in overt and covert ways. Their relationships with other mothers with young children were particularly important because cultural notions of motherhood took on meaning and became concrete for the women through a process of "checking out" their feelings and comparing their experiences with those of other mothers.[26] Pam, for example, struggled physically and emotionally after her daughter's birth. She felt lonely and isolated in her experiences and turned to other mothers seeking reassurance. However, neither her neighbor, who had a similar aged child, nor other mothers she met at a postnatal group appeared to share her emotions. This exacerbated her sense of difference from other mothers, and sense of deviance from cultural ideals.

Relationships with male partners, family, friends, and health professionals were equally important. For women like Sonya, who described receiving little emotional or practical support from their partners, these relationships reinforced their sense of failure and inadequacy. Other women described very positive relationships with their partners whom they found supportive, helpful, and understanding. However, these women still found it difficult to disclose their feelings of ambivalence and depression. They felt that admitting their needs and feelings was a sign of weakness and failure. They also feared burdening their partners, and being misunderstood, rejected and morally condemned. Petra, for example, withheld her depression from her husband despite describing him as supportive and caring. "I could tell him," she said, "It's just that I think he'd never been depressed. He didn't understand depression. . . . So I mean he probably wasn't as understanding as someone that has been depressed would be." Penny described her partner as "a dream husband" who gave her complete practical and emotional support. Nevertheless, she felt that "another mother . . . whose children are the same age, going through the same feelings as you, gives you someone to talk to." Thus, irrespective of the quality of their relationships, the mothers concealed their feelings from partners and other people.[27]

An important question is why, given that mothers live in the same cultural context, some become depressed while others do not. There are likely to be many answers to this question. My research suggests that one reason might be that mothers who do not become depressed do not experience a conflict between their expectations and their experiences of motherhood, either because their expectations are not high or "unrealistic" to begin with, or because their experiences are largely positive ones. A more likely explanation is that the majority of mothers living in Western societies do experience this type of conflict, but resolve it in different ways. Mothers who do not become depressed may find it easier to modify or "let go" of their standards. Their ability to do so is likely to depend on their ability to accept their feelings and discuss these within responsive and nonjudgmental interpersonal, professional, and cultural contexts. Anna, for example, was a mother I interviewed who found motherhood difficult but did not develop postpartum depression. She attributed this largely to her earlier experience of depression as a teenager, and how she learned the importance of accepting rather than fighting her feelings. "You have to have room for your feelings," she explained, "and there are times when you don't feel happy or you feel angry or you feel sad, and . . . you shouldn't pretend that you don't feel those feelings." Depression, she said, was "having the same feelings that I was having [after the baby was born] but really not being able to . . . come to terms with them." "Being depressed," she concluded, "is feeling low and feeling really bad about feeling low."

The birth of a child is likely to create some problems and ambivalent feelings for most women. However, for a combination of individual, interpersonal, and cultural reasons, women may find it more or less difficult to acknowledge and disclose their feelings. Some may struggle to accept their feelings and may feel they do not have access to supportive relationships within which to confide. They may withdraw into silence, and their feelings give way to more serious and debilitating feelings of depression. Others may come to terms with their feelings and discuss them early on. Consequently, there might be a critical time of withdrawal and silence which marks the transition from feelings of low mood to feelings of depression. If health professionals, mothers and their relatives and friends are aware of this critical period, if mothers are given time and permission to talk about their feelings early on and provided with supportive, nonjudgmental and accepting relationships within which to do so, postpartum depression might be prevented. This relational reformulation of postpartum depression points to the importance of creating cultural, social, and interpersonal contexts in which the stresses and strains of motherhood, and the *range* of feelings mothers experience, are accepted and acceptable.

Notes

I am deeply indebted to the mothers who agreed to take part in this study and share their experiences with me. Financial assistance for the research in Britain was provided by a doctoral studentship from the Medical Research Council. In the United States, my work was supported by an International Fellowship from the American

Association of University Women, and Wingate and Fulbright Scholarships. I am grateful to Martin Richards and Carol Gilligan for supporting and encouraging my research. I also wish to thank Janet Stoppard and Linda McMullen for their guidance and patience.

1. Sonya's real name, and that of her husband and daughter, have been changed for reasons of confidentiality.

2. The terms "postpartum depression" and "postnatal depression" have the same meaning, the former being used in the United States and the latter in Britain.

3. See B. Pitt, "'Atypical' depression following childbirth."

4. N.S. Mauthner, *The darkest days of my life: Stories of postpartum depression.*

5. For further details on the methods I have used, see N.S. Mauthner, ibid.

6. For further details on how I used relational theory and methodology see N.S. Mauthner, "'It's a woman's cry for help': A relational perspective on post-partum depression"; "'Feeling low and feeling really bad about feeling low': Women's experiences of motherhood and postpartum depression"; *The darkest days of my life*; and N.S. Mauthner and A. Doucet, "Reflections on a voice-centred relational method: Analysing maternal and domestic voices." Also see N.S. Mauthner, O. Parry, and K. Backett-Milburn, "The data are out there, or are they? Implications for archiving and revisiting qualitative data"; and N.S. Mauthner and A. Doucet, "Reflexive accounts and accounts of reflexivity in qualitative data analysis" for a lengthier discussion of reflexive issues in my research.

7. S. Wilkinson, *Feminist social psychologies: International perspectives*, 13.

8. See J.B. Miller, *Toward a new psychology of women*, and C. Gilligan, "In a different voice: Women's conceptions of self and of morality" and *In a different voice.*

9. C. Gilligan, *In a different voice.*

10. J.B. Miller, *Toward a new psychology*, 83.

11. J.L. Surrey, *The "self-in-relation": A theory of women's development.*

12. D.C. Jack, *Silencing the self: Women and depression.*

13. I.P. Stiver and J.B. Miller, *From depression to sadness in women's psychother-apy*; D.C. Jack, ibid., L.M. Brown and C. Gilligan, *Meeting at the crossroads: Women's psychology and girls' development*; J.M. Taylor, C. Gilligan, and A. Sullivan, *Between voice and silence: Women and girls, race and relationships.*

14. J.B. Miller, I.P. Stiver, J.V. Jordan and J.L. Surrey, "The psychology of women: A relational approach."

15. A.G. Kaplan, *The "self-in-relation": Implications for depression in women*; I.P. Stiver and J.B. Miller, ibid.; Jack, *Silencing the self*; C. Steiner-Adair, "The body politic"; A. Willard, "Cultural scripts of mothering."

16. Relational aspects of women's experiences of postpartum depression have tended to be neglected within existing feminist thinking, in which postpartum depression is linked to the loss of identity, autonomy, independence, power, and paid employment seen to result from the transition to motherhood (P. Nicolson, *Postpartum depression: Psychology, science and the transition to motherhood*; A. Oakley,

Women confined: Towards a sociology of childbirth; P. Romito, *La naissance du premier enfant: Etude psycho-sociale de l'expérience de la maternité et de la dépression post-partum*). See N.S. Mauthner, "'It's a woman's cry for help'"; and "'Feeling low and feeling really bad about feeling low,'" for further details on how a relational perspective on postpartum depression differs from current feminist thinking.

17. S. Freud, "Mourning and melancholia," 157.

18. D.C. Jack, *Silencing the self.*

19. S. Hays, *The cultural contradictions of motherhood.*

20. In Britain, a health visitor is a nurse who has responsibility for the welfare of mothers and children up to the age of five years old, and visits families on a regular basis during pregnancy and in the months following childbirth.

21. N.S. Mauthner, "Postnatal depression: how can midwives help?"

22. N.S. Mauthner, "Postpartum depression: The significance of social contacts between mothers."

23. See J.B. Morris, "Group psychotherapy for prolonged postnatal depression"; S.A. Elliott, M. Sanjack, and T.J. Leverton, "Parent groups in pregnancy: A preventive intervention for postnatal depression?"; J. McKears, "Group support for young mothers"; and C. Jones, "A postpartum support group."

24. N.S. Mauthner, "Postnatal depression: how can midwives help?"

25. H. Marshall, "The social construction of motherhood: An analysis of childcare and parenting manuals"; A. Phoenix and A. Woollett, "Motherhood: Social construction, politics and psychology."

26. N.S. Mauthner, "Postpartum depression: The significance of social contacts between mothers."

27. N.S. Mauthner, "Re-assessing the importance and role of the marital relationship in postpartum depression: Methodological and theoretical implications."

References

Brown, L.M., & Gilligan, C. (1992). *Meeting at the crossroads: Women's psychology and girls' development.* Cambridge: Harvard University Press.

Elliott, S.A., Sanjack, M., & Leverton, T.J. (1988). Parents groups in pregnancy: A preventive intervention for postnatal depression? In B.H. Gottlieb (Ed.), *Marshaling social support: Formats, processes and effects* (pp. 87–110). Newbury Park, CA: Sage.

Freud, S. (1995). Mourning and melancholia. In E. Jones (Ed.), *Collected papers, Volume IV: Papers on metapsychology. Papers on applied psycho-analysis.* London: Hogarth Press.

Gilligan, C. (1977). In a different voice: Women's conceptions of self and of morality. *Harvard Educational Review, 47,* 481–517.

Gilligan, C. (1982). *In a different voice.* Cambridge: Harvard University Press.

Hays, S. (1996). *The cultural contradictions of motherhood*. New Haven: Yale University Press.

Jack, D. (1991). *Silencing the self: Women and depression*. Cambridge: Harvard University Press.

Jones, C. (1984). A postpartum support group. *Birth, 11*, 244.

Kaplan, A.G. (1984). The *"self-in-relation"*: Implications for depression in women. Work in Progress, No. 14, Wellesley, MA: Stone Center Working Paper Series.

Marshall, H. (1991). The social construction of motherhood: An analysis of childcare and parenting manuals. In A. Phoenix, A. Woollett, & E. Lloyd (Eds.), *Motherhood: Meanings, practices and ideologies* (pp. 66–85). London: Sage.

Mauthner, N.S. (1995). Postpartum depression: The significance of social contacts between mothers. *Women's Studies International Forum, 18*, 311–323.

Mauthner, N.S. (1997) Postnatal depression: how can midwives help? *Midwifery, 13*, 163–171.

Mauthner, N.S. (1998a). Re-assessing the importance and role of the marital relationship in postpartum depression: Methodological and theoretical implications. *Journal of Reproductive and Infant Psychology, 16*, 157–175.

Mauthner, N.S. (1998b). "It's a woman's cry for help": A relational perspective on postpartum depression. *Feminism and Psychology, 8*, 325–355.

Mauthner, N.S. (1999). "Feeling low and feeling really bad about feeling low": Women's experiences of motherhood and postpartum depression. *Canadian Psychology, 40*, 143–161.

Mauthner, N.S. (2002). *The darkest days of my life: Stories of postpartum depression*. Cambridge: Harvard University Press.

Mauthner, N.S., & Doucet, A. (1998). Reflections on a voice-centred relational method: Analysing maternal and domestic voices. In J. Ribbens & R. Edwards (Eds.), *Feminist dilemmas in qualitative research: Public knowledge and private lives* (pp. 119–146). London: Sage.

Mauthner, N.S., & Doucet, A. (in press). Reflexive accounts and accounts of reflexivity in qualitative data analysis. *Sociology*.

Mauthner, N.S., Parry, O., & Backett-Milburn, K. (1998). The data are out there, or are they? Implications for archiving and revisiting qualitative data. *Sociology, 32*, 733–745.

McKears, J. (1983). Group support for young mothers. *Health Visitor, 56*, 16.

Miller, J.B. (1986). *Toward a new psychology of women*. London: Penguin Books.

Miller, J.B., Stiver, I.P., Jordan, J.V., & Surrey, J.L. (1994). The psychology of women: A relational approach. In J. Fadiman & R. Frager (Eds.), *Personality and personal growth* (pp. 159–179). New York: Longman.

Morris, J.B. (1987). Group psychotherapy for prolonged postnatal depression. *British Journal of Medical Psychology, 60*, 279–281.

Nicolson, P. (1998). *Postpartum depression: Psychology, science and the transition to motherhood*. London: Routledge.

Oakley, A. (1980). *Women confined: Towards a sociology of childbirth.* Oxford: Martin Robertson.

Phoenix, A., & Woollett, A. (1991). Motherhood: Social construction, politics and psychology. In A. Phoenix, A. Woollett, & E. Lloyd (Eds.), *Motherhood: Meanings, practices and ideologies* (pp. 13–27). London: Sage.

Pitt, B. (1968). "Atypical" depression following childbirth. *British Journal of Psychiatry, 114,* 1325–1335.

Romito, P. (1990). *La naissance du premier enfant: Etude psycho-sociale de l'expérience de la maternité et de la dépression post-partum.* Lausanne: Delachaux and Niestle.

Steiner-Adair, C. (1990). The body politic. In C. Gilligan, N.P. Lyons, & T.J. Hanmer (Eds.), *Making connections: The relational worlds of adolescent girls at Emma Willard School.* Cambridge: Harvard University Press.

Stiver, I.P., & Miller, J.B. (1988). *From depression to sadness in women's psychotherapy.* Work in Progress, No. 36, Wellesley, MA: Stone Center Working Paper Series.

Surrey, J.L. (1985). *The "self-in-relation": A theory of women's development.* Work in Progress, No. 13, Wellesley, MA: Stone Center Working Paper Series.

Taylor, J.M., Gilligan, C., & Sullivan, A. (1995). *Between voice and silence: Women and girls, race and relationships.* Cambridge: Harvard University Press.

Wilkinson, S. (1996). *Feminist social psychologies: International perspectives.* Buckingham, UK: Open University Press.

Willard, A. (1988). Cultural scripts for mothering. In C. Gilligan, J.V. Ward, & J.M. Taylor (Eds.), *Mapping the moral domain: A contribution of women's thinking to psychological theory and education* (pp. 225–243). Cambridge: Harvard University Press.

5

■　　■　　■　　■　　■　　■　　■　　■　　■

Postpartum Depression

Women's Accounts of Loss and Change

Paula Nicolson

It's been more difficult than I thought it would be. It's not being able
to do anything. Not even to put the washing in the washing machine or
cook a meal except when my partner's here.

—Norma

When Jenny was five months old I finished breast-feeding completely
and for a week after that I felt down. I felt as if I had lost some of the
closeness.

—Samantha

BECOMING A MOTHER is expected to be a "happy event" in family
life, and it is assumed that somehow women have the natural ability or in-
stinct to cope with all the challenges of new motherhood. But women's
lives change a great deal during the postpartum period. Although for most
women the changes are positive in the longer term, many feel unprepared
and they lack the support for managing the emotional ups and downs of
new motherhood and the burdens of infant care.

In order to better understand this phenomenon, it is important to attend to the way women *themselves* describe and try to make sense of their

experiences following childbirth and in the first six postpartum months. The fact that a significant number of women routinely become depressed over that period of their lives[1] is frequently portrayed in the scientific literature as a psychological problem, that is, postpartum depression. The implication of the label is that the problem lies within the woman herself. *She* is the one who gets depressed and that is not psychologically or emotionally *normal*.[2] The meaning or interpretation that the women *themselves* might seek to place upon their experiences has been curiously absent from the research or clinical literature until a very few years ago.[3]

What Is Postpartum Depression?

Postpartum depression is still seen by many experts and lay people as distinct both from the social context of childbirth and motherhood and from any other kind of depression.[4] It is frequently described as an irrational, inevitable response to the hormone fluctuations following childbirth.[5] However, there is currently little empirical support among researchers for a biological basis for postpartum depression[6] and although a link has been established between the "maternity blues" and subsequent depression, this link is not considered to be hormonally based.[7]

The research literature on postpartum depression is extensive.[8] Between 1980 and 1990 more than one hundred studies were published[9] and this trend seems to have continued into the twenty-first century. Women's mental health during the postpartum remains an issue that intrigues scientists, but even so, relatively few of them take serious notice of women's own voices. The emphasis and focus of these studies has varied from concern with severe psychiatric illness to clinical depression, "maternity blues"[10] and, most recently, the impact of maternal depression on the family.[11] Notwithstanding this increasing and abundant knowledge, many questions remain unanswered. For example, it is unclear why, if postpartum depression is brought about because of hormone changes at the time of birth as some suggest,[12] considerable numbers of women do *not* get clinically depressed at that stage. Further, are psychological problems following childbirth, from psychosis to mild depression, part of a continuum or a series of different, unrelated conditions?[13] Are there any qualitative differences between depression at this time and other times in a woman's life?[14] Or indeed are there any qualitative differences between postpartum depression and depression suffered by *men* on entering fatherhood?[15]

It is also evident now that socially isolated women[16] from low socioeconomic status backgrounds, who live in poor housing and have marital difficulties,[17] are more likely to experience depression at this stage of their lives than women who have good social support networks and who come from affluent backgrounds.[18] Psychological background, personality factors, and the experience of childbirth itself also have an impact upon a woman's potential vulnerability to depression over the postpartum period.[19] Others have argued that postpartum depression is an individual reaction, on entering motherhood, toward women's role, both in society and the family, in relation to men.[20] Despite the attention of experts, until 1992, neither the Diagnostic and Statistical Manual of the American Psychiatric Association nor the World Health Organization identified postpartum depression as a distinct diagnosis.[21] Clinical practice and popular knowledge about postpartum depression appear to be based on belief, myth, and a body of contentious empirical evidence.[22]

Asking Women about Their Experiences

I initiated a longitudinal study comprising a series of in-depth interviews over the course of the transition to motherhood.[23] The interviews took place during pregnancy and then one, three, and six months after the baby was born.[24] The aim was to enable women to talk about their feelings and moods over this time period. I wanted to find out what the experience of being a mother meant to them. If they did become down or depressed, then why did they think it had happened? And what did *they* think might prevent or alleviate the depression?

The participants (see Table 2) were contacted through several sources (prenatal clinics, health centers, British National Childbirth Trust[25] classes, and personal contacts). These organizations were contacted with a request for women in the last few weeks of their pregnancy to volunteer for the study (details were provided).[26] Recruitment also took the form of "word of mouth" with some of the early volunteers recommending friends, who in turn did the same.

Table 2

Pregnancy, Reproductive, and Social Information

Name	Number of interviews	Weeks pregnant at first interview	Number of previous children	Terminations and miscarriages	Type of delivery	Age	Marital Status	Occupation prior to pregnancy	Occupation after the baby	Partner's occupation
Jane	4	35	0	0	normal	21	single	telephonist	none	machinist
Lynn	4	33	0	0	normal*	31	married	local politics	consultancy	optician
Isobel	4	35	0	0	normal	30	married	dietician	dietician	teacher
Gwen	3	30	0	T**	normal	27	married	secretary	none	contracts manager
Francis	3+	35	1	0	normal	35	married	publisher	publisher	solicitor
Dion	1	36	1	0	-	23	single	shop assistant		driver
Matilda	3+	35	0	0	caesarean	26	married	student	student	student
Samantha	3+	35	0	0	normal	27	married	computer supervisor	computer supervisor	postman
Shirley	4	25	0	2 T	planned induction	35	single	press officer	press officer	antique dealer
Meg	3	33	2	0	normal	33	married	none	none	bank manager
Adrienne	2	22	1	1 M^{M}	normal	30	married	none	none	barrister
Sylvia	4	32	0	0	normal	29	married	antique dealer	none	solicitor

Name	Number of interviews	Weeks pregnant at first interview	Number of previous children	Terminations and miscarriages	Type of delivery	Age	Marital Status	Occupation prior to pregnancy	Occupation after the baby	Partner's occupation
Sharon	4	29	0	0	normal	33	married	none	none	businessman
Penelope	4	32	0	0	premature	41	single	lecturer	lecturer	surveyor
Sarah	3+	28	0	0	normal	32	married	social worker	social worker	social work manager
Natasha	4	36	0	1 T	caesarean	23	single	payroll supervisor	none	printer
Angela	4	36	1	0	normal	32	married	none	none	lorry driver
Hilary	3	24	0	0	normal	34	married	housing officer	housing officer	academic
Jerri	4	31	0	0	caesarean	29	single	none	none	plumber
Ruth	3+	19	0	1 T	normal	31	married	lecturer	none	industrial manager
Melanie	4	31	0	2 M	normal	35	married	civil servant	civil servant	lorry driver
Norma	4	36	0	0	normal*	27	married	midwife	midwife	hospital technician
Wendy	3+	16	0	0	normal	32	married	caterer/trainer	caterer/trainer	council worker
Felicity	4	22	0	0	normal	31	married	scientist	scientist	economist

* = Delivery took place in hospital although a home delivery had been planned

T** = Termination

*3+ = 3 interviews plus a completed and returned questionnaire

M^M = Miscarriage

Altogether, twenty-four women participated in the study. Their ages ranged from twenty-one to forty-one years at the first interview (average age 30.3 years). For eighteen women it was their first baby, for five their second, and for one her third. All of the women had a permanent relationship with the baby's father. Two women were black (one from Zimbabwe, the other born in London of West Indian origin), another was Irish, and the remainder were white, British-born, and lived in London, although several had their origins outside the capital. All but one of the women had had a previous experience of depression and most volunteered because they felt they might be depressed after the birth. The aim of the study was to examine what women had to say about their experiences in a systematic and rigorous manner, but without losing the sense of the woman's experience. I examined the transcripts from each interview to identify descriptions and discussions of "depression," related words which referred to emotion and mood, such as "down," "low," or "upset," or behaviors typically associated with negative affect such as "crying," "being too tired to move/carry on," or "weeping." I then examined the surrounding, relevant paragraphs to make sense of how depression was talked about and the extent to which it was related to meaning, experience, and the biographical context of the woman's life. From examining several transcripts, I was able to identify common themes.

My intention was to develop a specific woman-centered (rather than clinician-centered) approach to understanding postpartum depression. I was also particularly interested in the context in which women make sense of their emotions after the birth of a baby. This meant that from the start I had *a sense of what I was looking for* and wanted to explore this with the participants. I believed, before I started the formal study, that women themselves do not necessarily see their postpartum experiences in the unitary fashion characteristic of research papers and clinical textbooks. Thus, I had a clear research agenda.[27]

Here I want to focus on one particular aspect of the women's accounts, and that is "loss." It became apparent from reading many of the transcripts that the participants' feelings were discussed in the context of what the woman had *lost*. For instance:

> I got really down—oh dear it's difficult to explain really—shut up—knowing you can't go out, even if you wanted to. I know it was cold and every-

thing and not everyone likes to go out—but I mean it's nice to be able to pack your things and go. (Jane)

Through trying to explain, both to me and to herself, why she felt so down on one particular occasion, when it had been snowing and she felt especially alone and isolated, Jane demonstrated that *there was something that would in the past have been easy that she could not do now*. This was because things had changed for her since she had become a mother. Leaving the house in inclement weather might be putting the baby's health at risk. Leaving her apartment and walking in the snow was simply not practical with a baby carriage. Independent outings, and being able to put herself first on her list of priorities, were no longer possible if she were to maintain her (desired) identity as a responsible mother. This change in social status led to a sense of being "down" or "depressed" when confronted with loss of time and autonomy in this way.

In a different example, Angela was concerned about getting employment and was very depressed when she had had two job interviews without success.

> I found it hard—I'm frightened I'm going to end up cleaning or stacking shelves in a supermarket because I know that's a job—but I want to use the skills I've got—I don't want to lose my typing.

She accounted for her depression as emerging from her anxiety that a suitable and desired type of employment was no longer available to her. She perceived herself as having lost opportunities in the course of early motherhood (this was her second baby, and the first was still under school age). She was further fearful of losing her skills altogether if she did not manage to gain employment, recognizing this might lead her toward a prolonged period of depression.

However, as with many of the participants, there was more than one reason for episodes of heightened depression. Angela again:

> I have had a bad spell since I saw you last which went on for a couple of weeks where I couldn't stop crying and I was very, very depressed—I think that was tied up with my weight. I hadn't lost any—and I was starting to creep up again. I then went back on a diet—the doctor said it was

a bit early—but I decided to do it and I've lost nearly seven pounds again.

Here, Angela is focusing upon the "loss" of her valued, pre-pregnancy body and her *failure* (as she saw it) to return to her old weight. She also acknowledged that the medical expert took a different view. It may be that she went against the expert advice because she resented being identified, by someone else, as a person who should accept a larger body than the one she saw and valued as her own.

Hilary demonstrated how the intensity of a particular experience (in her case recovering from extensive tearing during delivery) can seem, at the time, to be a permanent change (or loss) and induce a sense of panic which leads to further depression.

> My body things are over now—I was miserable but you feel you have to be all right. So I was quite miserable—not only being ill—but being depressed about it. It has gone now, although it was bad for a couple of weeks. You think you'll never get your body back together really.

Almost every woman who took part in this study had found the experience of becoming a mother, whether for the first, second, or third time, changed her life in more than one way and on several levels. This originated from having to put another (or yet another) individual's needs first, to having lost a valued identity in order to incorporate that of "mother" (for the first time or as mother of one more child). Some changes were permanent and some transitional, though, at the time, the intensity of the feeling of loss frequently meant the woman was unlikely to be able to distinguish or predict which was which. Any experience of change initially was described, or understood, as the "loss" of what had been their previous experience. For most, in some way, this experience of change gradually became integrated into a new sense of identity as "mother."

Melanie and Natasha, for instance, specifically expressed the view, in the later interviews, that becoming a mother made them feel that they were "growing" as people. However, they acknowledged that it often took time to meet the new challenges that this altered status brought. Growth and maturity were recognized as positive, but their acceptance also meant the loss of youth or at least of the "carefree" self-centered behaviors that youth sometimes represented. While not specifically discussing depression in this part of the interview, Melanie expressed a version of this kind of loss.

> I think I've calmed down a bit. I'm not so emotional as I was. I think I'm more ambitious. That comes with the responsibility. I think I must go out and earn a crust for the family.

Natasha, however, who was relatively young (aged twenty-three) when first interviewed, deeply regretted some of the changes to her sense of identity and how she believed she should behave. Motherhood, in her view, brought with it a weight of responsibility.

> *Natasha:* I went out the other night but she's [the baby] on my mind the whole time. I don't act any differently. I don't think—maybe a little more grown-up.
>
> *Interviewer:* What exactly is it?
>
> *Natasha:* Whereas before I'd probably be really "mad," I won't so much now. Like on Saturday—I wanted to wear my leather miniskirt. But I had second thoughts. . . . I'm a mother now.

First-time mothers appeared to experience the changes as more significant than those who were mothers already, although this was not always the case. After having had her third baby, Meg said that this new baby represented a significant change for her because it meant a loss of her "expected future," especially the loss of the expectation of a return to work. The new baby's arrival further eliminated time for her and her husband to be on their own together. This reduced time together potentially stretched ahead for another eighteen years, and she sometimes felt very depressed about this.

The theme of "loss" comprised the subthemes: "loss of autonomy and time," "loss of appearance," "loss of femininity/sexuality," and "loss of occupational identity."

Loss of Autonomy and Time

The postpartum period is expected to be exhausting. Most participants, even so, were taken unawares by the *extent* to which this had an impact on their moods and emotions. Caring for a demanding infant consumes time and energy and the demands are relentless. Not having time for self-care or to recover from the work of caring for their families and themselves results directly in tiredness, exhaustion, and occasionally resentment, which were seen by the participants as the main reasons for depression and low moods during the early weeks. Time to consider oneself, and to process everyday experiences, enables a feeling of control.

> Although everyone says it's a full-time job, I hadn't realized. Until it happens . . . this is a twenty-four-hour full-time job! I didn't realize I'd have no time. I do need support. I'm now in the fifth week and have had constant support and I have needed that. (Lynn)

There are specific incidents that make this experience more acute. Jane reported:

> You've not only got yourself to think about—you've got the baby and she had a bad bout of bronchitis and she went through it—she nearly went into hospital—yeh [just a little while before Christmas] she was really bad up with it and I had to walk the floor with her, and had the doctor in the night and he kept a check on her. Then I couldn't go out either. No—you've got to put the baby first—she just couldn't sleep—that was getting me down.

Time to oneself and time to do things, other than for the baby or the family, was a major issue in the early days and months of motherhood. This loss of time for oneself is likely to remove that sense of control and can lead to depression. Some interviews, however, provided evidence of reflection upon the early postpartum weeks, through which the woman had managed to gain a sense of perspective on the changes, and to develop a coping strategy, which enabled a degree of integration of those changes into her new life. Hilary, who had one child already, knew to expect to have very little of her own time. That did not stop her *feeling* down, but she could be philosophical about it, which helped her to cope a little better.

> I've re-adjusted what I consider time to myself. I suppose I've lowered my definition of what that really means.

Felicity similarly realized when her baby was around one month old that

it takes monumental powers of organization in order to actually do anything.
. . . Time just disappears. . . . It's all more consuming than I expected. I was
unprepared for the fact that you can't do anything else.

Time also seems to take on a different significance. Aspects of this shift
made Sharon reflect on her past life and experience a sense of difference,
both from others of her age and background and from her "old" self. By
the time of the fourth interview, she was not particularly depressed about
the change—but curiously "outside" of what she had been in the past.

The days go by—and you're completely unaware. We're almost a little back-
water here and you go out and think—"oh God the world is still going on
outside." But you can't be part of it in the same way.

Adapting to the sudden changes that the baby brings is difficult because
the changes are so dramatic. Although the women experienced what are
sometimes extreme bouts of anxiety, fractiousness, and depression, on the
whole these are offset by the recognition that motherhood is positive for
them and that the exhaustion is temporary.

Loss of Appearance

Loss of autonomy and time conspired, along with physical strain and exhaustion, to provoke a sense for some participants that they had lost their
former *appearance*. Participants expressed varying degrees of anxiety that
their appearance had changed in a negative way, which was a source of
upset and depression. Wendy remarked, however:

I think I look an awful lot older than I did one year ago. I'm not worried
about it, but it does concern me. I don't want to look gaunt and haggard.

She felt that she often smelled of "baby" and was worried about this. However, in her questionnaire response (see endnote 24), she emphasized the
point that she couldn't "interest my husband in having sex with me." She
declared though that none of this particularly depressed her; she was only
depressed through sheer exhaustion. Loss of time in itself reduces the ability to pay attention to appearance, as Jane found:

> I don't bother with myself as much as I did. Sometimes that gets me down—toenails, hair and so on. But it's not always that bad because sometimes she'll [the baby] lie on the floor and I can get my hair done.

Appearance, especially body size, was on everyone's mind at some stage during and after pregnancy. At five weeks postpartum, Francis was

> longing to be thin again. The last part comes when you stop breast-feeding. I want to be nice and flat again.

And Dion had anticipated it would be

> a nice relief to be thin and get rid of that big stomach . . . but I keep thinking "God, no shorts this year!"

Samantha, who had become quite heavy in the later stages of pregnancy, had lost weight by the twelfth postpartum week. However, she began to feel a bit down when she tried to buy some clothes and found she was still too big to fit into the ones she wanted. Penelope, who had been so pleased about her weight reduction prior to pregnancy, had put on twenty-eight pounds more than she had wanted to while she was pregnant, and was very unhappy about this. However, she did not want to believe that she was so concerned with her appearance that she could be considered vain. Rather she suggested that the excess weight itself was making her tired and that was why she was depressed.

> I'm carrying around twenty-eight pounds too much. I've got to do something about this. I've got no energy. Things just aren't working and I know I've got to get energy from somewhere. If one has energy one can accomplish a great deal. It's the permanent tiredness—that's the problem.

Loss of Femininity and Sexuality

Some women were worried about their body shape because their self-image had changed, and others were caught up in a complex set of emotions about the loss and change of their sexuality in relation to their sense of identity and their relationships with their partners, as with Wendy's comment above. Natasha provides another example:

> *Interviewer:* Have you thought any more about how you've changed?
> *Natasha:* No I can't say I have, but I can say how I feel. I feel a lot older. I don't feel right in certain things I wear, and I feel like I've got to be a lot more respectable.

Natasha was very concerned about the relationship between her new identity, her social life and the image that her appearance portrayed in relation to sexuality, and the specific anxiety that her partner would find other women more attractive.

> Like once I rang Mary and said "shall we go out?" and I got my leather miniskirt, leather jacket, red stilettos and black net tights and waited on the corner of the road for her. And I hated it because it didn't feel right. Wearing this. But I just wore it to make him [partner] jealous.

Disentangling motives about appearance is a complicated process. The loss of the pre-pregnancy body shape and the image of a "mother" both contribute to the sense that femininity and sexuality have been lost.

To give birth to and to breast-feed a baby mean that a woman has to experience her body in a different way from that of being a sexual and sexually attractive individual. The body functions differently and the sensations are different. Sometimes this is because of physical damage. For example, Sarah had difficulties with sexual intercourse because of scar tissue: "My stitches remained sore for a long time. Each failed attempt at sex made me feel very depressed and hopeless" (Sarah).[28] Other women, such as Ruth and Francis, had problems with their breasts, including engorgement, infection, and sore nipples. It often takes up to twelve months before a woman feels "sexual" after childbirth.[29] In addition, feeling feminine and good about one's self, which corresponds with positive sexual feelings, changes over the transition to motherhood. Becoming a mother for Isobel meant becoming womanly rather than feminine, which was depressing.

> I suppose I feel less feminine—more matronly or womanly in some way that's hard to express. I definitely feel different about myself . . . maybe the

way I look at things and feel about myself. I know I'm not as young looking. I know I'm not the same shape as I used to be.

Loss of Occupational Identity

The loss of occupational identity for the participants was, in various ways,
seen as loss of an important part of their *sense of who they had been before
the baby*—as successful and/or independent, as powerful, with work-re-
lated friends and practical or intellectual competence. Several welcomed
the return to their former situation as an escape from depression. Others
were ambivalent or approached a return to work with trepidation. Having
a young baby increased their private and public responsibilities, which in
turn influenced the *meaning* of their occupational identity. For some, this
identity was now a burden. They had lost the identity connected to their
occupation, which could not be retrieved, because so much else had
changed and these changes provided the potential for (and frequently the
reality of) depression.

Hilary reflected, while pregnant with her second child, that there are
pros and cons to being a professional woman and that motherhood can be
an "escape route."

> *Hilary:* In giving up the treadmill, I'm also giving up the money and
> prospects of promotion. It's hard to catch up afterwards—and I knew I'd
> find it hard to keep up. So I think some of it's—laziness or it was until you
> realize how much work is involved in child-care.
> *Interviewer:* How do you see your future at work when the second baby ar-
> rives?
> *Hilary:* I've got very mixed feelings about that—when I'm at work I really
> enjoy it, and I always did—especially the power—not that I have it now—
> although there are still some people who ask my advice. There's no doubt
> about the power thing and at any one time—I have more experience in
> terms of years than new staff. It's a very pre-organized job—and I'm a bit
> of an old hand.

Expression of loss changed in some cases over the course of the study, as an
integration of the changes occurred. Matilda, a student whose baby was

born during the summer, found the return to university after a short maternity break, stressful and depressing. She no longer knew whether she was "like" the other students.

Some participants had ambivalent feelings toward their occupational identity and motherhood. Meg, trained as a math teacher, felt that the pregnancy was one of the biggest mistakes she had made. This was because she had a clear view that mothers of young children should not work outside the home. "I had spent eight years being a mum and wanted to do something else. I'd just started supply teaching."

Eight women left work permanently to have their babies and remain as full-time mothers. They did so intentionally, believing that they had made a positive choice. However, some found that full-time motherhood and the loss of their role in the workplace turned out be a complex change in lifestyle, which gave rise to emotional reactions, particularly depression, loneliness, and panic and not simply a decision about child-care. Natasha and Jane, who both experienced deteriorating relationships with their partners after the birth, missed work for the companionship it provided. However they did not feel supported enough domestically to apply for work during the period I was in contact with them.

Gwen, Sylvia, Jerri, and Sharon all intended to remain at home until their families were in school, and all planned to have more children in the short term. Sylvia, however, expressed extreme discomfort at not having her own income and, in conjunction with her perception that her partner neither pulled his weight in the household tasks, nor appreciated her efforts, she had bouts of depression. She attributed these feelings of depression to a combination of exhaustion and guilt.

Sylvia: When the money in the purse is mine—I'd just go and do it [buy the baby a new cot]. But because I have to ask him for money, I don't like doing that.

Interviewer: He doesn't feel he's giving you money, does he?

Sylvia: It's that *I* feel I'm *asking* for it. He's quite happy to spend it. I just feel guilty because I've never been in that situation before. I had a house and my business and my own money. If I had money I'd spend it. If I didn't, I didn't.

Interviewer: But you're bringing up the baby and you said it was his choice that you should be at home.

> *Sylvia:* It's funny. It's just me. Even *with* the baby I feel guilty. . . . I feel I'm not contributing to the finances. I want to say "Oh I've earned the money to do this."

Most women who had been away from their work outside the home found, after the first few weeks, that they missed the companionship of colleagues and that the sense of isolation was depressing. Samantha had the opportunity to attend her office Christmas party. "It was the first time I had left her [the baby]. It was a really nice afternoon. . . . It was nice to see them all again, and quite a lot had happened since I had left. But I shall be going back in March." Felicity was ambivalent about her friends connected with her work, and although they had been to visit her, she did not go to see them because "a lot are either single or don't have children." Ruth found that an opportunity to return to work posed an excruciating dilemma for her. She left her lecturing post, which was stressful and involved a great deal of traveling. Unexpectedly, however, she was offered a local, part-time post. This led her to feel ". . . panicky. When I came to interview the people for the job of nanny, there were a couple of days when I felt I couldn't cope."

Other participants also were very anxious about working outside the home, specifically because they had a young baby. Isobel had formerly been very conscious of her professional status and did not want to lose it, but by the fourth interview, she felt:

> I'll never be able to cope with getting up at six o'clock every morning. Beforehand I used to tumble out of bed at eight and out of the door at five past! But I've got to be a bit more organized than that. As soon as I get home it's going to be bath time. Then we've got to start to think about meals and all sorts of things. Thinking about it more positively, I can cope with that aspect. What worries me is the baby.

Sarah, a social worker, had thoughts of work "looming," which bothered her during the early postnatal weeks. At three months, though, she began to see work as possible once again.

> I kept thinking about going back to work and leaving him. This was so much that I no longer enjoyed my time with him. I was really

churned up with peaks that made me feel very bad. But it has passed I think.

At six months postpartum, however, once she had begun to work part-time, she felt ambivalent about her return to work, because of guilt about child-care. Felicity could not decide whether she wanted to return to work or not. She felt she had done "everything in the house I could be bothered with. But I really want to be back at work." However, she also admitted she was "daunted by the prospect" and "unsure about how much stress I'll be under." Norma, a midwife, had been terrified and angry about returning to work. This was partly because she did not like midwifery and had planned to leave and retrain as a health visitor before she discovered she was pregnant. Once she had found a child-minder, however, and found she could work the hours of her choice, she said, "I am really happy. It worked out so well. It just shows you. I had built all this up." Prior to that, she had felt that she might not be able to pick up her life again until her son started school.

For Melanie, the return to work presented no practical problems, as John, her husband, had been the one to give up work. She felt she had little time to think about returning to work as an issue because she returned from maternity leave after only three months. When she did return to work, she felt that nothing much had changed, although she did feel more ambitious than before, because of her sense of responsibility as bread-winner.

Loss of occupational identity for this group of women provoked a variety of responses reflecting the many different ways that new motherhood intersected with their working and domestic lives and their sense of identity. It is worth noting also that many of the women found it difficult to predict accurately how they would react to both leaving and returning to work. The relationship between occupational identity, motherhood, and overall sense of identity is clearly complex.

Re-Integration and Change

Loss is an inevitable part of any change, but most human beings survive a series of losses, which if recognized and handled properly, lead to psychological re-integration and the development of increased competence and strength. Poor mental health only follows loss when the potential impact of the loss is ignored or repressed; or an individual's psychological history indicates that there have been unresolved difficulties surrounding loss or bereavement in the past.[30] Loss, however, can lead to degrees of change for most people. Following such varied experiences as bereavement, divorce, or childbirth, many report that they no longer know who they are. People forget simple things, and find planning their day and organizing their lives very difficult. They may feel they are "all over the place."

In this study, several emotional and psychological changes were notable, particularly between the third and fourth occasions when the women were interviewed. At the first meeting, we talked about the woman's past and her aspirations for the future. At this stage we were strangers, although each woman knew that I wanted to talk to them about depression and their views and expectations relating to postpartum depression. The interview itself allowed them time to reflect on who they were and how they expected to change. When we met the second time, the baby had arrived, and the memory of the birth, social and emotional disruption, and sometimes trauma, had occurred for each of them. Many had difficulty holding their thoughts and their sense of themselves together. My arrival and the focus of the discussion on themselves (rather than as a mother to the baby) was acknowledged by many as "therapeutic." It was almost as if the opportunity to talk things through enabled reflexivity and psychological development. The research process in this case did not just extract information; something beneficial and healing seemed to be incorporated. This process was particularly evident during the later interviews. Time had passed since the emotional turmoil of the early days following the birth, and a recognition and acceptance of personal change came about through a re-integration of the "self" to include some of the new experiences, skills, and responsibilities that the recent situation had precipitated.

The ways in which women changed depended very much on their personal experiences, life stories, events surrounding the birth, and early postnatal months. For instance, Francis felt split between her two children, her husband, and trying to make time for herself, something which Hilary dismissed as an impossible aspiration. Others, such as Isobel and Natasha, felt older but not in a particularly positive way. Norma expressed the view that she felt able to separate herself from some of the "pettiness" of her former life and in certain ways saw some of her friends as immature, which she had not done before. Sarah said that being a mother has "made me feel much more adult. I always felt not properly grown up . . . I always felt as if I'd been a daughter, and a little daughter until I had a family of my own and then I could be an adult daughter." Melanie felt the baby made her more contented. "I think I'm much happier than I was before. It's a difficult thing to put into words. But I think I'm more content. I feel 'rounded off.'"

Jerri felt that she no longer had to prove herself to others: "Now I couldn't care less what they think of me." Having the baby gave her that extra edge of confidence. She said that she felt more "herself." Becoming a mother may enable a greater sense of maturity: "I feel more separate from my parents. I feel I have joined a 'secret club' of women who have children" (Sarah). Sometimes, it is only after having a second baby that this feeling is experienced: "You feel more of a mother. More at ease. More complete" (Angela).

It was not necessarily the case that achieving motherhood and a greater sense of maturity or adulthood made someone more secure in their identity.

> In theory I'm the same. In practice I'm probably slightly less confident than I thought I'd be. . . . I've changed very little—perhaps I feel a little more grown up now. (Francis)

Some women do experience a sense of psychological *fulfillment*, which is unmistakable and directly connected to motherhood.

> Fundamentally there is something about being a mum that is quite magical really. . . . You can say it's love, motherhood, or whatever! (Meg)

In the excerpt from Sharon's interview, shown below, it is clear that the reintegration and adaptation to motherhood is a compromise. As Sharon sees it, she has *lost* her freedom and autonomy but *gained* the social status that goes with being a mother.

> *Sharon:* The difficulty for me is "freedom"—Not being able to go off with my husband. If we want to go out, having to have prior notice so we can have a baby-sitter and then. . . . Oh yesterday I was asked to stand in as a

Godmother—and previously I would have gone off and bought a new dress. But I haven't yet worked out how to go off and buy clothes with one like this [the baby] in tow!

Interviewer: How does that make you feel?

Sharon: Well I had a good time—because when you go out you make much more of it because you go out less. So I really didn't feel upset that I was wearing something five years old! That's not the point now. I go out to see people and talk to them—and I think I get a lot more out of such occasions.

Interviewer: That is like you were saying last time about dinner parties.

Sharon: Yes—you have friends round—you haven't the time to spend getting the meal ready—you're just pleased to see them as long as the meal's passable.

Discussion

Pregnancy and childbirth in themselves are disruptive life events. This has been acknowledged by experts for over thirty years.[31] However, there is less specific understanding of the complex psychological issues surrounding this experience in the context of women's lives. Expert clinicians and researchers still focus upon the idea that women are, or should be, happy and fulfilled when they become mothers. Traditional research, which searches for "facts," fails, however, to take account of the contradictions and paradoxes that occur in women's lives at this time. They may be happy and fulfilled but they may also be tired, anxious, confused, and frustrated, and it is sometimes this very *mixture* of emotions that leads to depression. As sociologists have made clear, depression is likely to be the result of the way women's lives are constrained by the early years of parenthood rather than any psychological problems. Postpartum depression may be a social rather than a psychological or psychiatric phenomenon.

It is important to ask why the transition to motherhood—the trauma of birth, the pain of its aftermath, hospitalization and then returning home to a whole new set of responsibilities—has *not* been portrayed by researchers as potentially disruptive and depressing in the same way as other life transitions have been. Women in contemporary Western societies are not permitted to grieve or mourn when they become mothers as they might be with other life changes. If they do, they are seen as "ill" or "unnatural" in some fundamental way. So strong is the taboo against appearing unhappy after having a baby, that women themselves frequently fail to admit their sense of loss to themselves, at least in a conscious way.

Having a baby, as I have indicated, is marked by a series of complex *losses* in women's lives alongside the *gain* of the baby and social status as a mother. Women are actively prevented from mourning such losses because of social constraints and the unconscious acceptance of those constraints. Grief, however, is potentially healing, as has been demonstrated by studies of people who have experienced disruption and loss in their lives in relation to other things.

Peter Marris, a sociologist and writer about human experiences of loss and change, argued that grieving is a "process of psychological re-integration, impelled by the contradictory desires at once to search for and recover the lost relationships and to escape from painful reminders of loss."[32] In other words, the experience of loss is a paradox. You *search* for the past, that is, the time before the loss, yet you also try to *forget* the past in order to escape from the pain of that loss. Individual psychology is driven toward healing, as is the individual body with a physical wound—unless that process is disturbed in some way.

When an essential thread of a person's life is broken, the individual struggles to repair it—both seeking and resisting change. So a woman might seek to have a baby and accordingly change her life. But this means disruption of her experience of continuity. To heal, an individual needs permission and space to mourn.

Conclusions

In doing this research it became clear that traditional studies of postpartum depression have failed to take account of women's own experience of the transition to motherhood. Through talking directly to women and inviting them to provide their own version of events, their experiences of the pregnancy, birth, and early days, weeks, and months of motherhood become center stage. Childbirth is not an isolated event that somehow "triggers" a hormonal or psychosocial response. Having a baby is part of a person's life. Thus, the baby's arrival and all that that entails needs to be understood by researchers as part of that context.

In women's accounts of depression in the postpartum months, they explain their experiences in terms that relate closely to accounts of depression following a major life event or trauma,[33] disruption and loss.[34] This contrasts sharply with the traditional clinical/medical discourse, which continues to describe pregnancy, birth, and the postpartum period as a "happy event" and portrays the women who find this transition stressful or depressing as "ill." The women I interviewed contextualized and gave meaning to their depression in the postpartum. They saw themselves as healthy but under immense pressure to cope, with a role and set of responsibilities that were difficult.

A central theme in all the women's accounts was that of *loss*, which is taboo in the expert literature on birth and motherhood, although it does correspond with some feminist literature on maternal ambivalence.[35] The linking of "loss" with successful childbirth also conflicts with everyday understanding of the transition to motherhood—the archetypal "happy event." Loss and motherhood appear paradoxical and contradictory. Of course they are not. Women who become mothers (each time) lose at least their autonomy, sense of identity, work, time, friends, relationship patterns, sexuality, sense of their own body, and health and comfort. These losses occur (like all such losses) in a complex way as part of life experience and in the context of each individual's subjective understanding of that experience.

The losses described here, which occur following childbirth and in the early postpartum months, are not all permanent, in the sense that "nothing will be the same again." The arrival of a baby means that nothing reverts to *exactly* as it had been before the birth. Some losses represent the first stage of the role or status change that occurs each time a woman gives birth—being a mother is very different from not being a mother, as the care of child(ren) engages a certain, and vital, amount of a woman's focus. Women's lives and the gains, losses, and mechanisms of psychological change and development are dependent upon personal history. Furthermore, the way an individual gives an experience *meaning* is dependent upon how they have made sense of their *biography* or life development.

Overall, therefore, depression is a normal part of the transition to motherhood for many women. Depression following childbirth to some extent should be considered the rule rather than the exception. It is also potentially a *healthy*, grieving reaction to *loss* and clinicians need to be aware of this. However, within contemporary Western societies, the image of the happy, healthy, and energetic new mother maintains its grip on both the public and clinical imagination and thus, unfortunately, depression remains a "case for treatment."

Qualitative research of this kind has provided invaluable insights into the experiences which surround postpartum depression. Over the course of time this type of research data has become increasingly accessible to women and others such as midwives and nurses who work closely with mothers. However, mainstream academic studies on postpartum depression still fail to pay heed to the findings from qualitative studies of this kind, which impoverishes their research agenda and the overall knowledge base of health professionals.

Notes

1. See C. Lee, "Social context, depression and the transition to motherhood."
2. See J.M. Ussher, *The psychology of the female body*; P. Nicolson, *Postnatal depression: Psychology, science and the transition to motherhood.*
3. Ussher, ibid.; Nicolson, ibid.; S. Lewis and P. Nicolson, "Talking about early motherhood: Recognising loss and reconstructing depression"; J.M. Stoppard, "Dis-ordering depression in women: Toward a materialist-discursive account."
4. World Health Organization, *The ICD-10 Classification of Mental and Behavioural Disorders.*
5. For example, K. Dalton, *Depression after childbirth.*
6. See M.W. O'Hara, "The nature of postpartum depressive disorders."
7. See B. Harris, "A hormonal component to postnatal depression."
8. Definitions of postpartum or postnatal depression seem to vary from researcher to researcher. However, it is broadly taken to be depression occurring during the twelve postpartum months. Some prefer to include only "clinically" identifiable depression, while others are happier with a broader category of any self-reported episode of depression during that time period (see V. Thurtle, "Post natal depression: The relevance of sociological approaches").
9. V. Whiffen, "Is postnatal depression a distinct diagnosis?"
10. Defined typically as transitory episodes of weepiness, irritability, and/or anxiety during the first 8–10 days after childbirth (see A. Oakley, *Women confined: Towards a sociology of childbirth*).
11. E. Boath, A.J. Pryce, and J.L. Cox, "Postnatal depression: The impact on the family"; P.J. Cooper and L. Murray, "Postnatal depression: Clinical review."
12. B. Harris, "Biological and hormonal aspects of depressed mood: Working towards strategies for prophylaxis and treatment."

13. L. Appleby, "The aetiology of post partum psychosis: Why are there no answers?"

14. J.M. Stoppard, "Dis-ordering depression in women"; J.M. Green, "Postnatal depression or perinatal dysphoria? Findings from a longitudinal community-based study using the Edinburgh Postnatal Depression Scale."

15. J.A. Richman, V.D. Raskin, and C. Gaines, "Gender roles, social support and post natal depressive symptomatology: The benefits of caring."

16. H. Gavron, *The captive wife*; V. Welburn, *Postnatal depression*.

17. G. Brown and T. Harris, *The social origins of depression*; S. Payne, *Women, health and poverty*.

18. S.A. Elliot, "Commentary on 'Childbirth as a life event'"; C. Jelabi, "A feminist perspective on postnatal depression."

19. A. Oakley, *Women confined*; V. Thurtle, "Post-natal depression"; P.J. Cooper and L. Murray, "Postnatal depression"; P. Nicolson, *Postnatal depression*.

20. S.E. Lewis and P. Nicolson, "Talking about early motherhood."

21. V.E. Whiffen, "Is postnatal depression a distinct diagnosis?"; J.L. Cox, "Introduction and classification dilemmas."

22. V. Thurtle, "Post-natal depression"; Nicolson, *Postnatal depression*.

23. A longitudinal study is one that follows the same group of people over time.

24. Twenty-four women were recruited to the study and interviewed during pregnancy. One dropped out after that, which left twenty-three to be interviewed at one-month postpartum, twenty-one at three months, and thirteen at six months. In addition, four women, unable to be interviewed at this stage, returned a postal questionnaire (for details see P. Nicolson, "Loss, happiness and postpartum depression: The ultimate paradox").

25. A voluntary organization providing support nationally (in the UK) for natural childbirth. The women would normally be in the higher socioeconomic groups.

26. Ruth, Wendy, and Felicity were only nineteen, sixteen, and twenty-two weeks pregnant, respectively, at the time of the first interview. It was difficult to recruit women to be interviewed within the time frame for the research. Thus, the criterion of "willingness to participate" was given priority over weeks into the pregnancy.

27. Some psychologists would argue that this was a form of bias, as the researcher is supposed to be neutral. I would dispute this. Traditional researchers all have an interest in a research topic and have hypotheses to test. My "hypothesis" was based upon my own experience of being depressed after my daughter was born, but knowing full well that this was connected more to isolation and personal circumstances at the time than to physiology.

28. This information was from the questionnaire that was returned instead of the fourth interview.

29. E. Alder, "Postnatal sexuality."

30. See, for example, P. Marris, *Loss and change*; C. Murray-Parkes, "Psychosocial transitions: A field for study."

31. T.M. Holmes and R.H. Rahe, "The social re-adjustment rating scale."

32. P. Marris, *Loss and change*, p. vii.

33. C. Murray-Parkes, "Psychosocial transitions."

34. P. Marris, *Loss and change*.

35. For example, A. Rich, *Of woman born*; R. Parker, *Torn in two: The experience of maternal ambivalence*.

References

Alder, E. (1994). Postnatal sexuality. In P.Y.L. Choi & P. Nicolson (Eds.), *Female sexuality: Psychology, biology and social context* (pp. 83–99). Hemel Hempstead, UK: Harvester Wheatsheaf.

Appleby, L. (1990). The aetiology of post partum psychosis: Why are there no answers? *Journal of Reproductive and Infant Psychology, 8,* 109–118.

Boath, E., Pryce, A.J., & Cox, J.L. (1998). Postnatal depression: the impact on the family. *Journal of Reproductive and Infant Psychology, 16,* 199–203.

Brown, G., & Harris, T. (1978). *The social origins of depression*. London: Tavistock.

Cooper, P.J., & Murray, L. (1998). Postnatal depression: Clinical review. *British Medical Journal, 316,* 1884–1886.

Cox, J.L. (1994). Introduction and classification dilemmas. In J. Cox & J. Holden (Eds.), *Perinatal psychiatry: Use and misuse of the Edinburgh Postnatal Depression Scale* (pp. 3–7). London: Gaskell/Royal College of Psychiatrists.

Dalton, K. (1980/1989 revised edition). *Depression after childbirth*. Oxford: Oxford University Press.

Elliot, S.A. (1990). Commentary on 'Childbirth as a life event.' *Journal of Reproductive and Infant Psychology, 8,* 147–159.

Gavron, H. (1966/1977). *The captive wife*. Harmondsworth, UK: Penguin.

Green, J.M. (1998). Postnatal depression or perinatal dysphoria? Findings from a longitudinal community-based study using the Edinburgh Postnatal Depression Scale. *Journal of Reproductive and Infant Psychology, 16,* 143–155.

Harris, B. (1993). A hormonal component to postnatal depression. *British Journal of Psychiatry, 163,* 403–405.

Harris, B. (1994). Biological and hormonal aspects of depressed mood: Working towards strategies for prophylaxis and treatment. *British Journal of Psychiatry, 164,* 288–292.

Holmes, T.M., & Rahe, R.H. (1967). The social re-adjustment rating scale. *Journal of Psychosomatic Research, 11,* 213–218.

Jelabi, C. (1993). A feminist perspective on postnatal depression. *Health Visitor, 66,* 59–60.

Lee, C. (1997). Social context, depression and the transition to motherhood. *British Journal of Health Psychology, 2,* 93–108.

Lewis, S.E., & Nicolson, P. (1998). Talking about early motherhood: Recognising loss and reconstructing depression. *Journal of Reproductive and Infant Psychology, 16,* 177–197.

Marris, P. (1986). *Loss and change.* London: Tavistock.

Murray-Parkes, C. (1971). Psychosocial transitions: A field for study. *Social Science and Medicine, 5,* 101–115.

Nicolson, P. (1998). *Postnatal depression: Psychology, science and the transition to motherhood.* London: Routledge.

Nicolson, P. (1999). Loss, happiness and postpartum depression: The ultimate paradox. *Canadian Psychology, 40 (2),* 162–178.

Oakley, A. (1980). *Women confined: Towards a sociology of childbirth.* Oxford: Martin Robertson.

O'Hara, M.W. (1997). The nature of postpartum depressive disorders. In L. Murray & P.J. Cooper (Eds.), *Postpartum depression and child development* (pp. 3–31). New York: Guildford.

Parker, R. (1995). *Torn in two: The experience of maternal ambivalence.* London: Virago.

Payne, S. (1991). *Women, health and poverty.* Hemel Hempstead, UK: Harvester Wheatsheaf.

Rich, A. (1984). *Of woman born.* London: Virago.

Richman, J.A., Raskin, V.D., & Gaines, C. (1991). Gender roles, social support and post natal depressive symptomatology: The benefits of caring. *Journal of Nervous and Mental Disease, 179,* 139–147.

Stoppard, J. (1998). Dis-ordering depression in women: Toward a materialist-discursive account. *Theory & Psychology, 8,* 79–99.

Thurtle, V. (1995). Post-natal depression: The relevance of sociological approaches. *Journal of Advanced Nursing, 22,* 416–424.

Ussher, J.M. (1989). *The psychology of the female body.* London: Routledge and Kegan Paul.

Ussher, J.M. (1991). *Women's madness: Misogyny or mental illness?* Hemel Hempstead, UK: Harvester Wheatsheaf.

Welburn, V. (1980). *Postnatal depression.* London: Fontana.

Whiffen, V.E. (1992). Is postnatal depression a distinct diagnosis? *Clinical Psychology Review, 12,* 485–508.

World Health Organization. (1992). *The ICD-10 Classification of Mental and Behavioural Disorders.* Geneva: WHO.

6

■　　■　　■　　■　　■　　■　　■　　■　　■

Legacy of Betrayal

*A Theory of Demoralization
from the Perspective of Women
Who Have Been Depressed*

Susan A. Hurst

Whoever it is who wrote this, have you really, really been down to our level? Do you know how we live? How we feel? Because so much of it is way up in the clouds, and just doesn't apply to us. And there's nothing we can use to help us.

THESE COMMENTS WERE MADE by Evelyn, a woman whom I interviewed about her understanding of how she became depressed. She was expressing her dissatisfaction with the "expert" theories of depression that she had read.

I decided to talk with women who had been depressed about their experiences because I wanted to develop a theory that would reflect how women who had been depressed understood what had contributed to their depressions. I wanted to understand the complexity of factors in their lives that had resulted in depression, including the social context in which their personal experiences were embedded. As was stated by Barbara DuBois, a feminist researcher, "to address women's lives and experiences in their own terms, to create theory grounded in the actual experience and language of women, is the central agenda for feminist social science and scholarship."[1] To develop a theory based on personal experience, I chose the research method known as grounded theory, which is ideally suited to the exploration of subjective experiences and personal meaning.[2] With this method, theory emerges from analyzing the actual words spoken by the participants, and is thus truly grounded in them.

Participants

All but one of the seven women whom I interviewed responded to an advertisement in a free newspaper that is delivered weekly to all the neighborhoods in one of the major cities in western Canada. The seventh woman who volunteered to participate was referred to me by an acquaintance. On the basis of responses to a standard clinical interview, I determined that each of these seven women had experienced at least one episode of a depressive disorder in the past.[3] In addition, none of the seven women had received counseling for depression. I specifically chose to interview women who had not received counseling because I wanted to know how the women, themselves, understood how they had become depressed. I reasoned that if I interviewed women who had received counseling for depression, I might hear accounts that were shaped by their counselors' understandings of depression.

The seven women ranged in age from late teens to mid-fifties, varied in education from less than high school to two years of college, were either employed, supported by a spouse, or on social assistance, represented the marital statuses of single, married, and divorced, and all were mothers. One participant was black, and one identified herself as a lesbian.[4] The following is a brief description of the participants, using pseudonyms.

Anne was in her mid-twenties, married with one child, and working full-time. She had two years of college education. Anne experienced one episode of major depression that followed her husband's decision, contrary to her wishes, to work out of town immediately after they moved to a new city. She had been depressed for about one year and had only recovered several months before I met her.

Barb was in her late teens, a black, single mother of one child, on social assistance, who had not completed high school. Barb had been depressed for three years in her teens while enduring ongoing sexual abuse.

Cathy was in her early forties, divorced, with one teenage child. She had a high school education and had taken some courses from a community college. She was currently on social assistance. She had been depressed many times in her life, beginning as a child when she was physically and emotionally abused. Several of her depressions followed the ending of significant relationships.

Debbie was in her mid-forties, married with one child, and had a high school education. She had worked full-time until her child was born, but she became depressed after her husband coerced her into quitting her job and staying home. Her depression of seven years had just recently lifted.

Evelyn was in her mid-fifties, divorced with two teenage children. She had a high school education, had taken some community college courses, and she worked full-time. She became depressed when she was a teenager and was forced to quit school to look after younger siblings after her mother died. She was depressed off and on during her marriage, and became depressed for about ten years after she left her husband. This depression had only abated in the last year.

Frances was in her early thirties, divorced with two teenage children, and on social assistance. She had a high school education. Frances was sexually abused by her father for many years, and was also physically and emotionally abused. She experienced numerous episodes of major depression, some of them precipitated by losses.

Gina was in her early thirties, married with one child, and pregnant. She had a high school education, had taken technical courses, and had been working full-time until recently. Gina had experienced sexual, physical, and emotional abuse as a child. She estimated that she had been depressed more than ten times off and on over the last seven years, usually without fully recovering each time.

Developing a Theory of Becoming Demoralized Based in Women's Accounts

I interviewed each of the women about their personal understandings of how they became depressed. Then, using a grounded theory approach,[5] I developed a theory of depression that both captured and summarized the women's views. What I discovered through this process was that these women shared a common experience—that of being betrayed within their most significant relationships—which led to their becoming depressed. The betrayals they experienced included being abused, being disrespected, and being left. These betrayals led the women to feel they were left out of the world, feeling that no one cared about them. It was being betrayed, often coupled with feeling left out of the world, that resulted in a process that I have conceptualized as *becoming demoralized*.[6] For the women I interviewed, the experience of demoralization involved believing that they were not worthy of love, that there was nothing they could do to change their situations, and that nothing was ever going to get better for them. When a woman is demoralized, she does not believe that she is of value or that she has the potential to exert control over her circumstances, both of which are necessary to have hope that she will experience intimate relationships and have a sense of purpose in her life. A woman can be demoralized to varying degrees. When the level of self devaluation and despair with her life is severe, a diagnosis of depression, which is defined in terms of a group of symptoms, may be applied.[7]

Not Worthy of Love

When these women were betrayed in their most significant relationships, they learned to believe they were not worthy of love. It was being devalued by others, especially by their parents, that led the women to believe they were unlovable.

Feelings of being unworthy of love are demonstrated in comments of Evelyn, who had been devalued by others throughout her life: "No one cares. I'm, I'm useless, no one wants me, no one loves me, no one cares about me. . . . Feeling that you're not worth anything, you can't do it." Evelyn did not feel like a loved and valued daughter in her family, but rather like she, as a female, was a second-class citizen. As a female child, she was expected to cook, clean, and care for her younger siblings. Her goals did not matter and she was forced to quit school against her wishes. Furthermore, Evelyn's family viewed her as a female who lacked any value because she had epilepsy, and it was assumed no one would marry her. When she did in fact marry, her husband also treated her with utter disregard.

Rather than believing that the central people in her life had been unloving, Evelyn believed that she was unlovable.

It was frequently the experience of being disrespected or being left (which can feel like a rejection of oneself as a person) that led these women to believe that they were seen as unworthy by others. Additionally, most of the women I interviewed had also been abused, sexually, physically, or emotionally, and these betrayals led them to feel unworthy of love. When a person is treated as an object rather than as a human being with inherent worth, she may come to believe that if others, especially her parents, have deemed her as unworthy of love, then she must be unworthy. At the extreme negative end of the continuum of worthiness, Frances, a survivor of incest, described an extreme level of self-loathing:

> To be coming from that place, to be coming from a very shy, voiceless place, to be feeling rotten inside to the point where I . . . felt like that inside was all black, hard and brittle like coal or something. . . . That I was rotten inside . . . nothing good. . . . Just rotten to, you know the old rotten to the core saying? . . . That there was no heart, that there was no insides, there was no anything. . . . Once they really get to know me they're going to hate me . . . because there's stuff to hate inside.

When a woman experienced betrayals in childhood that interfered with the development of a view of the self as worthy of love, this self-view was firmly entrenched and made it difficult for her to develop relationships that were validating of her worth. Similar betrayals as an adult reinforced feelings of being unlovable.

Two of the women, Anne and Debbie, did not report feelings of unworthiness prior to experiencing betrayals as adults. They did, however, identify betrayals in childhood that were similar to the betrayals they experienced as adults. These earlier betrayals may have sensitized them to attribute these later betrayals to unworthiness. For Debbie and Anne, it was when they were betrayed by being disrespected by their husbands that they lost their sense of worth. They described their depressions as a loss of self. For example, Debbie stated: "My whole self was taken away from me. . . . I lost my identity. I just felt that I lost everything. . . . I was just dead, I was a whole dead person, my whole, my whole self." For Anne as well, it was the loss of who she thought she was that made her feel unworthy. She saw herself as an independent and very capable person until she became depressed when she felt betrayed by her husband. When she saw how much the disruption of this relationship affected her, she interpreted this as a sign that she was a dependent person. This altered view of herself led her to lose her sense of self-worth. Perhaps depression is experienced as a loss of self in individuals who had previously developed a sense of worthiness, and so could experience its loss.

An additional form of unworthiness is believing one is not of use. Some of these women's abilities had been denigrated since childhood, such as Gina's: "Feeling inadequate, not good enough. . . . My mother instilled them in me. She always said you can't do anything. I was always put down and criticized. It made me insecure. I hated myself." Other women began to feel they were not of use when they lost important roles, such as their work roles, or when their feelings of success in their relationship roles were undermined by being left. In addition, when the women became depressed and were not functioning as well as they usually did, this further reinforced feelings that they were not of use. Feeling that one does not have valuable abilities and purpose in life and, additionally, missing the acceptance from others that these qualities elicit, is demoralizing.

There Is Nothing I Can Do to Change Things

When these women were demoralized, they believed there was nothing they could do to change their situations. They believed they could not exert control over their lives and could not, therefore, change negative circumstances. The primary way in which the women developed this belief was when they lived in circumstances in which they experienced a lack of control because someone was abusing power and they were being abused or being disrespected. In these situations, attempts by the women to exert control were punished by the abusers, further entrenching the belief that it was futile to try to exert control over their lives. It was also common for the women to develop feelings of powerlessness when they had experiences of being left because they had lacked control over decisions that so altered their lives.

An additional way in which the women reported feeling powerless was when they were unaware of why they were depressed and unaware of what their feelings and behaviors reflected. Being unaware in this way was distressing in itself as well as rendering them powerless to take action to overcome their depressions. Frances stated, "I was sucked right into it [depression] before I even knew what was happening. And I was so deep in I was scared I wouldn't get out." Similarly, Gina stated, "behavior that you can't explain—and that in itself is weird that you can't explain it—when you can't label it, it is hard to fix it."

Once a woman developed the belief that there was nothing she could do to change things, she was less likely to exert control in situations where she might have done so. She was more apt to tolerate situations or relationships in which she had to conform to others' wishes. A few women became involved in relationships in which they believed they were dependent on a romantic partner for their well-being. Therefore, believing there was nothing she could do to change things sometimes led a woman to become involved in repeated situations in which she was powerless, thus exacerbating her demoralization. Frances spoke in the most depth about the significance that this belief had in her life:

> I'm an adult child of an alcoholic and an incest survivor and those two things together I think produce a whole feeling of very low self-esteem and lack of control. 'Cause you know, from a very young age I didn't have any control over my body, I didn't have any control over, anything really. So that, that kind of builds up. . . . The lack of control that I felt I had . . . to be coming from a very shy, very insecure, very voiceless place. Like what control, I didn't perceive myself as having any control over events, any control over anything that happened to me. And so I didn't try and exert control in any way either.

Nothing Is Ever Going to Get Better

When these women were demoralized, they believed that the negative circumstances of their lives were never going to improve. Without the hope that life will get better, it is harder to persevere through painful experiences. The belief that there was nothing they could do to change things often contributed to the belief that nothing was ever going to get better for them. When one believes that one does not have control over one's life, it means there is less reason to hope that one's life will improve. An exception exists when uncontrollable negative circumstances are perceived to be transitory. For example, if a woman experiences the loss of a relationship, but believes the pain of grieving will pass with time, then she might feel hopeful about the future. If she believes, however, that it is her personal inadequacies that led her unavoidably to continue patterns that doom her to being left repeatedly, she will feel hopeless about the potential for future satisfying relationships. For example, Cathy believed that her failed relationships stemmed from her troubled relationship with her father. When her partner was unfaithful, as her father had been to her mother, her interpretation was that it was "like this was a sewer, and this was a manhole. . . . And all this old junk from the sewer . . . just started coming up." She stated, "That's how far I got with my dad and that's how far I get, and I can't go one step past." Her belief that nothing would ever get better led her to avoid relationships and to despair that she will "spend the whole rest of [her] life alone."

For the women who were repeatedly betrayed throughout their lives, the belief that nothing was ever going to get better became deeply entrenched. Several of these women had periods in their lives when their circumstances had improved, but became demoralized again when they encountered further betrayals. They were then no longer able to believe that they would not become depressed in the future. These women experienced more hopelessness than the women who had experienced one depressive episode.

Another powerful source of hopelessness is the belief that one has a genetic predisposition to depression, so that becoming depressed is viewed as inevitable. As Cathy said, "They don't put the worst horses in the world to mate and then expect a thoroughbred." She believed that her whole family was genetically destined to be depressed. It was Cathy and Gina—who both believed they were genetically vulnerable to depression—who expressed the strongest belief that they would struggle with depression throughout their lives.

Regardless of the reason why a woman believed nothing was ever going to get better, this belief resulted in her being less likely to try to take active charge of her life. Cathy felt that no matter how well a period of her life went, it was just a matter of time until she became depressed again. The more a woman believed in a negative fate, the more pointless it seemed to try to change the relationships and situations that were further demoralizing her. Rather, these experiences further confirmed her belief that nothing in her life would improve, thus exacerbating her demoralization.

Being Betrayed

There is an expectation inherent in significant relationships that one will be treated with love and respect and that the relationship can be relied on for support. When this expectation is breached by someone from whom you expect love, you have been betrayed. The types of betrayals these women experienced included being abused, being disrespected, and being left. The legacy was that they believed they were unworthy of love, that there was nothing they could do to change things, and that nothing would ever get better for them.

Being Abused

Cathy attributed her depressions to "being a woman and being abused." Being abused includes sexual, physical, and emotional abuse. Four of the seven women were sexually abused as children. Three of these four, and two who were not sexually abused, were physically and emotionally abused. Only one woman, Anne, did not link being sexually abused to the depression she experienced years later. Anne was sexually abused by strangers rather than family members, and, therefore, was not betrayed by people she trusted and on whom she was dependent.

Two women, Barb and Frances, experienced prolonged sexual, physical, and emotional abuse by their fathers. In Barb's case, the betrayals began when she was abandoned by both parents as an infant. Then, when she was eleven years old and began living with her parents, her father began sexually abusing her regularly. Barb was further betrayed by her mother, who not only failed to protect Barb, but also blamed her for the sexual abuse. She told Barb that if her father wanted to return home, she would have to move out. At one point her mother sent her to live with her father, who abused her further and threatened her life. Barb later cut off contact with her mother, and said that, as far as she is concerned, her mother is dead.

When a person who is supposed to love you disregards your feelings and your rights and, instead, harms you, it can make you feel that you are not worthy of love. In addition, when these women were abused by their parents and partners, they experienced a lack of control that fostered the belief that there was nothing they could do to change things, and gave them reason to believe that nothing was ever going to get better. An additional consequence of prolonged abuse was the experience of never being safe. Frances stated that she grew up feeling "my thoughts are the only part of me that are safe."

Abuse occurs when those who have some form of power abuse that power. For many of these women, their relation to power was that they did not have it and others did, and more often than not it was used against them. Their parents had power of authority in addition to physical power. Their spouses and lovers often had physical power. If the women stayed home with children, they lost financial power. In these situations, powerlessness was an outcome of gender.

Being Disrespected

Although abuse is obviously disrespectful, for the purposes of this discussion, being disrespected refers to treatment other than being abused. I think that it would be an understatement to label abuse disrespectful. The theme being disrespected refers to experiences in a significant relationship in which one is not treated with respect and in which there is little consideration of one's needs.

The betrayals that occurred when the women were adults frequently involved being disrespected by spouses or lovers. Three of the women, two of whom had no prior history of depression, became depressed in the context of marital relationships in which they were treated disrespectfully. Debbie, for example, realized after she married that her husband was an alcoholic and that he would not help with any domestic chores or child rearing. Despite the importance to her of her work role, her husband relentlessly pushed her to be a stay-at-home mother. Debbie was unhappy in this role, but when her husband told her that she was a bad mother if she did not want to be home with her child, and she had no right to feel the way she did, she doubted the legitimacy of her feelings and blamed herself. After quitting her job, Debbie became depressed and her husband continued, relentlessly, to invalidate her feelings. When she did not want to have sex with him, he coerced her by threatening to leave her. Once Debbie had become financially dependent on him, she felt she could not defy him, which intensified her feeling that there was nothing she could do to change things. Being disrespected made Debbie feel unvalued, and as she lost her sense of self-worth she no longer trusted her perceptions. Debbie stated: "He wasn't there for me. He just hung me out to dry, he just abandoned me. . . . Emotionally, I was abandoned. I was abandoned by my mother. I was abandoned by him." Debbie's reference to her mother's emotional abandonment demonstrates how previous betrayals can contribute to demoralization even if the person did not become depressed after the initial betrayal.

Women who were in marriages in which they were being disrespected felt trapped when they were financially dependent on their husbands as a result of staying at home. Debbie's fear of impoverishment if she left her marriage was realistic, as Evelyn's experience attests. When Evelyn left her husband, she and her children faced chronic poverty. Contrasting Debbie's and Evelyn's experiences highlights the double bind women are in when they are in an abusive or disrespectful marriage, do not have the education or training to adequately support themselves and their children, and are not likely to receive adequate child support payments. For the women I interviewed, impoverishment resulted from being pressured into traditional gender roles. Some of the women followed the societal expectation that they stay at home with their children and rely financially on their partners, which left them vulnerable to impoverishment when the relationship ended. In addition, some of the women were denied education or were discriminated against at work because of their gender. Impoverishment contributes to demoralization because of the accompanying powerlessness, sense of hopelessness, and, in our society, the presumed association between wealth and worth.

It was societal pressure to adopt a traditional gender role that contributed to three of these women becoming ensnared in unhappy marriages. Frances, a lesbian, described how social pressures led her into an unsuccessful marriage:

We know that women in our society get married and settle down to people, men who they hopefully love, but they don't really have to, but they do have to tolerate, you know, and that at eighteen I never wanted to get married, but at nineteen I was married. Why? Because I bought into the trap, but I mean part of it is the trap is there, and part of it is me accepting it, right?

Frances had learned from being abused that there was nothing she could do to change things, and for her, being a woman meant being submissive and feeling emotionally dependent. Even when Frances was in a lesbian relationship she said she played the role of a dependent housewife.

Being devalued as female was a form of disrespect these women experienced frequently. Cathy grew up in a home in which her father consistently conveyed that he didn't "have any sense of a woman being of value other than sex." Cathy was further devalued when she was discriminated against at work because of her gender. Cathy learned to believe: "[I am] too woman to have a place. . . . I'm not respected, I'm not valued. . . . Like what I am as a person who nurtures and loves and believes in God, what value does that have in the world? It has no value."

Evelyn grew up in what she described as a "traditional European home." She was taught that

> little girls are to be seen and not heard, girls are made to take care of men.
> . . . My father wouldn't let me get the education I wanted because I was only
> gonna get married, "you cook, you clean, you have kids et cetera." . . . I had
> no right to want anything. I had no right to even talk. . . . They put more
> importance on the men. And I just really did not have any right to question,
> to have my own feelings and opinions.

When Evelyn's mother died, her father forced her to quit school to look after younger siblings, which meant abandoning her educational goals. Her father's demand conveyed the message that she and her wishes were unimportant. She said that when it was discovered that she had a disability, her aunts said to her father, "Now what are you going to do with her? No man is going to want her, so what are you going to do with her now?" Evelyn said, "That hurt me and left me feeling, you're not worth anything."

When these women were disrespected, they learned to believe they were not worthy of love and that nothing was ever going to get better. As Cathy stated: "The only time mutts win is when somebody loves them beyond a shadow of a doubt. . . . But I don't feel like I have anybody who is loving me enough to help me get to the next step and I also feel like I have people whipping me and hurting me. . . . It's very depressing, very, very, very depressing."

Being Left

Some of the women were abandoned by their parents as infants or young children, resulting in either no bond or a very conflicted relationship. The lack of parental relationship left them vulnerable to abuse and, throughout their lives, the experience of feeling unworthy of love from their parents.

As adults, two of the women became demoralized when they were left by romantic partners. The lack of control the women had over the ending of these relationships complicated the experience of loss, contributing to the feeling that there was nothing they could do to change things. This belief, and the message that one is not worthy of love implied by rejection, often contributed to the belief that nothing was ever going to get better. It was the interpretation that being left meant one was not worthy of love and, therefore, would never be loved, that was crucial to demoralization. Women who had numerous similar experiences that included their parents were especially vulnerable to this belief.

Being left is more specifically demoralizing than are losses of relationships for other reasons. Although the women had experienced losses through death, including death of a parent, and they often experienced sadness and lost important sources of support, they did not necessarily become depressed. The exception was if the relationship with the deceased was complicated in some way, and/or there was a co-occurrence of losses. For example, Frances became depressed when her mother became seriously ill because it brought up many intensely ambivalent feelings about her mother, who had been emotionally abusive. She said that when her mother died two years later, she felt that she would cope because she had the support of her partner. When her partner left her a short time later, at a time when she was very vulnerable, she felt profoundly betrayed. This relationship failure left her questioning her own ability to maintain relationships and feeling unworthy of love. The loss of her mother was thus complicated by a co-occurrence of losses. Frances became depressed again.

The more times a woman experienced being left, the more entrenched her beliefs were that she was not worthy of love and that she would experience further relationship failures, and that nothing would ever get better. Some women then avoided relationships because of fear of further injury. It seems probable that some of the women's relationship choices were likely to lead to further betrayals, and, thus, were decisions that ultimately confirmed their expectations of relationships in the form of a self-fulfilling prophecy.

Left Out of the World

Feeling left out of the world, which refers to being isolated without supportive relationships, emerged as a common and central experience that resulted from being betrayed and further contributed to demoralization. Betrayals were sufficient in themselves to result in demoralization, but because feeling left out of the world involves believing that no one cares about you, and that is interpreted to mean that you are unworthy of love, it also contributes to demoralization. When one sees oneself as not worthy of love, and believes there is nothing one can do to change being unlovable, then there is no reason to hope for future supportive relationships. In other words, one is demoralized.

The experience of being abused, being disrespected, or being left frequently led the women to feel left out of the world, whether it was complete isolation from other relationships or emotional isolation, in which one did not feel cared about within any existing relationships. Examples of feeling left out of the world include the following. When Cathy experienced being left, she would tell herself that she was "nobody to anybody ever." She came to believe that "nobody's gonna love me and I'm gonna be just alone out there all by myself all the time. . . . If I can't even want somebody in the door, I know I'll spend the whole rest of my life alone." Evelyn, who experienced being disrespected in all her significant relationships, except those with her children, stated she would have "sold my soul to the devil for a shoulder to cry on," for somebody just to "sit and have a cup of coffee or tea and just be there." Debbie felt left out of the world after she was pressured to stay at home, with her husband interfering in all her relationships. She reported that "I withdrew from even wanting to have anyone around because I just knew he would take it, he would just take it away from me." When Barb was sexually abused by her father, he isolated her from others and her family members shunned her. Barb emphasized the significance of feeling left out of the world: "[Being isolated] That's depression, that's what in my opinion is depression. You have nobody to talk to, you're there, you feel left out . . . left out of the world. Because to me, locked up in that room, depression is, when I was locked up in that room and nobody to talk to."

Feeling left out of the world also resulted from discrimination, such as when Barb experienced racism from other children. Staying at home with children and impoverishment were also conditions that contributed to isolation, but if the women had not been betrayed in their relationships, they would not have felt so utterly alone.

For Anne and Frances, geographical moves contributed to their feelings of isolation because they had less access to their support networks. In both these cases, however, betrayals by the people they most relied on for support immediately followed their moves. Although the physical separation from their usual support networks increased their sense of isolation, it was evident in these women's accounts that it was the betrayals in their most significant relationships that made them feel left out of the world. In fact, for these two women, support from others was not enough to avert depression. The sad truth for many of these women was that most of the time there was no available support, but there were also situations in which the women withdrew from potential sources of support. When a betrayal in a central relationship leads a woman to believe that nobody cares about her, her withdrawal is not surprising. When a woman feels demoralized she does not trust that others will be supportive or that support would make a difference anyway.

Demoralization Is Self-perpetuating

The process of *becoming demoralized* is essentially the same whether it begins in childhood or adulthood, except that when it begins in childhood the effects on the woman's view of herself and her life occur at an early stage of her development, and thus, can be profound. Five of the women I interviewed were demoralized in childhood, and thus, to varying degrees, believed throughout their lives that they were not worthy of love, that there was nothing they could do to change things, and that nothing was ever going to get better. These beliefs can then become a self-fulfilling prophecy.

Women who have had childhood experiences that made them feel not worthy of love have difficulty establishing intimate and nurturing relationships because they do not believe they are worthy of having such relationships. They are apt, instead, to choose partners who will fulfill their expectations, just as Cathy chose a man who was unfaithful like her father. They are also apt to interact with others in the way they learned in childhood, as Frances did by being submissive and dependent in her adult relationships. When a woman's relationships involve additional, often similar forms of betrayals, her belief that she is unworthy of love is reinforced, which increases her demoralization. The woman then frequently withdraws from potential sources of support because she does not expect to get it, but this contributes to her feeling left out of the world, which also perpetuates demoralization.

Women who believe that there is nothing they can do to change things adopt a passive approach to life in which they neither pursue opportunities nor exercise control when it is possible to do so. They are more likely to become involved in situations and relationships in which they experience a lack of control, such as relationships in which they are abused or disrespected. Further experiences of being powerless entrench the belief that one has no control, as well as the belief that nothing is ever going to get better. The latter belief is confirmed every time there is a further betrayal. The self-perpetuating effects of demoralization thus have the tendency to bring about further betrayals, exacerbate demoralization, and result in chronic or recurrent depression.

Anne and Debbie were the two women who were not demoralized in childhood, but became so as a result of later betrayals. It should be noted, however, that they recounted childhood experiences that resulted in sensitivities to particular betrayals as adults. Given the self-perpetuating nature of demoralization, it is possible that they could be vulnerable to becoming demoralized again if they experience betrayals in the future.

Reflections on the Research Process

This theory of demoralization is based on the accounts these women gave about how they became depressed, which were essentially narratives reflecting how they had made sense of their experiences.[8] The group of women who chose to pursue this opportunity to talk about their experience with depression may have had more developed views than is typical of people who have been depressed. It is also possible that the information they shared was influenced by my research question. Asking women about their understanding of why they became depressed conveys the assumption that there are identifiable reasons for depression, and that those reasons go beyond biological explanations. I assume that individuals who felt their depressions were purely biological in nature would have been unlikely to respond to my ad. The choice of the research question reflects my assumption that depression is not purely biological, at least not for all people, and that those who have experienced depression will have useful and meaningful theories about it, even though some of the factors that contributed to their depressions may be outside of their awareness. The focus of the research, therefore, probably encouraged psychological explanations. Furthermore, it is possible that these women placed greater emphasis on experiences in which they sensed I was more interested, something I might have indicated subtly without realizing I was doing so.

My goal was to avoid shaping the women's views so that I could learn about their personal understandings. In general, when a woman talked about an experience, but did not link it to being depressed, I would not pursue more information about that experience, even if I thought it might be relevant. So, for example, when Evelyn talked about her mother dying when she was a teenager, without linking her mother's death to becoming depressed, I did not ask her whether there was a connection. As a result, the theory that emerged reflects the participants' understanding of depression, which is a description of the influences that they had been able to observe, recognize, infer, understand, and of which they were aware, and so cannot be assumed to account for all the factors at play in their depressions.

This theory also does not account for the experiences of all depressed women, but rather, reflects my understanding of the views of the seven women I interviewed. Nevertheless, this theory provides the opportunity to reflect upon what is revealed by a perspective that is based on personal experiences.

Reflections on the Theoretical Findings

The primary conclusion of this study is that demoralization stems from profound betrayals by the most significant figures in one's life. Betrayal is experienced as piercing rejection, a shattering of trust, and disillusionment. Feeling unlovable, utterly alone, and without hope is the crux of the experience of *becoming demoralized*. Life loses its meaning when one feels that there are no meaningful relationships in one's life and one believes that, because of fundamental personal flaws, the future will be one of isolation. This theory emphasizes the importance of relationship experiences on a woman's development of her views of self, and her ability to value herself even when relationships falter, which is consistent with other feminist theories of depression.[9]

Also of relevance to this theory of demoralization is the concept of existential losses, which have been described as experiences that lead one to question three assumptions: that one is invulnerable, that the world is meaningful, and that one has positive qualities.[10] These assumptions help people to function day-to-day and to plan for the future. When a person ceases to believe that the world makes sense, that what happens to her or him is controllable, and that being a good person protects one from misfortune, the world may no longer seem meaningful. One's view of self can be altered. People frequently think "if misfortune happens to *me*, there must be something wrong with *me*." The concept of existential losses seems strikingly relevant to the experiences of the women I interviewed.

Also consistent with other feminist research is the finding that a focus on the personal experiences of participants did not preclude their identifying social conditions that contributed to those personal experiences. The participants either directly spoke about societal influences or, in talking about their lives, revealed such influences. The themes of impoverishment, lack of power, being devalued as female, being pressured to adopt traditional gender roles, and lack of safety were identified. The women also talked about experiences of discrimination on the basis of race, disability, and weight. Most of the social conditions they identified are interrelated and directly associated with being female. The majority of the experiences described under the theme "being disrespected" directly stem from gender-related social conditions. For example, societal pressure to adopt traditional gender roles, especially the expectation to marry, stay at home with children, and take care of others, constricts women's options. Several women talked about having married simply because they felt it was expected of them. If the roles of wife and/or mother are not desirable to a woman, and she is denied access to the activities from which she derives satisfaction, it can lead to loss of gratification and meaning, despondency, and anger. I believe that being pressured to fit a role, especially when that role is a devalued one, is depersonalizing and inherently disrespectful. Even the women who wanted to stay at home with their children felt the effects of this role being devalued. They also experienced a loss of financial power that left them with less control and vulnerable to impoverishment. The themes of power and never being safe were directly related to being abused, which, in adulthood, is an experience that is strongly linked to gender. Although the women did not always draw direct links between the social context and their own experiences, they did refer to experiences that revealed these underlying conditions.

The fact that the women were able to identify social conditions defies what many sociological thinkers believe: that individuals do not recognize the effects of social influences on their personal lives.[11] It is possible that the women who volunteered to be interviewed had more awareness of social influences than is typical. It is also possible that these social conditions were identified because they have been brought to societal consciousness by feminist theories and social critiques. It may be that these women's lives were affected by additional social influences of which they were unaware because these influences are less recognized in our culture. We also cannot assume that all women are influenced equally by the same social conditions.

Despite the significant impact of social influences, however, the predominant factor in the demoralization of these women was betrayal in their most significant relationships. It is our most intimate personal relationships that form our most fundamental beliefs about ourselves and about what we can expect in our lives.

Concluding Comments

A particularly difficult dilemma I faced during the research process was finding a balance between reflecting the participants' views as closely as possible and interpreting them further to develop a conceptual framework. I made interpretations using grounded theory analysis, and so the present theory goes beyond the explanations of the participants. Yet, the source of these ideas was the women's personal stories, and the theory closely reflects their views. I think I achieved my objective of developing a theory of depression that reflected the experience of participants. After the women read my analysis, they told me that they felt understood, and that it was meaningful to read a theory based on their own experiences. They also told me they benefitted from relating to the similar experiences and feelings of the other women. Cathy stated that others made statements that "could all have been said by any of us." When you feel left out of the world, realizing others feel like you do can reduce that sense of isolation. Knowing that others have overcome depression can directly counter the demoralizing beliefs that there is nothing you can do to change things and nothing is ever going to get better. Reflecting upon the experiences one has managed to survive can be therapeutic in itself. Frances wrote to me, expressing this view:

> I started this "experience" wanting only to help you—and yet I am constantly discovering ways in which this has enriched my own life. . . . So, in helping you I have helped myself as well. My involvement with your project has been a tremendously empowering force in my life—a kind of measuring stick by which to measure—and celebrate—my own progress. . . . It has been an opportunity to think about certain concepts, to examine and discover (or rediscover) facets of myself and the world I live in, and it has left me with a certain pride of accomplishment. . . . Thanks for helping me see myself in a positive way—and for the strength and inspiration that gives me!

The process of constructing a narrative about our experience, of reflecting on how key life experiences have affected our view of ourselves and approach to life, can bring about change. Sometimes this process involves recognizing unexamined beliefs, which provides an opportunity to rewrite our personal stories, to find new meaning in our experiences. For example, when we are betrayed by a loved one, we may start to believe that we are unworthy of love, sometimes without realizing we believe this, or even while knowing that it is not true. It is difficult but important to remember that a betrayal reflects on the betrayer, not the betrayed. A betrayal is the action of another person, not a result of unworthiness of the person betrayed. Even when we think we have "evidence" of our unworthiness in the form of a list of people who have not valued us, that history reflects what we have learned to believe about ourselves, not our true worth.

It can also be helpful to broaden our personal narratives by purposefully thinking about the types of social factors that have affected us. People easily focus on individual, psychological explanations, but identifying the social context of our experiences can also decrease self-blame. It is when people come to see themselves as deficient rather than recognizing how social influences or the actions of others have affected them that they are apt to become demoralized.

When a person is depressed and wants to find a therapist who will be helpful in the process of understanding, it is important to find someone who—in addition to having appropriate training—asks about one's understanding of one's experiences, and who values one's point of view. *We are all authorities on our own experiences!* Sometimes it takes several tries to find the therapist who feels like the right fit.

I hope that women who are, or have been, depressed will find this theory relevant and useful. I know that was the hope of the women whom I interviewed.

Notes

The research on which this chapter is based was funded by the Social Sciences and Humanities Research Council of Canada (SSHRC) in the form of a Doctoral Fellowship. I would like to acknowledge the contributions of Dr. Linda McMullen to the research. I would also like to thank the women who shared their experiences and understanding with me.

1. B. DuBois, "Passionate scholarship: Notes on values, knowing, and method in feminist social science," p. 108.

2. J. Corbin and A. Strauss, "Grounded theory research: Procedures, canons and evaluative criteria"; B. Glaser and A. Strauss, *The discovery of grounded theory: Strategies for qualitative research*; D.L. Rennie, J.R. Phillips, and G.K. Quartaro, "Grounded theory: A promising approach to conceptualization in psychology?"; A. Strauss, *Qualitative analysis for social scientists*; A. Strauss and J. Corbin, *Basics of qualitative research: Grounded theory procedures and techniques.*

3. I used the Structured Clinical Interview for DSM-III-R-Outpatient Version (SCID-OP, 4/11/87) by R.L. Spitzer, J.B.W. Williams, and M. Gibbons.

4. Although this group of participants was reasonably diverse, it did not include women with a university education or professional occupation, and it did not include women who were not mothers.

5. See S.A. Hurst, "Legacy of betrayal: A grounded theory of becoming demoralized from the perspective of women who have been depressed," for a more detailed description of the research method.

6. The experience of demoralization has been described by J.D. Frank as follows: "'[t]o demoralize' as to 'deprive a person of spirit, courage, to dishearten, bewilder, to throw [her] into disorder or confusion.' . . . To various degrees the

demoralized person feels isolated, hopeless, and helpless, and is preoccupied with merely trying to survive" (*Persuastion and healing*, p. 314).

7. The criteria for a diagnosis of depression are described in the *Diagnostic and statistical manual of mental disorders*, 4th ed.

8. D.A. Karp states that "everyone suffering from depression inevitably becomes a theorist as they try to give order and coherence to their situation" (*Speaking of sadness: Depression, disconnection, and the meanings of illness*, p. 166).

9. See D.C. Jack, *Silencing the self: Women and depression*, and R. Schreiber, "(Re)Defining my self: Women's process of recovery from depression."

10. See S.H. Budman and A.S. Gurman, *Theory and practice of brief therapy*.

11. According to Karp:

With rare exceptions, the themes they generate locate the cause(s) of depression somewhere either in their biographies or their biologies. Occasionally, respondents spin out more complex theories that see depression as resulting from the subtle interplay of personal history, recent life events, and chemical imbalances. However, even those who name situational causes for their emotional problems typically restrict their conceptual vision to the immediate and local circumstances of their lives. Only rarely do sufferers of depression relate their condition to the kinds of broad cultural trends that, I believe, influence our consciousness about everything. *Speaking of sadness*, p.166.

References

American Psychiatric Association. (1994). *Diagnostic and statistical manual of mental disorders* (4th ed.). Washington, DC: Author.

Budman, S.H., & Gurman, A.S. (1988). *Theory and practice of brief therapy*. New York: Guilford.

Corbin, J., & Strauss, A. (1990). Grounded theory research: Procedures, canons and evaluative criteria. *Zeitschrift fur Soziologie, 19(6),* 418–427.

DuBois, B. (1983). Passionate scholarship: Notes on values, knowing, and method in feminist social science. In G. Bowles & R.D. Klein (Eds.), *Theories of women's studies* (pp. 105–116). Boston: Routledge and Kegan Paul.

Frank, J.D. (1974). *Persuasion and healing*. New York: Schocken Books.

Glaser, B.G., & Strauss, A.L. (1967). *The discovery of grounded theory: Strategies for qualitative research*. New York: Aldine de Gruyter.

Hurst, S.A. (1999). Legacy of betrayal: A grounded theory of becoming demoralized from the perspective of women who have been depressed. *Canadian Psychology, 40,* 179–191.

Jack, D.C. (1991). *Silencing the self: Women and depression*. Cambridge: Harvard University Press.

Karp, D.A. (1996). *Speaking of sadness: Depression, disconnection, and the meanings of illness.* New York: Oxford University Press.

Rennie, D.L., Phillips, J.R., & Quartaro, G.K. (1988). Grounded theory: A promising approach to conceptualization in psychology? *Canadian Psychology, 29(2),* 139–149.

Schreiber, R. (1996). (Re)Defining my self: Women's process of recovery from depression. *Qualitative Health Research, 6(4),* 469–491.

Spitzer, R.L., Williams, J.B.W., & Gibbons, M. (1987). *Structured Clinical Interview for DSM-111-R-Outpatient Version (SCID-OP, 4/11/87).* New York State Psychiatric Institute: Biometrics Research Department.

Strauss, A.L. (1987). *Qualitative analysis for social scientists.* Cambridge: Cambridge University Press.

Strauss, A.L., & Corbin, J. (1990). *Basics of qualitative research: Grounded theory procedures and techniques.* Newbury Park, CA: Sage.

7

■　　■　　■　　■　　■　　■　　■　　■　　■

"I Just Went On. . . . There Was No Feeling Better, There Was No Feeling Worse"

Rural Women's Experiences of Living with and Managing "Depression"

Yvette Scattolon

NOT ALL WOMEN SEEK PROFESSIONAL HELP when depressed.[1] Women who live in rural communities are particularly likely to confront barriers to help-seeking, including lack of services, inability to access services (because of lack of money), and social stigma. Rural communities also tend to be characterized by conditions, such as economic instability, geographic isolation, and traditional attitudes about the roles of women, known to increase risk of depression.[2] How do women living in rural communities understand, experience, and cope with being depressed on their own, without professional help? To answer these questions, I talked to women living in rural communities in New Brunswick, a province in the eastern part of Canada (adjacent to Maine).

The fifteen women[3] I talked to lived in rural areas in central New Brunswick and also described themselves as depressed or under a great deal of stress. None of the women had sought professional help to cope with their distress. The backgrounds of the women were diverse. Their ages ranged from early twenties to sixty, with the majority of the women being in their thirties and forties. Four women were married, three were in common-law relationships, six were divorced, and one was single. The women had, on average, three children, and all but one woman had at least one child. Almost half of the women had graduated from high school or had high school equivalency, almost one third had university courses or an undergraduate degree, and the remainder completed junior high or grades ten and eleven. Less than half of the women were on Income Assistance, with the majority working on a part-time basis, three had full-time employment, and one was retired.

Participation in the study was strictly voluntary. Contact with participants was made through a number of sources, including "Letters to the Editor" in various rural newspapers, a community development worker (i.e., she helped women on Income Assistance receive retraining), and flyers posted in community settings (e.g., libraries, community recreational centers). Women who were interested in participating in the study either called me directly or were contacted by telephone after their names were received from the community development worker. Interviews lasted approximately sixty to ninety minutes, averaging seventy-five minutes. The majority of interviews were conducted at each of the women's homes and their accounts were then transcribed verbatim. Following the interview, each participant completed a standard questionnaire for assessing degree of depression.[4]

The women were interviewed individually by me and asked about how they came to understand that they were "distressed" or "depressed," how they explained their depressive experiences, whether they thought of themselves as "depressed" or something else, and what it felt like to be "depressed." The women also were asked to talk about how their depressive feelings affected their everyday lives, the nature of their coping methods, whether they disclosed their feelings to others, and their views on professional treatment for depression. I introduced myself as a graduate student in psychology who was interested in talking to women who lived in rural areas about the hardships and distress they may have experienced in their everyday lives and how they coped with such experiences.

Exploration of Findings

The women's accounts were transcribed and analyzed using a qualitative methodology that combined the constant comparative procedure of grounded theory and discourse analysis.[5] I explored the validity of this qualitative research through the method of "reflexivity" or adopting a reflexive viewpoint, which involves exposing and examining the central role of the researcher in this process. It is based on the premise that all findings are constructions or personal views of reality that are subject to change, and in order to understand research findings, we need to understand how the researcher arrived at her or his conclusions. Adopting a reflexive style entails reflecting on and critically evaluating the entire research process, including why the topic was chosen, how the information was gathered and analyzed, and the influence of the researcher's personal experiences (e.g., background, thoughts, feelings, ethics, morals) on the carrying out of research. I incorporated reflexivity into my research process through writing notes about anything that may have affected the process (e.g., any emotional reactions or preliminary interpretations), and incorporated them at the analysis stage. Through the analysis, I identified five main themes in the women's accounts of their experiences of depression. Within each of these themes, I also identified a number of subthemes. The main theme of "Making sense of and dealing with depressive experiences" is highlighted because I believe it to be most germane to the women's lives and feel that it most fully captured the meaning reflected in their accounts. Within this main theme there are five subthemes, three of which are highlighted in this chapter, namely, how women experience "depression," how they understand and explain these experiences, and how they cope with their depressive feelings.[6]

How Women Experience Depression

Depression and Feelings of Isolation and Aloneness

The women described their experiences of depression in various ways; however, a theme common to their accounts was that of isolation and aloneness. For these women, depression was felt as an emotional experience that was private in nature and not shared with others, particularly family members. Jane (age thirty-three), who was living in a common-law relationship and had six children, and who had recently become the sole supporter of the family, described her depressive experiences in the following way:

> I don't know, I just go in the room and cry . . . and go in the bathtub and read . . . if I get too depressed or just stay in my room. . . . I don't want no one around me at all. The kids will come for one reason or another, and I'll just tell them . . . I don't want no one around me at all. . . . I just go in my little space wherever I can get and be by myself. . . . I know I'm depressed when I don't want no one around me. I mean I could be sitting there and smiling and still know that I'm depressed because I don't want them [children] around me.

Jane experienced her depressed feelings as time when she chose to be away from her children ("I don't want no one around me"), whether it was in her "room" or in the "bathtub." Thus, her depression left her feeling distressed (i.e., crying), as well as detached from her daily activities with her children. She also experienced this sense of detachment when her children were with her, when she was "sitting there and smiling" with them.

Gina (age forty-two), who was married for nine years with three small children and was employed on a part-time basis, also talked about her depressive experiences as involving isolation.

> So I used to go to parks, just public parks and sit down, cry as much as I could . . . Or sometimes when some church . . . that is open during the day, just cry you know, sometimes feeling so lonely, so lost, so isolated, I just didn't feel like coming home. . . . For weeks I would cry. . . . I wouldn't stop, like if I let myself stay here from morning til three o'clock, that was weeping, weeping, and then when the children come home from school, I try to you know, children are come, but the next day, same thing again.

Gina's account suggests that, for her, being depressed was something that was to be experienced alone, not only personal in nature, but also hidden from public view. Despite the fact that she went to public places (i.e., parks, church) to cry, the idea of being around others did not comfort her or reduce her isolated or lonely feelings. Being in these public places allowed her to get away from her home ("I just didn't feel like coming home"), which suggests there was no place in which Gina did not feel isolated and, thus, there was no place in which she felt better. The chronicity of her crying seemed to reflect the hopelessness of her situation ("for weeks I would cry. . . . I wouldn't stop"). Gina admitted that despite her distressing feelings, she still tried to be there for her children ("I try to you know, children are come"), thereby suggesting the centrality of child-care in her life and the importance of maintaining this care despite her own distress.

Depression and Inability to Carry On as Usual

The women interviewed talked about how their depressive experiences interfered with their daily activities. Many of the women gave accounts of trying to maintain their daily routines, although their feelings of distress made it sometimes difficult to continue with their day-to-day activities. Cara (age forty), who was in a common-law relationship and had two teenage daughters, was employed part-time. Her feelings of depression interfered with her ability to perform household duties to the extent that her husband carried out these responsibilities: "He [name of partner], he took care of everything, he did everything. He made sure that the youngest one had her meals, he made sure that everything was done here. He answered the phone, and he would take the messages whether I wanted to talk or not, he always took messages."

Cara's account of her husband preparing "meals" and "answering the phone" and "taking messages" implied that these things were normally Cara's responsibility. What she did not say, but what could be inferred from her account, was the assumption that taking care of "everything" was her job, and the only reason she was not doing this was that she was depressed. Thus, for Cara, a sign of her distress was not only her inability to carry out these activities, but the fact that her husband took care of them. Underlying her account seemed to be taken-for-granted ideas about how women should behave as mothers and wives. According to Cara, she should have been taking care of "everything," which seemed to mean household responsibilities such as organizing meals and taking phone messages and, perhaps, keeping the house in order. These practices seemed to be shaped by underlying beliefs in which taking care of things in the home and meeting the needs of family members were perceived as the responsibility of women.[7] According to these beliefs, the "good" woman is expected to organize her daily activities around taking care of her family's needs. Thus, having her husband temporarily take over her responsibilities was viewed by Cara both as a sign of her depression and as evidence of her failure to live up to cultural ideals of what it means to be a good mother and wife.

Mary (age fifty-four), who was on Income Assistance, had been divorced four times and had five adult children. She reported that her feelings of depression led her to neglect her physical health and self-care: "I always took great pride in my appearance but that depression. . . . I didn't cover up those grey hairs . . . and I didn't cut my bangs. . . . I let my appearance go and my hygiene. . . . There would be days and days that I wouldn't get dressed."

For Mary, feeling depressed was about not taking care of her physical appearance, particularly her hair, and how she was dressed (e.g., "I let my appearance go"). Here, she seemed to be drawing on taken-for-granted ideas about femininity that perceive physical appearance and maintenance of a youthful look (e.g., "I didn't cover up those grey hairs") as important for women.[8] According to Mary's account, such feminine practices as having her hair professionally styled allowed her to "feel good" about herself and take "great pride" in her appearance. Her way of experiencing distress, in terms of her inability to maintain an outwardly feminine appearance, suggested the centrality of physical attractiveness to women's sense of self.

Depression and "Going On" for the Sake of Others

Jane spoke about how she could not allow her feelings of depression to interfere with the care of her children: "No, I guess I just went on. There was no feeling better, there was no feeling worse. I mean I had no choice, I had to go on for the other ones." Susan (age forty-eight), who was divorced with four adult children and supported herself with a part-time job, described her everyday life as follows: "And I still make their supper, and I would still do their laundry, and I would still do whatever I feel is my duty to do for them."

For the women interviewed, the experience of being depressed was something that interfered with many aspects of their lives as mothers and wives. At the same time, many of these women continued to carry on with work in the home, despite their depressive experiences. Both Jane and Susan reported that they maintained their household responsibilities, despite their depressed feelings. By describing their experiences of depression in a matter-of-fact way, through use of terms such as "just" (e.g., "I guess

I just went on") and by drawing on moral language ("I had no choice," "my duty") to explain their actions, these women were able to present a picture of themselves as being good wives and mothers, despite their feelings of distress. Both women "constructed" their accounts around the assumption that a woman's main responsibility is to meet the needs of family members. Thus, women's everyday activities, such as preparing supper and doing the laundry, seemed to be regulated by taken-for-granted ideas of these practices as part of being a "proper" woman, mother, and wife.

Gina's account provided a clear indication of how she viewed her depressed feelings as being secondary to meeting her responsibilities as a wife and mother.

> And then as always just keeping strong and trying to be happy for both of us [she and her husband] . . . that was very stressful . . . but always trying to cope because the children were young. . . . During the day you had to cope because at the time I had no washer, no dryer, we lived very poor, and um, I had to do everything by hand and the children. . . . So you keep busy you know, changing diapers, and feeding and crying and put them to sleep. . . . I wasn't doing anything for myself. . . . It's my family, I'm going to keep up, I'll never finish . . . because my family, it's not going to be me, couldn't have them go through that.

By drawing on underlying or taken-for-granted beliefs about femininity, Gina was able to portray herself as a good wife and mother, caring for and about her children, "always trying to cope," despite her depressed feelings. She utilized moral language ("as always just keeping strong and trying to be happy") and associated depression with "stress" and always keeping "busy" to paint a picture of herself as someone able to keep up with the demands of being a mother and providing for her children (e.g., "changing diapers," "feeding and . . . put them to sleep"). Gina's frequent use of the pronoun "I" when speaking about her responsibilities (e.g., "I had no washer," "I had to do everything," "I'm going to keep up," "I'll never finish") indicated that she saw herself as having sole responsibility for her family's well-being. She seemed here to draw on the taken-for-granted idea that the good woman makes sacrifices and copes for the good of her family (e.g., "it's my family, I'm going to keep up"), thereby placing the well-being of her children and partner before her own ("I wasn't doing anything for myself").

How Women Make Sense of and
Explain Their Depressive Experiences

Depression as a Result of "Normal" Life Stressors

The women in the study attempted to make sense of their depressive experiences by drawing on a variety of explanations, with the majority articulating psychological and social understandings of depression. Lucy (age thirty-nine), a single mother with two children who were supported by Income Assistance, explained her depressed feelings by talking specifically about financial problems:

> I still think that my problem would have been that I had no money, I don't even care for help. I know what my problem is. But if I went to the doctor, he probably would have said, well, you're depressed or something. And I probably would have said, yeah, and said, what's the use, whatever, you know. I know I am depressed and I don't know how you can help there. Are you going to give me some money?

Jane also spoke about how her depression was partly explained by financial stress: "Or one thing, you're sitting on welfare, you're bound to get stressed out. You're alright for about two weeks and then everything comes crashing down and . . . you're bound to be depressed and stressed out."

The women in the study used various strategies to justify their experiences of depression in ways that defended them against the idea that they might be "insane" or mentally ill or inadequate as women. Both Lucy and Jane were adamant in identifying their financial difficulties as a reason for their depression (e.g., "I know what my problem is"). Lucy framed her reasoning, in part, as a hypothetical dialogue between herself and her doctor in which she admitted both that she was depressed and that she knew the reason for these feelings, that is, "no money." Lucy's refusal of help from a medical doctor ("I don't know how you [doctor] can help there") suggested that she did not believe that she was medically ill or that her depression needed to be treated by a professional. In fact, her question of "are you going to give me some money?" implied that she felt her depressive experiences resulted from practical issues within her everyday life. Jane's reasoning was similar to Lucy's, in that she depicted her problems in terms of being on "welfare" and having "everything come crashing down" on her. Jane associated her depressed feelings with "stress" and being "stressed out," as she talked about the inevitability of experiencing depression when she was financially unstable ("you're bound to be depressed and stressed out").

Both Lucy and Jane's situations of being on Income Assistance and having financial difficulties were representative of the circumstances of a number of the women in the study. Almost half of the women interviewed were receiving Income Assistance, and thus, providing the basic necessities for their families and home was an immediate and practical struggle for them. Having a low socioeconomic status shaped the way these women lived their everyday lives and also their subjective experiences, including their depressed feelings. For these women, being depressed seemed like a normal and accepted part of life, partly because their economic circumstances prevented them from providing for their families.

Jane talked about her depressed feelings as being a consequence of the strain of caring for six children:

> Because the kids are going to be the kids. They are at the age where they are going to make you depressed. And like I said, whether it's rich or poor, they are at the age where they are never going to be satisfied anyway, so of course, I'm the one that's gonna end up depressed or upset. . . . I imagine still the kids would find something to bicker about, and I'd end up depressed.

Here, Jane appears to argue that she would be depressed even if she did not have financial problems ("whether it's rich or poor"). According to Jane, the very nature of children and child-care ("because the kids are going to be the kids") were sufficient reasons for becoming depressed. Her use of the pronoun "I" (e.g., "I'm the one . . .") and her use of phrases such as "so of course" and "I'd end up depressed," suggested that she saw herself as having sole responsibility for her children's welfare and that both this responsibility and her depressive experiences were an inevitable part of being a mother.

The women's accounts indicated that they explained their depressive experiences in terms of the impact of external stressors in their lives, rather than a sign that they were "insane" or needed professional help. Thus, these women believed that their depressed feelings were a normal and to-be-expected part of their lives. Louise (age sixty), married for over forty years with five adult children and currently retired, talked about the frequency of her depressed feelings and how she took such experiences for granted as an expected part of life: "I'm not saying, I'm not, a healthy person's going to get depressed once in awhile. . . . I think that there are times when we are depressed. Boy, we wouldn't be too normal if we didn't get depressed once in awhile."

By normalizing her depressed feelings (e.g., "we wouldn't be too normal if we didn't get depressed"), Louise portrayed her experiences as a "natural" and, therefore, unexceptional part of life. Louise justified her depressed feelings by suggesting that even "healthy people" sometimes get depressed. In addition, she implied that people who did not get depressed may not be "too normal." By identifying her experiences of depression as normal or natural, she was able to defend herself against the idea that she was abnormal or that such feelings were a sign of illness. Based on these women's accounts, it appeared that they struggled to reject the perception of depression as defined by the medical model, in which people who are depressed are perceived as mentally ill and unstable, and having something biologically "wrong" with them.

Searching for Alternative Ways to Understand Depression

In explaining their depressive experiences, the women in the study drew mainly on two types of explanations—external life stressors, and to a lesser extent, hormonal or medical reasons. The majority of women talked about their depression as resulting from stressors in their lives, such as financial problems, child-care responsibilities, and abusive relationships with partners. A smaller number of women talked about "baby blues" and "hormones." For example, Bridget (age twenty-six), who had her first child as a single parent, and who was now married approximately five years with two small children and working part-time, talked about her depression in the following way:

> Mom called them the baby blues or postpartum whatever, and maybe that, maybe that you know, but I don't think they were. I mean I was just over-all, everything I was, from you know, not having a man, not having a boyfriend, not having a husband, to it wasn't just the baby. Like, I wasn't just focused on him and that. You know, I had a baby, and oh, you know, it wasn't that, it was everything.

Bridget initially acknowledged her mother's medical explanation of "the baby blues or postpartum whatever," but then rejected this as the reason for her depressed feelings. For her, depression was not hormonally based, but rather the result of "everything," meaning external stressors such as "not having a man." Thus, Bridget did not accept the medical model view of the female body that constructs women's experiences and actions as closely tied to hormonal influences. Instead, she viewed her depressed feelings as due to a combination of external life stressors, rather than solely the effect of hormones.

After rejecting the label of depression, Gina had difficulty thinking of another way to describe her experiences: "I would love to find another word, but I just don't know . . . women's issues, stresses of life, something like that." The women appeared to have difficulties in identifying their experiences as depression and finding a satisfactory way to explain these experiences. The choices that seemed to be available to them were limited to bodily pathology or inability to cope with external stressors, neither of which fit comfortably with their identities as mothers and wives, as caregivers and nurturers of others. The majority of women did not draw on a medical or hormonal definition because it did not seem to fit with their experiences and also implied that they were ill or suffering from a mental illness. Instead, they explained their depressive experiences by referring to external stressors, particularly those linked to their child-care responsibilities and financial difficulties. At the same time, this type of reasoning also posed a threat to their identity as a good woman because admitting that they were depressed implied that they were inadequate in coping with everyday sources of stress, including their children. The women in this study, however, did not talk about being unable to cope and, generally, they did not blame anything or anyone, including themselves, for their depressed feelings. Instead, they "normalized" their depressive experiences, viewing them as a normal reaction to longstanding circumstances. They tended to attribute their experiences to "stress" and depicted their lives as not being unusual, but as "the way things were."

Women's Ways of Coping with Depressive Experiences

Getting On with Life

Pat (age thirty-five), who was a disabled mother with one child, unemployed and living on Income Assistance, and Cara, whose daughter had recently moved out of the family home, described their experiences of coping with depression in the following way:

> But I just said, somebody's got to look after the house, somebody has got to look after the lawn, and it was me who had to do it. . . . I got through that by realizing that somebody had to do stuff around here, you knew it, stuff wasn't getting done. (Pat)

> Well, I laid in bed for about a week and then after that week, I started moving around and then I just said, I have to do something. So that's what I started doing, packing [the rest of] her [daughter's] stuff away. (Cara)

The tendency of women to normalize their depressive experiences was reflected in the coping strategies that Pat and Cara adopted. For many of the women, coping involved ignoring their distress and continuing with their lives as usual. The women talked about "moving on" or "carrying on" with their lives, despite their depressive experiences, using phrases such as "I had to go on" to describe how they coped. Pat's account implied that she was drawing on ideas about the good wife and mother as someone who "had to do stuff around here," as responsible for looking after the home ("and it was me who had to do it"). Cara described coping as a type of sequential process that involved laying in bed for a week, followed by "moving around," and then "doing something," which involved "packing" her daughter's stuff away. Her use of the phrase "I just said, I have to do something" minimized her agency by suggesting that coping in this way was almost second-nature, rather than requiring effort on her part.

Susan talked about how part of her coping involved becoming more financially stable: "I went on Income Assistance and got my act together and got a job and got you know, a life, and got on with life. . . . So I was forced on Income Assistance, which was another, in my eyes at that time, was another step down to the bottom of the barrel." Susan coped with her depressive experiences by trying to get her life back together after her divorce so that she could care for her children. Coping meant "getting her act together," "getting a job," and "getting on with life." In using the metaphor "another step down to the bottom of the barrel," she portrayed her situation as one of falling deeper into despair, first with her depression and then with having to go on Income Assistance. Thus, having little money was a sign for Susan that she was "down." Although she talked about coping in a somewhat matter-of-fact way (e.g., "got my act together"), her struggle over needing money yet not wanting to accept Income Assistance suggested that coping and "getting a life" were not always easy things to do.

Jane coped with her depressed feelings by giving priority to her activities as a mother: "No matter how depressed or stressed out you are, for me, I know I still have to get up every morning and I still have to get them their breakfast. . . . I don't know if you'd say they were my anchor, but I guess that's the way you'd put it. . . . For me it always comes down to the kids." As Jane's account indicates, many of the women felt that they had no choice but to get on with their lives, in part because of the needs of family members. For women such as Jane, continuing with life as usual took precedence over attending to their own depressive feelings. Jane said "it always comes down to the kids," implying clearly that she put her children's needs ahead of dealing with her depressed feelings. Thus, for her, coping with her depression did not entail looking after herself and her feelings, but rather, carrying on with her normal routine so as not to disrupt the lives of her family members. Getting up every morning and making sure her children had breakfast were taken for granted as part of Jane's daily activities.

Seeking Support from Similar Others

One of the ways in which the women attempted to cope with their depressed feelings was by seeking support from family members, friends, and sometimes, strangers who had similar life experiences. For instance, Susan turned to a friend for support: "Thank god I had a friend two doors away. . . . Before she went to work, and then when she came home, she'd run over and have a cup of tea or something. . . . I give her all the credit for pulling me through that because I didn't go to a doctor." For Susan, confiding in a friend was what she identified as coping or "pulling through." Like the other women in the study, Susan had not sought help from a mental health professional ("I didn't go to a doctor"). Rather, comfort was sought from other women who were experiencing similar situations and who could be expected to understand what they were going through. To whom a woman chose to talk depended somewhat on what she believed was happening in her own life. Few women chose partners as confidants, preferring instead women who had shared similar depressive experiences and who could, perhaps, relate better to what they were feeling.

In order to manage her depressive experiences, Bridget turned to a friend whose situation was similar to her own.

> Once and awhile, like I say, my friend down the road, we need to just get out. Her and I just need to after the kids are in bed . . . because you get too busy and you get caught up in things. . . . You're already stressed out from . . . the daily routine. . . . You know you still need that time for yourself. I used to do a lot of toll painting. . . . I don't do that anymore, but yet once in awhile . . . I call her and say, let's go out for a coffee . . . and you both need that. . . . You still need that out away from it all for like an hour. That's, that's a big, that to me, keeps my sanity, I think, even though it should be more often.

For Bridget, spending time with a friend once a month helped her to cope and kept her "sane." Her use of phrases such as "you get too busy" and "you get caught up in things" suggested that she had little time for herself because of household and child-care demands. Being a good mother meant that the "kids" came first and Bridget had no time for herself and her own hobbies ("toll painting"), and barely enough time to spend with others. This daily routine left her feeling "stressed out" and wanting to get out of the house. Bridget's use of the term "need" ("we need to just get out," "you still need that time for yourself," "you still need that out") implied that spending time away from home and children was not only something that enabled her to manage and carry on with her life, but also something to which she was not really entitled.

Talking to other women in similar circumstances also was identified by Gina as something that would have been helpful to her: "If you have another woman to talk to, I could go to a meeting and see if other women experienced the same . . . you feel that you know you're not lonely . . . the feeling to think that you are alone and you are getting crazy, that's what frightens me." Although Gina seemed to be drawing on underlying beliefs about depression espoused by the medical model, knowing that she was not the only one who was depressed ("the feeling to think that you are alone") would have at least alleviated her feelings of loneliness and her fear that she was alone and "crazy."

Both Mary and Jennifer (age thirty-eight), who was married for twenty years with four older children and employed part-time, had attended support groups and found them useful:

> They'd have these support groups and there'd be women there that were from all walks of life that were different nationality, they could hardly speak English and they were different ages and ah, and they were there for different reasons. . . . It was exhilarating, my god. . . . Like it wasn't all depressing, but it just made you realize how vast the problems in life are and you see how they coped and how they survived. (Mary)

> They meet once a week and the idea is mothers come . . . just to socialize with each other . . . but a number of them have said to me this has been a life saver . . . just to talk to another adult. (Jennifer)

For Mary, support groups were a tool that provided her with advice and information on how to cope with her depressed feelings. She seemed to have benefitted from gaining advice from women who were like herself and who had experienced and managed similar feelings. In contrast, Jennifer did not rely so much on the advice of others; rather, she spent time with other mothers to have a break from household duties and to be among other adult women ("just to socialize"). Thus, in seeking out similar others, these women were given a reprieve from their normally "busy" lives, in addition to receiving confirmation that they and their depressive experiences were "normal" and that they were not the only ones feeling depressed. By talking about and sharing their depressive feelings with other women, these women were able to validate their own experiences and to avoid the implication that their feelings were a sign of "mental illness."

Withdrawal and Social Isolation

Although some women turned to friends or family members for support, others coped with their depressed feelings on their own. Jane treasured her moments alone when feeling depressed: "I wanted my own little quiet." For Jane, isolating herself from her family members was a positive experience, because she was able to withdraw to her bath and relax and forget her problems for a while. In this sense, being alone provided a form of sanctuary, something Jane preferred in order to cope. This notion of withdrawal, of isolating themselves from others, was a common theme in the women's accounts. The idea of coping on their own without help was, for some women, directly tied to the negative stigma associated with depression in rural communities. Not wanting other people in their small community to find out that they were depressed, many women concealed their depressive experiences. Gina gave the following reason for not seeking help for her depressed feelings: "I don't feel comfortable to go to the doctors here because I know their wives and so we don't want to expose ourselves . . . especially some of the doctors go to our church, nobody wants to talk about it." Jane commented:

> I mean I went like for medical reasons, but no . . . I liked her [doctor] medical-wise, but to sit and talk to her, I wouldn't. . . . There is no one to talk to unless you have a lot of friends . . . good friends, there's definitely no one. . . . My neighborhood is all his family. I mean there's not that I could say, well, my girlfriend, you know, or my buddy that I go out. . . . As far as friends go, no I have no one. I have his family, I don't have no family of my own.

The negative connotations associated with the term "depression" combined with the lack of anonymity that is an inherent part of living in a rural community prevented some women from seeking any kind of professional help. Gina talked about coping on her own because she did not want to seek help from anyone whom she knew personally (e.g., "I know their [doctor's] wives"). Although she did not talk about the negative stigma surrounding depression, it was implied, for instance, when she said "nobody wants to talk about it." For Jane, the combination of not having any friends ("I have no one"), her social contacts being limited to her husband's family ("I don't have no family of my own"), and not seeing her doctor as someone she could talk to ("I liked her medical-wise, but to sit and talk to her, I wouldn't"), left her feeling that she had no one with whom to share her experiences.

Conclusions

The women's accounts of their depressive experiences provided a wealth of information for understanding depression among women. Through these accounts, the social and cultural influences that form the context of women's lives and shape their depressive experiences could be explored. Through my adoption of a qualitative methodology, and in particular, a reflexive standpoint, I was also able to see how my subjectivity as a researcher affected all aspects of the research process, thereby shaping the findings of the study. My personal background was reflected in my research topic, questions, and reactions during the interviews and in what I said or did not say. As a woman, I was concerned with the predominance of depression among women. As a graduate student in clinical psychology within the Maritime Provinces region of Canada, I was concerned with the inadequacy of research that either pathologized women's experiences or neglected to ask women, particularly those in rural areas, about their depressive feelings. Before I began the interviews, I had not realized the extent of the pain and hardships within participants' lives. I somehow felt "privileged" for not having to deal with such hardships, and also for being able to be a graduate student, not working, and living a fairly comfortable existence devoid of any comparable degree of distress. I felt conflicted by thinking about how resourceful and strong these women were and, at the same time, wanting to comfort them for what they had endured on their own. When some of the women spoke about their hardships, I became more emotionally involved, perhaps empathizing more, asking more questions, and taking more time to "debrief" or process the interview than I did with other women. Thus, I may have been perceived as more caring and sympathetic to these particular women, and in turn they may have felt more comfortable with me, disclosing more than other women interviewed. The attention paid to these issues affected how I interacted with participants, what they said to me, and how I interpreted and analyzed their accounts in the write-up of the research.

By providing a forum for women to speak about their depressive experiences, findings were generated that would have been difficult or impossible to derive by asking women to fill out questionnaires. Analysis of the women's accounts suggested that their experiences of self and everyday lives were regulated by taken-for-granted ideas of what is femininity. The "good woman" was defined in terms of the practices of the "good" mother and housewife providing services and caring for others. Such practices, which permeated all aspects of the lives of the women interviewed, were integral to how these women experienced depression, how it was understood and explained by them, and the coping strategies they drew on to deal with their depressive experiences. According to the women's accounts, depression and recovery from depression were associated with women's perceptions of their adequacy to perform motherly and housewifely duties.

Although the women interviewed in the present study were cognizant of both external sources of stress in their lives and the link between these stressors and their distress, they were still uncomfortable identifying themselves as depressed. One reason for this was that doing so would have implied that their coping skills were inadequate, something which would further suggest that they were unable to meet the culturally constructed standards defining the good woman. Instead, the women tended to interpret their depressed feelings as "normal" and understandable and, therefore, as acceptable reactions to stressors that were external to themselves and originated in the demands of their lives as mothers and housewives. By "normalizing" their experiences, the women painted a picture of themselves as managing their depressed feelings in an appropriate manner, and as coping as effectively as they could under the circumstances. The women did not view their depressive experiences as in any way "pathological" or "abnormal" when considered in the context of the hardships, particularly economic, they faced in their everyday lives in a rural community.

The women's coping methods, as well as their understanding of the relevance of mental health services to their lives, were also linked to these normalizing processes. Neither desiring nor believing they needed professional services, they engaged in coping strategies that made sense to them in the context of their lived experiences, and that enabled them to "go on" with their daily lives despite their depressive experiences. The theme that seemed to underlie all of the coping strategies used by these women was a determination or will to "get on with life." This idea of moving on despite feelings of distress seemed to be fueled by the women's desire to meet their own, others', and societal expectations of being a good woman.

The women were quite resourceful in their coping without the aid of antidepressants or therapy. Some of the women coped with their depressive experiences on their own, not only to avoid stigma, but because they preferred to be by themselves. For other women, coping was facilitated by seeking reassurance from others in similar circumstances that they were not the "only one." The sharing of experiences, either with friends or in informal support groups, enabled them to see commonalities among the difficulties each experienced and, thus, to have their own experiences and feelings validated. The exchange of personal histories among women also may have allowed them to interpret their experiences as understandable reactions to stress from burdensome family responsibilities coupled with financial hardships, rather than the result of personal inadequacy.

The women in the study were also quite vocal in their beliefs and suggestions about what they felt would make their lives easier and lessen their depressive experiences. They spoke about increasing the availability of support groups for single moms, stay-at-home wives, and working mothers, as well as leisure or recreational groups where they had the option of taking their children. More accessible and affordable daycare services were identified as a key to allowing women to get out of the house and possibly to find some form of paid employment, thereby decreasing financial dependence on male partners. The women also talked about better transportation to surrounding areas or urban centers to help combat loneliness and feelings of isolation. Although they did not utilize professional mental health services, their reasons for not doing so provide valuable information for mental health professionals. Educating these professionals on women's perceptions of mental health services, as well as their beliefs about depression and the context of their lives, will increase awareness among professionals, allowing them to be better prepared to talk to women about their distress and to suggest coping methods that make sense within the context of women's lives.

By talking to these women about their depressive experiences, I was able to gain an understanding of their lives and the conditions that gave rise to their distress or "depression." Few studies have explored depression among women living in rural communities, or focused on women's experiences of depression in the absence of contact with mental health professionals. This study represents one contribution to knowledge about depressive experiences in this group of women.

Notes

The research on which this chapter is based was supported by a grant from Mind-Care New Brunswick and a Hyde Graduate Student Research Grant awarded by the Psychology of Women Society of the American Psychological Association. I would also like to acknowledge the support provided by a Doctoral Fellowship awarded by the Social Sciences and Humanities Research Council of Canada.

1. The majority of women who have symptoms meeting diagnostic criteria for depression have neither sought nor received professional help. See P.J. Leaf and M.L. Bruce, "Gender differences in the use of mental health-related services: A re-examination."

2. M.J. Graveline, "Threats to rural women's well-being: A group response."

3. Although fifteen women were interviewed for the study, one woman's interview was excluded from the analysis after she revealed that she was receiving treatment for depression from a mental health professional.

4. See Y. Scattolon and J.M. Stoppard, "'Getting on with life': Women's experiences and ways of coping with depression" for details on the participants' scores on the Beck Depression Inventory.

5. Scattolon and Stoppard, ibid.; K.L. Henwood, "Women and later life: The discursive construction of identities within family relationships"; D.C. Jack, *Silencing the self: Women and depression.*

6. The two additional subthemes, that is, how women identify their experiences as "depression" and how they recover from their depressive experiences, are discussed in Y. Scattolon, *Perceptions of depression and coping with depressive experiences among rural women in New Brunswick.*

7. J.M. Ussher, *Women's madness: Misogyny or mental illness?*

8. S. Bordo, *Unbearable weight: Feminism, western culture and the body.*

References

Bordo, S. (1993). *Unbearable weight: Feminism, western culture and the body.* Berkeley: University of California Press.

Graveline, M.J. (1990). Threats to rural women's well-being: A group response. In V. Dhruvarajan (Ed.), *Women and well-being* (pp. 169–179). Montreal and Kingston: McGill-Queen's University Press.

Henwood, K.L. (1993). Women and later life: The discursive construction of identities within family relationships. *Journal of Aging Studies, 7,* 303–319.

Jack, D.C. (1991). *Silencing the self: Women and depression.* Cambridge: Harvard University Press.

Leaf, P.J., & Bruce, M.L. (1987). Gender differences in the use of mental health-related services: A re-examination. *Journal of Health and Social Behavior, 28,* 171–183.

Scattolon, Y. (1999). *Perceptions of depression and coping with depressive experiences among rural women in New Brunswick.* Unpublished doctoral dissertation, University of New Brunswick, Fredericton, New Brunswick, Canada.

Scattolon, Y., & Stoppard, J.M. (1999). "Getting on with life": Women's experiences and ways of coping with depression. *Canadian Psychology, 40,* 205–219.

Ussher, J.M. (1991). *Women's madness: Misogyny or mental illness?* Hemel Hempstead, UK: Harvester Wheatsheaf.

8

■ ■ ■ ■ ■ ■ ■ ■ ■

"Your Heart Is Never Free"

Women in Wales and Ghana
Talking about Distress

Vivienne Walters, Joyce Yaa Avotri,
and Nickie Charles

OUR FOCUS IN THIS CHAPTER is women's understandings of their emotional and psychological health and how it is embedded in the circumstances of their lives. Women's main health problems include tiredness, stress, disturbed sleep, lack of time for self, anxiety, depression, and thinking or worrying too much.[1] In seeking to make sense of these problems, women develop understandings of their state of mind which often emphasize the social bases of ill health—the social and economic circumstances in which they live and the nature of gender relations. This differs from the dominant approach to women's health which has often emphasized the definitions of experts, reflecting a medical model and underlining the value of medication in the treatment of problems such as depression.[2]

The studies we report on here grew out of research begun in Canada.[3] In a study of 356 women in Hamilton, Canada, participants were asked about the health problems they had experienced in the preceding six months.[4] The most frequently mentioned problems were: tiredness, stress, disturbed sleep, lack of time for self, anxiety, arthritis, and depression. Money problems were a worry for over a third of the women. Depression was more likely to be reported by women in their twenties and thirties, those who had fewer years of education, who were not employed or who worked part-time, whose family income was low and who more often said that they worried about money and about unemployment. They were more likely to experience problems in their relationship with their partner and with other family members, and they also reported disturbed sleep and loneliness.[5] We used statistical analysis to identify the main problems the women experienced and to investigate whether they were associated with women's work and family life. Such an analysis does not convey the ways in which women think about their health and whether they feel their health problems are related to the nature of their day-to-day lives. For this reason, we then embarked on in-depth interviews, in an attempt to explore women's own accounts of their health. We were also curious to know whether the patterns would be similar in a comparable setting in another industrialized society and in a third world context and so, using our links with each country, we chose Wales and Ghana.

We conducted in-depth interviews with women, in each of these two settings—south Wales, in the United Kingdom, and Ghana, in West Africa—enabling them to talk about their health in the context of their day-to-day lives. The main emphasis in the women's accounts was on the enduring and pervasive features of their daily lives, rather than on periods of exceptional stress or the problems associated with a particular life event. There is a marked similarity in the issues of which women spoke and these point to the importance of both material deprivation and gender relations in understanding women's experience of distress. Women described money problems, their work roles in relation to production and social reproduction,[6] and problems in their relationships with their partners. These wove together to create or amplify the mental health problems women experienced. It would be unwise to overemphasize the similarities in women's lives across such different countries, yet the common strands in our interviews do suggest that it is important to examine shared experiences and the ways in which the structure of women's lives influences their well-being.

The Studies

The women lived in countries at very different levels of economic development, and the contrast between an advanced industrial society and a largely rural economy was apparent. The Welsh research was based in an industrial town in south Wales—an established working-class community characterized by strong family ties and a lack of geographical mobility.[7] Many of the women had lived in the area for their whole life and several generations live in close proximity. Throughout much of the twentieth century, south Wales was dominated by heavy industry, largely steel and coal, but since World War II these industries have been in decline. In recent years the decline has been more rapid and instead of high male employment and low female employment, the area has seen an increase in male unemployment while jobs for women have expanded.[8] Nevertheless, the area still has lower rates of female participation in the work force than other parts of Britain[9] and this is reflected among the women we interviewed; only one was employed full-time. In all, we interviewed thirty-five women, a relatively high proportion of whom had low incomes, reflecting the large number of households dependent on welfare benefits or pensions. Only fourteen women had access to a full-time wage and for only one was it her own. Five women were working part-time and three were looking after other people's children in their own homes. Two-thirds of the participants (twenty-four women) were married or living with a partner, while the others were single, widowed, divorced, or separated.[10]

The other study was conducted in a town in the Volta region of Ghana, West Africa. The area is characterized by subsistence and commercial farming of maize, cassava, yam, and vegetables. Following a long tradition in West Africa, women play important roles in the informal sector and they are the main producers of vegetables; they process and preserve fish, make clay pots and bowls, are very much involved in trading, and often control the many small local bars and eating places.[11] In the past decade or so Structural Adjustment Programs have created further impoverishment in Ghana[12] affecting women in particular and closing off some employment opportunities for them in the formal sector.[13] Of the seventy-five women we interviewed, most were engaged in economic activity. Typically they were traders or farmers. Part of the produce from their farms was usually sold in the local market for cash and was thus a source of income for them. A few of the women indicated that they were teachers, secretaries, nurses, hairdressers, and seamstresses, though many of these women engaged in multiple economic activities. For instance, one was formally employed as an accounts clerk, but she was also a farmer and a trader. Another was a housewife, a trader, a hairdresser, and she also cracked stones in the quar-ries. Just over half of the women (thirty-eight) were married or living with a partner and another nine had absentee husbands. The others were sin-gle, widowed, divorced, or separated.

In both studies women were asked about their main health concerns and what they felt influenced their health. We chose an open-ended ap-proach because it shows how women experience their world and how they talk about their health. The interviews were conducted by women who had strong links with the areas of study; both had been brought up in the areas and in this sense were regarded as "insiders." This meant that they were able to draw on some of their ties and their familiarity with the com-munities in initiating samples.[14] Each of them had also moved away for ed-ucation and had thus become "outsiders" too; the Ghanaian interviewer had moved to Canada and a very different culture.[15]

Because of their knowledge of the communities, the interviewers were more easily accepted, language and culture were familiar, and it was possi-ble for them to explore issues that emerged in the interviews and to do this in a culturally acceptable way. It is difficult to assess their effect on the women who were interviewed. The depth of the interviews and the rap-port that was established in many instances suggest that women found it easy to talk to and trust the interviewers. Their dual identity as both "in-sider" and "outsider" may have fostered the belief that the research might be beneficial—both to the interviewers themselves and to the participants insofar as the interviewers could convey their experiences and views to a broader audience. Women appeared to welcome the chance to talk at length, and several commented that they seldom had this sort of opportu-nity to reflect on such issues. Of course, it is possible that the interviewers' familiarity with the social and cultural context of the participants may have led them to take for granted themes in the interviews, themes that another researcher might have found more striking. However, our careful reading of the interview transcripts suggests that this was not a problem. On bal-ance, we feel that the interviewers' identity as "insiders" was an asset and that this was matched with their experiences outside the communities and their training as social researchers, which enabled them to step back and view the content of the interviews with a sense of distance—to be an "out-sider."

In addition to the role of the interviewers/research assistants, two of us (Charles and Walters) were principal investigators and as such played a major role in designing and supervising the research and analyzing the interviews. As sociologists we have been trained to interpret individuals' experiences in the light of their social context. We look for evidence of social influences, while psychologists might focus on individual traits and a physician would assign priority to the biological bases of ill health. Recognizing this element of selectivity, we have sought to rely on women's own words in this chapter rather than "putting words into their mouths."

In the following sections we show how women described the aspects of their lives that created or exacerbated the forms of distress they reported. It is noteworthy that the features of their day-to-day lives which they emphasized are often neglected in discussions of mental health, the dominant models being medical or approaches which emphasize lifestyle (diet, tobacco, alcohol consumption and so on) and blame the individual for her health problems.[16]

Distress

The majority of participants in south Wales and Ghana described various forms of distress. Women in south Wales spoke of tiredness, stress, disturbed sleep, a sense of little hope, feeling that they were not coping, and just over two-fifths said they were depressed. In Ghana, almost three-fourths of the participants spoke of thinking and worrying too much, which appeared to be the main form of expressing mental health problems. The importance of looking at women's own understandings of their sense of well-being is highlighted by their comments. One of the women in south Wales said: "The doctor says I've got stress, but to me stress is like you see on the television with these high living people and you know, like people who are living in London." Another woman asked, "Is worrying the same as stress?" Others were reluctant to say they were "depressed," and yet they described problems that other women might regard as examples of depression.

There was often a sense of despair in their responses: "I just think sometimes, you know, well what's the point? Why bother to go on?"; "I just feel sometimes as if I'm on a merry-go-round and there's no getting off, it's all the same and nothing to look forward to"; "I just don't want to get up and do anything when I'm that down"; or "You just think that, well, everything's coming to an end." This last woman was seeing a stress counselor and that seemed to help; at least she had someone to talk with.

> I didn't know what the problem was, I just felt I was going mad, like. I was having this pulsing all the time, and giddiness and racing and everything and just, well you do tend to think the worst of everything anyway, and I was just really freaked out about it. And then a doctor said, well, there's nothing wrong, and that freaked me out even more. . . . Well, it's not so bad now. I'd say about ten months in all I've been having treatment. But it's not so bad now as it was, definitely. . . . I wouldn't say it is severe. You know, I'm not suicidal or nothing like, thank goodness, 'cause they asked me that.

Several women spoke of an element of unpredictability, as the symptoms might vary from day to day and sometimes this gave false hope:

> One day I might feel really good and think, oh, it's gone now, it's over with, I'll get back to normal now and I think what I'm going to do and the next thing, I'm like black. Everything's turned black like as if something really bad, something have happened to hit it off, but it haven't like.[17]

Even though there were moments of respite, the general impression was of a constant cloud over these women: "I get quite a lot of depression. . . . I get quite a lot of feeling down, you know. Life always seems one long chore and there's no let up."

Among the Ghanaian women there was a very strong emphasis on "thinking too much" and "worrying too much" together with the related problems of tiredness and being unable to sleep. In addition, many women complained of headaches, bodily aches and pains, tiredness, and said they were always sad or referred to similar problems with mood. The following is a typical account:

> Because you see right now, when I worry or think too much, I get this severe headache. When my head is aching like that, then my neck also starts paining me, then I start experiencing the pain at my back, then my stomach,

and this will continue to pain me for a long time before I feel better. Because I have thought about the issue too much, my heart will not be free, so when I lie down and sleep and wake up like that around 12 midnight, I won't sleep again until day breaks.

Some women also spoke of their loss of weight which in this culture is a symbol of illness, malnutrition, or distress.

I get very worried, sister, it's not easy. I will be there aaaah [for a long time][18] thinking and thinking, I'll be worried, what can I do? When it happens that way, I'll just end up becoming something [not being myself]. I'll just be there, because as I am here now, there's nobody to go to and say "this is what is worrying me, what can I do?" So me alone, I'll be there, I'll go and lie down in bed like that, and be thinking and thinking, and then I grow thinner and thinner.

One of the women, a trader, became bankrupt and found she could no longer sleep. She turned to her doctor for help, though medication may well have intensified her problems.

When I go to bed, I can't sleep. I'll go and report to the doctor and he'll give me Valium, ten milligrams. I can come and take three tablets, but still I can't sleep. . . . I have even taken four tablets before . . . even then I couldn't sleep. . . . I realized that I was no longer myself. I can stand up here and walk all the way to [a nearby village] and then just walk back, and wouldn't know why I went there.

The interviews contain rich descriptions of the conditions of women's lives and in these we find clues to what impairs their emotional and psychological well-being. The following sections trace women's accounts of their money problems, the nature of their roles as wife and mother, and their relationships with their husbands. They often cited these aspects of their lives as the source of their distress. While there are important differences in the day-to-day lives of these women, the common threads in the interviews point to the importance of both material deprivation and gender relations in understanding women's health and well-being in Ghana and in south Wales.

Money Problems

A theme which ran through many of the interviews in south Wales and especially those in Ghana was money problems. The majority of the women
in each group of participants faced financial hardship. In south Wales most
were working-class women and they and their partners were often unemployed. Welfare benefits provided a financial "safety net," but women
faced major problems in juggling scarce resources in order to be able to
buy necessities. Their experience of hardship is different than in Ghana because there are few opportunities to earn income other than through a job.
The problems they faced as a result of their impoverishment included isolation, boredom, and loneliness.

In Ghana many of the women lived a precarious existence and they
faced the enormous challenge of creating ways to earn money. Isolation
was not a problem, instead the Ghanaian women spoke of how they moved
from one income-generating activity to another, working long and demanding days. Thus, the emphasis in the two sets of interviews is different, reflecting differences in levels of economic development, but women's
accounts in each country illustrate the effects of material deprivation.

In south Wales women lived from week to week and had to budget care-
fully. Speaking of her worries about money one woman said that she was
"always worrying that there's never going to be enough, to go and pay
everything." Their children could not expect the things that those from
more prosperous families might have. One mother described how she just
could not send her son to karate classes at the local Community Center because they cost the equivalent of $3.50 and were just too expensive. Oth-
ers felt defeated that there was so little to spare for even modest treats:
"We're so skint [poor]. Sometimes we can barely afford to just pay bills.
We're just constantly paying bills, paying for food, rent and what have you.
And you've no money left for yourself then, at all." This last woman, a
young unemployed mother whose partner was also unemployed, said "I'm
depressed because I'm bored and, well, lack of money." She was constantly
tired and described what sounded like a vicious circle of inertia:

> I think it's because I'm not doing anything. If I'm busy, I'm busy all day and
> I've got loads of energy, but if I get up in the morning, I sit down and have
> a fag [cigarette], I'm there for a couple of hours then, and then I'm sort of

dragging my feet about and doing things half-heartedly for the rest of the day.

She described how everything had to be counted and watched: "Even staying at home costs money anyway, 'cause I've got a token meter [for the electricity] and I can see the pennies just ticking away just by watching telly [television] and having a cup of tea and what have you." Welfare benefits cushioned people, but few wanted to rely on them:

Especially when both of us was working, coming down to none of us working, it makes a big difference like . . . and I don't like to be on Income Support. . . . I like to be earning, you know what I mean like, to be independent, get your own money. I don't like taking off the state.

One of the most important measures of poverty and whether or not one can manage to be a good parent seems to be the ability to afford Christmas presents. Women in south Wales often relied on buying things from "the catalogue" because it was cheaper than the shops (though also lower quality) and they tried to put aside money for this, though it was difficult.

With Christmas coming up now, what I got to try to do as best I can on the Family Allowance [child benefits]. I try not to touch that throughout the year so I know they got for Christmas then. Because, I used to do it when I was working, but now I could do with it through the month. But I try not to because I don't think they'd have much for Christmas otherwise, although I'm going to get a lot of things off the catalogue.

Women in Ghana spoke at length about their money problems and these were severe. Sometimes there was just no money for the next day.

You can't sleep, it happens to all women, because like me, I have three children and sometimes, common 10 Cedis [roughly $.01], I won't have at home. Tomorrow by all means I have to give the children money to take to school, I know that, but what can I do? Sometimes, you have corn, but you cannot roast corn for the children to chew, so you'll be thinking, "Jesus, when I wake up tomorrow, where am I going? What am I going to do?"

Even though women worked hard, they still could not pull themselves out of poverty.

> Poverty, some women work very hard, but they can't make ends meet. You are worried, you force yourself to do this and that at the same time. You'll be thinking, when you go to bed, you can't sleep. . . . For example, you see what I'm selling right now, if this were enough to take care of the home, I won't lie down in bed and be thinking about what else I should do to get money, or where will I go to get more money? But this alone is not enough, so I'm always thinking about other things to do. I farm too.

Some fell into the trap of borrowing money and, while providing temporary relief, the debts intensified their worries.

> This money that I've gone to borrow, how am I going to pay it back? How am I going to do this or that? How would I see to it that the children are okay? All these things make us think a lot, it's a whole lot of problem, you think and think and think. Day and night, you're thinking, you can't sleep.

Here, too, Christmas was an important measure of a woman's ability to care for her family. An unemployed woman talked about how she had frequent headaches and grew thinner as a result of thinking too much about her money problems. She mentioned that Christmas was fast approaching, but so far she had not even been able to buy her children "obroni wawu" (literally, "a dead white man," meaning second-hand clothes). This was a source of worry for her.

> Now Christmas is coming. We live in a big house, everybody is making preparations for the children, but it's only me who has never bought even "obroni wawu." . . . I can even take this [pointing to her dress] to church, so as for mine it's not a problem. It's the children I worry about, because there's nobody I can talk to for help, so I "hanu" [worry] a lot. I think a lot. . . . Sometimes when I think for a long time I, my head and my whole person become "basaa" [mixed up or confused], you won't know exactly where you are [she becomes absent-minded].

The women who were employed in jobs were also concerned about not earning enough to care for their families. Many pointed out that even though they had a wage, they did not earn sufficient to make a decent living. "Whatever you get, it goes into the cooking pot"—all their earnings are spent on food and other basic needs for the household. They believed that jobs in the formal sector would provide them with a steady, predictable income and improve the conditions in their households, yet in order to make enough money to care for their children, they had to engage in many different types of work, sometimes starting their day as early as 3:30 or 4:00 A.M. A thirty-six-year-old single mother of three, who was braiding another woman's hair during the interview, talked about how she juggled her work activities as a mother, farmer, hair braider, and stone cracker:

> Sometimes when I wake up at 5:30, I wash the dishes, I see to the children and then they leave for school, and then I make lunch and leave it behind for them. I have a small farm. I go to the farm and work. On some days, I have a place [the quarries] where I go to crack stones. So when it's not market day here or T—— market day where I go to braid hair, I go to the quarries to crack stones.

Many other women were also engaged in several different income-generating activities.

Relationships with Men

Both the Welsh and the Ghanaian women talked at length about gender roles and the nature of their relationships with their husbands or partners. Men in Wales often appeared to limit women's opportunities to go out and to be independent; gender roles were very traditional and younger women, in particular, railed against this. In Ghana there is a tradition of economic independence among women and less emphasis on the couple relationship. Ghanaian women often seem to play the role of both mother and father to their children.

The vehemence with which many women in south Wales spoke of husbands or partners was striking, although this is part of the local, gender-segregated culture. One woman in her forties said:

> I think we'd all be far happier if there were no men about. . . . I think
> women's biggest problems are their husbands . . . my age group especially.
> . . . We're married to selfish men, very selfish men then. . . . Like I make a
> joke of it and say, "well, once you've had your kids you might as well get rid
> of them, don't want them." . . . Lack of understanding, lack of compassion,
> and selfishness. . . . There's no such thing as equality. They can say there is
> as much as they like, but there isn't.

Women received little help with domestic chores. Even when both of
them were unemployed, women could not rely on their partners to help
around the house. "Who cleans the toilet? Me. Who cleans the bath? Me.
Who picks up all the socks and pants on the floor? Me." Another mother
spoke of having to look after the children when they are sick with no
help from her husband. Several of the women felt that their partners
were not unusual and they often spoke disparagingly of men in general.
One said that "as long as there are men on this earth it will be the same,
because they expect the women to do everything, and there aren't
enough strong women, to tell them no way, we're not going to do it."
A young mother said, "They all seem to be the same. I don't think anybody's happy. I mean, I'd rather be on my own any day of the week. I'd
rather have a dog, I think." In general, men were often viewed as providing neither emotional nor practical support. Some participants felt it
was women's fault for not standing up to them. Some others said that
they helped to create these patterns at the beginning of relationships.
Men became dependent on them and—a theme that appeared in the interviews in both countries—men became simply another child to look
after.

> I just think that we do too much, and I think we try to do too much at the
> beginning of relationships a lot of the time because we think they'll like us
> for it. And then before you know where you are, we've carried, we're taking,
> carrying that burden for them. . . . I do think this is a sort of thing a lot of
> women do and then, before you know where you are, you are his mother,
> aren't you?

No matter how they explained the nature of their relationships with men,
there was little sense of supportive relationships; indeed, men often

seemed to undermine women, belittle them, and restrict their opportunities to go out. A young mother said of her husband:

> He doesn't think that I'm a person. I'm his wife and their mother and, you know, get on with it. I'm not allowed—he goes out to work and yet I'm stuck here all day, so then if I want to go out when he's off work, he doesn't like it because he thinks I should be here with him.

Another woman commented that "it's the general atmosphere with the Welsh men . . . they like to keep their women in their little patch, nice and tidy and you know, don't go out too often." This, along with the relatively isolated nature of their lives, undermined women's confidence. A mother of two children said that men seem to make you question yourself all the time and she felt that her husband was always undermining her, both in front of others and when they were alone.

> I don't know, I just think really when I'm in my more lucid moments, I always think that he's really jealous of me and he really resents me. And at other times I tell myself "Oh, you're being stupid," but I really do think he resents me. . . . I just think sometimes he dislikes me. Sometimes I really do feel that, you know, the way he treats me and the way he speaks to me, I think he really must hate my guts, you know. Why does he stay with me? Why does he stay around?

But not all women described their husbands in this way. Some relied on them as confidants, but it was more often older women, typically widowed, who looked back on their relationships with a certain wistfulness and an apparent acceptance of traditional gender relations.[19] For older women, nursing a terminally ill partner or the death of their husband were often the events that precipitated feelings of depression or loneliness.

One Ghanaian woman said, "You just look at our work and see if you have any freedom on earth." Women carry a heavy workload and often assume much of the financial responsibility for their children. She talked about how she spent a typical day.

> You go to the farm, you come back, then you come and go to the market, come back and put food on fire. Yes, we do a lot of "tukara" [work], even

more than men, because when a man comes back from the farm, he sits in "akpasa" [easy chair] and does not do anything, but you will come back and move about and do everything. The only freedom you have is the sleep you go to sleep. You will go to the farm, carry your baby at your back, you can't put the baby down, so the baby is at your back, and you're working, weeding, collecting firewood "aaah . . ." [for a long time] like that. You carry the firewood on your head, the baby is at your back, you'll walk all the way back home, before you come and do more "tukara" at home. You'll never be free, oooh. If you come back, if you don't have [older] children, then you go to the market, then you come back, you come back and cook. . . . When you wake up, there you go again, you're never free!

Another woman made reference to her husband as having become her "firstborn," as his farm was not doing well and he was bringing no money into the house.

So when it happened that way and my husband wasn't doing anything, I was getting fed up. And it was not raining too [so the crops were not growing well]. . . . Now that I have taken him [her husband] as my firstborn, I can stand the problems . . . because when it's day break I have to see to it that he also eats, he takes his bath and everything. The children too the same. So I've taken it that he is my eldest child, so we are there [that is how it is]. We are fine anyway. But it's my wish that he'll get a job soon, that'll be good. . . . For the meantime I'm responsible for everything, the children's school fees. Now that Christmas is coming, I have to buy clothes for the children.

But it was more than the gendered division of labor that bothered women. They feared that their husbands might desert them, or be having casual affairs (with the associated risk of AIDS). One participant believed that the shock of being abandoned by their husbands created mental health problems for some women: "and the man will move out, leave you and go and stay with his girlfriend. . . . The man will not care whether you and the children have eaten or not." Others worried about the possibility of their husband taking another wife. The worst situation, according to one woman, developed when both partners were unemployed and the husband insisted on taking another wife. She said that in such circumstances women felt helpless because tradition continues to permit men to marry more than one wife even when it is not economically feasible and aggravates the burden on the first wife.

> Yes, what worries we women is your husband is not doing any work, the woman too is not doing any work, so you're hustling to make ends meet, and upon this, the man goes in for another wife! That is our problem in Ghana—he goes for another wife, and this wife will start bringing forth children. So these are worrying, but because of our tradition, um, I mean, if you talk no one will listen.

In some instances women spoke of the threat of violence from their husbands.

> He beat me and stumped his feet on me. By then I was six months pregnant, and I got very sick and was rushed to the hospital. . . . I lost the baby. . . . Oh! He beats me, he beats me very well [laughing]. People won't tell you, they beat us.

Relationships with husbands were a common theme in the interviews with Ghanaian women. As one woman reflected, "We women worry a lot about our husbands."

Yet there was an ambivalence in women's comments—paradoxes that were recognized by women in Ghana and south Wales. While some of the women, especially those who were single, brooded over their plight and were worried because they were lonely, some of those who were married were contemplating leaving their husbands. For many women marriage was a necessary evil. It brought social respect and sometimes companionship, comfort, and advice in times of crisis, though it could also bring challenges and problems which affected women's health. One Ghanaian woman summed up the contradictions:

> This marriage problems ooh, if you don't get married too, it's a problem, when you get married too it becomes a problem. As for marriage, it's like "hlomade Kotoku, kpakpla ha dor ye, makpla makpla ha dor ye" [a sack used to carry food and, as useful as the sack may be, it is very bulky and uncomfortable to carry, so using it causes as much discomfort as not using it].

The same contradiction was expressed by women in south Wales: "Well, most of my women friends and myself are not satisfied with the men in their lives. If they haven't got one, they seem to want one, and if they've got one, they want to get rid of them!"

Motherhood

Motherhood is at the center of traditional definitions of being a woman, more central than the role of wife. Here too, we see how gender shapes women's sense of well-being and how women face contradictions. As Doyal argues, women's "idioms of distress" can be traced to the "contradictory and demanding reality of so many women's daily lives."[20] Women wanted children and were expected to have them, yet at the same time some of them resented the way children tied them down; they found child-care difficult because they lost their sense of self and they faced a much increased workload or worried about their children's behavior.

Women in both countries spoke about their roles with respect to their domestic and caring work. They carry a heavy workload, the demands are constant, and the work has an essential quality. In Ghana, activities such as cleaning, collecting water, cooking, child-care, and the generation of income were not activities that could be postponed; they were necessary for the survival of families. A thirty-nine-year-old woman who was the main bread-winner for her household regarded her roles as a wife, mother, farmer, and office worker as "compulsory."

> But a woman, there's no rest, if you're doing your housework, you can't say that your children's clothes are dirty but you won't wash them, you can't say that you're tired so you won't fetch water, it's "compulsory" [said in English] that you go for water. You can't say you're tired so you won't go to the market, or you won't cook.

Other Ghanaian women said, "You're always worried, your heart is never free" or "if you get married right now, you'll never be free again." A similar sentiment was expressed by a woman in south Wales when she described how her husband could go to bed when he was ill, but said that bed-rest would be impossible for her: "I mean if [my husband] wanted to go off sick for work, if he was bad, he could just go to bed and that would be it. I couldn't. . . . The woman is still the one who's got to carry the can with the family and that, definitely." Another Welsh woman said:

> Well, I know how . . . hard it is for people to live. I mean with shopping, I mean women have got all the added worry haven't they, of making ends meet and worrying about the family. Oh, I think women have always had more worry than men. . . . I mean a woman never shuts off, do they really, when they've got a family.

In particular, the responsibility of bringing up their children was a focus of women's lives. One of the young women in south Wales had been feeling really depressed and said, "It was all the stress of my family and marriage like. Crying all the time and taking it out on them." She felt she could barely cope.

> I don't want to be this wife and mother I am at the moment. Just feel like going and leaving them—you know, my mother have them and look after them for me like . . . I feel like running. I couldn't, I haven't got the guts to do that to be honest, but sometimes I think well I'll have to go or I'm going to hurt someone like, you know.

Others, too, spoke of the way that motherhood changed them: "I don't think you're a mother if you don't worry. . . . If you're a mother, you'll worry always. You'll worry if there's nothing to worry about, I think." And another woman said: "Nearly everybody you speak to is usually stressed out, one way or another, harassed, run down, with screaming kids. I just think it's part and parcel of the job, isn't it, being a wife and mother or what have you." They put their children first and the relentless demands, with little help from their husbands, "got them down." Yet not to do this and to put themselves first was to fail as a mother. Thus, women in south Wales were caught in a vicious circle—they craved time for themselves, resented their husbands for refusing them this, but felt that to meet their own needs would be selfish. One mother, speaking of her sister-in-law, said, "You know she can't cope with being a mother. She wants her own life more than she wants to be a mother. . . . I don't think she's a good, no, not a good mother. In some ways she is, but, you know what I mean, she puts herself first." Ironically, this woman was one of the participants who described most graphically how motherhood seemed to be destroying her, she did not want to be the person she had turned into and felt like leaving her children.

As we have seen, women in Ghana bear the bulk of the responsibility for their children and this is an important source of worry for them.

> All these responsibilities make them [women] think too much, "where am I going to get food for these children today? What are they going to eat today?" You see that you are alone but you are talking to yourself. . . . Sometimes you don't even know that you are talking loudly, but someone who overhears you will say "Ei! Is this woman tying a yam [behaving strangely]?"

The importance of motherhood as a source of worry and a threat to women's mental health was brought out by a story told by one Ghanaian woman. It illustrates the cultural recognition that having children is stressful for women.

> Two childless women went to see a medicine man for help to have children. The medicine man asked them if they wanted to become mad. One of them said "yes," while the other one said "No." He treated both of them and sent them back home. Later on, the woman who said she was willing to become mad got pregnant and had a child. The other woman who was unwilling to become mad could still not have children. The childless woman went back to the medicine man and asked why she was not having children. She argued that her friend who was willing to become mad was still not mad and had even had a child. The medicine man explained: "Telling children, 'Don't do this! Don't do that!' is the madness I was talking about. The reason why you have not been able to have children is because you don't want to become mad."

In sum, themes of material deprivation, relationships with men, and the strains of motherhood were among the most striking features of women's lives as they talked in the interviews. These were aspects of their lives that helped them to explain the problems they encountered with tiredness, disturbed sleep, anxiety, thinking too much, worrying too much, and feeling sad or under stress. Such problems indicate the distress that characterized the lives of many of the women we interviewed in each country. They also led to a changed sense of self—women spoke of "the old me," "I'll just end up becoming something [not being myself]," and "I don't want to be the person I've turned into."

Discussion

The women in these studies come from countries at very different stages of economic development, yet common themes emerged in the interviews, suggesting that there is something about the structure of women's lives that creates distress. Material deprivation and gender relations are both important, constraining women and limiting the control that they can assert over their lives. While there are differences in women's day-to-day lives, the broad features of their productive roles, their lack of access to material resources, and their responsibility for domestic labor and caring work produce similar feelings of distress. Despite cultural differences in the expression of distress, we see how relations of production and social reproduction can influence women's experiences.

In their comments about their money worries we also see the central role of work in women's lives. Apart from the obvious financial importance of work, it represents independence, social integration, and social support. In south Wales lack of work was soul-destroying and women faced a sense of isolation, boredom, and loss of confidence; they were divorced from the mainstream of life. In Ghana, on the other hand, where women are very much engaged in income-generating work, the interviews show how heavy workloads and insecurity created relentless demands.

The gendered division of labor and women's ambivalent feelings toward men are key themes in each study; the problems women described appear to be intimately linked with the nature of their roles as women. They sometimes turned to family and friends for social support, and religion might also provide solace. Several women also relied on medication, and paracetamol (similar to Tylenol) appears to have been consumed in large quantities in both countries. But women's hopes for the future involved education, jobs and, in Ghana, access to credit. All these could give them a measure of independence and control over their lives. They would alleviate their financial problems, help women to transcend some of the limits of gender, and counter the sense of powerlessness that pervaded many of the interviews.

The women's emphasis on the link between their distress and the social and material conditions of their lives is at odds with the very strong emphasis in recent years on the development of new drugs for problems such as depression and anxiety. Such medications have proved to be among the most lucrative in the pharmaceutical repertoire and are widely prescribed in the developed world.[21] In the same period, we also see growing unemployment, a proliferation of low-paid, part-time, and insecure jobs, welfare cutbacks, and growing poverty. The contradiction is striking.

The dominant emphasis in relation to health has been biomedical and, more recently, explanations which focus on lifestyles have gained greater currency.[22] The latter approaches represent a change insofar as they focus on behavioral rather than biological aspects of health, and on the promotion of health in general rather than the origins and treatment of specific diseases and disorders. Nevertheless, lifestyle explanations dwell on individual responsibility for health and often neglect the broader structural and cultural determinants of health and illness. Were the change of emphasis to be taken a step further, one useful starting point would be the material and social conditions of women's lives, exploring the ways in which they influence women's health. A similar argument is made by Doyal:

> [T]raditional epidemiological methods have to be turned on their head. Instead of identifying diseases and then searching for a cause, we need to begin by identifying the major areas of activity that constitute women's lives. We can then go on to analyze the impact of these activities on their health and well-being.[23]

It is important that in adopting such an approach, we incorporate women's own understandings of their health and the ways in which their day-to-day lives influence their sense of well-being. In this regard women are experts.

The arguments we have developed here have implications for both policy makers and practitioners. Above all, we suggest that it is not sufficient to consider mental health problems simply in terms of physiology (with an attendant emphasis on medication) nor can we view them as primarily individual problems (with a focus on counseling, behavioral therapy, and medication). While we do not discount the value of such approaches, there are compelling reasons to turn our attention to the *social* bases of distress. In so doing, mental health becomes a political challenge rather than an individual misfortune attributable to biology, personality traits, or lifestyle. Once we focus attention on the social bases of mental health, it is clear that the onus lies with politicians and other policy makers to change the social and economic conditions that impair mental health. Rather than individuals feeling a sense of culpability, practitioners could help women to see the social roots of their distress and ways in which they might seek to change the immediate conditions of their lives.

Notes

The research reported here was funded by the Social Sciences and Humanities Research Council of Canada, the Economic and Social Research Council in the United Kingdom and the Faculty of Graduate Studies of McMaster University. The authors wish to thank all the women who so willingly gave up their time to participate in the study. The first author also thanks the School of Social Sciences and International Development, University of Wales Swansea for the facilities they provided for her as an Honorary Research Fellow.

1. For more information on the studies, see J.Y. Avotri, *"Thinking too much" and "worrying too much": Ghanaian women's accounts of their health problems,* J.Y. Avotri and V. Walters, "'You just look at our work and see if we have any freedom on earth': Ghanaian women's accounts of their work and their health"; J.Y. Avotri and V. Walters, "'We women worry a lot about our husbands': Ghanaian women talking about their relationships with men"; N. Charles and V. Walters, "Age and gender in women's accounts of their health: Interviews with women in south Wales"; V. Walters and N. Charles, " 'I just cope from day to day': Unpredictability and anxiety in the lives of women."

2. J.M. Stoppard, "Dis-ordering depression in women: Toward a materialist-discursive account"; J.M. Stoppard, "Women's bodies, women's lives and depression: Towards a reconciliation of material and discursive accounts"; V. Walters, "Beyond medical and academic agendas: Lay perspectives and priorities."

3. V. Walters, "Stress, anxiety and depression: Women's accounts of their health problems"; V. Walters, "Women's views of their main health problems"; V. Walters and M. Denton, "Stress, depression and tiredness among women: The social production and social construction of health."

4. V. Walters, "Women's views of their main health problems."

5. V. Walters, "Stress, anxiety and depression"; V. Walters and M. Denton, "Stress, depression and tiredness among women."

6. We use the term social reproduction to refer to the work involved in caring for children, partners, and others and the domestic and other labor undertaken by women to ensure that their families are fed, clothed, and cared for.

7. C.C. Harris, *Redundancy and recession in south Wales*; L. Morris, *The workings of the household*; C. Rosser and C.C. Harris, *The family and social change*.

8. N. Charles, "Women—advancing or retreating?"

9. T. Rees, *Women in the Welsh workforce: 21 years of equality legislation*.

10. The interviews in south Wales took place between July and December 1993, and those in Ghana were conducted between November 1994 and March 1995. For further details of the methodology in each study, see V. Walters, J.Y. Avotri, and N. Charles, " 'Your heart is never free': Women in Wales and Ghana talking about distress."

11. E. Ardayfio-Schandorf, "Household energy supply and women's work in Ghana"; T. Manuh, "Ghana: Women in the public and informal sectors under the Economic Recovery Programme." In the developing world it is common for many women to work in the informal sector, often providing services (such as hair braiding) or trading goods (vegetables, prepared foods, clay pots) they have produced. This economic activity is unregulated, in contrast to work in the formal sector which is within a capital-labor relation and regulated by the state. However, wages may be so low that women have to supplement their income with work in the informal sector.

12. Structural Adjustment Programs which have forced reductions in public expenditures have been mandated by the International Monetary Fund to reduce the fiscal crisis in developing countries. Loans have been contingent on the introduction of such programs. This has led to a reduction of health and public services and the loss of jobs in these sectors.

13. C.A. Anyinam, "The social costs of the International Monetary Fund's adjustment programs for poverty: The case of health care development in Ghana."

14. In both studies women were selected for interview by using social networks. The interviewers used their own links with the community (mothers' groups, churches, women's organizations) to recruit participants, and each woman who was interviewed was then asked to suggest two others who might be willing to talk to us. We took care to ensure that women of different ages and different circumstances were included in the studies.

15. In south Wales, the interviews were conducted by a post-doctoral research assistant, Jackie Lucas. Joyce Yaa Avotri, a doctoral student in Canada, originally from Ghana, used the data she collected for her Ph.D. dissertation and is a co-author of this chapter.

16. H. Graham, "Behaving well: Women's health behaviour in context"; S. Nettleton, "Women and the new paradigm of health and medicine."

17. The phrasing in this quote is an example of a south Walian dialect.

18. Words in brackets serve as a translation or clarification.

19. N. Charles and V. Walters, "Age and gender in women's accounts of their health: Interviews with women in south Wales."

20. L. Doyal, *What makes women sick? Gender and the political economy of health*.

21. N. Angier, "Drugs for depression multiply, and so do the hard questions."
22. S. Nettleton, "Women and the new paradigm of health and medicine."
23. L. Doyal, "Women, health and the sexual division of labour: A case study of the women's health movement."

References

Angier, N. (1997). Drugs for depression multiply, and so do the hard questions. *The New York Times*, June 22, WH 11.

Anyinam, C.A. (1989). The social costs of the International Monetary Fund's adjustment programs for poverty: The case of health care development in Ghana. *International Journal of Health Services, 19*, 531–547.

Ardayfio-Schandorf, E. (1993). Household energy supply and women's work in Ghana. In J.H. Momsen & V. Kinnaird (Eds.), *Different places, different voices: Gender and development in Africa, Asia and Latin America* (pp. 15–29). London: Routledge.

Avotri, J.Y. (1997). *"Thinking too much" and "worrying too much": Ghanaian women's accounts of their health problems.* Unpublished doctoral dissertation, McMaster University, Hamilton, Ontario, Canada.

Avotri, J.Y., & Walters, V. (1999). 'You just look at our work and see if we have any freedom on earth': Ghanaian women's accounts of their work and their health. *Social Science and Medicine, 48*, 1123–1133.

Avotri, J.Y., & Walters, V. (2001). "We women worry a lot about our husbands": Ghanaian women talking about their relationships with men. *Journal of Gender Studies, 10*, 197–211.

Charles, N. (1990). Women—advancing or retreating? In R. Jenkins & A. Edwards (Eds.), *One step forward? South and west Wales towards the year 2000.* Llandysul, Wales: Gomer Press.

Charles, N., & Walters, V. (1998). Age and gender in women's accounts of their health: Interviews with women in south Wales. *Sociology of Health and Illness, 20*, 331–350.

Doyal, L. (1983). Women, health and the sexual division of labour: A case study of the women's health movement. *International Journal of Health Services, 13*, 373–387.

Doyal, L. (1995). *What makes women sick? Gender and the political economy of health.* London: Macmillan.

Graham, H. (1990). Behaving well: Women's health behaviour in context. In H. Roberts (Ed.), *Women's health counts* (pp. 195–219). London: Routledge.

Harris, C.C. (1987). *Redundancy and recession in south Wales.* Oxford: Basil Blackwell.

Manuh, T. (1994). Ghana: Women in the public and informal sectors under the Economic Recovery Programme. In P. Sparr (Ed.), *Mortgaging women's lives: Feminist critiques of structural adjustment* (pp. 61–72). London: Zed Books.

Morris, L. (1990). *The workings of the household*. Oxford: Polity Press.

Nettleton, S. (1996). Women and the new paradigm of health and medicine. *Critical Social Policy, 48,* 33–53.

Rees, T. (1999). *Women in the Welsh workforce: 21 years of equality legislation*. Bristol, UK: School for Policy Studies, University of Bristol.

Rosser, C., & Harris, C.C. (1983). *The family and social change*. London: Routledge and Kegan Paul.

Stoppard, J. (1997). Women's bodies, women's lives and depression: Towards a reconciliation of material and discursive accounts. In J.M. Ussher (Ed.), *Body talk: The material and discursive regulation of sexuality, madness and reproduction* (pp. 10–32). London: Routledge.

Stoppard, J. (1998). Dis-ordering depression in women: Toward a materialist-discursive account. *Theory & Psychology, 8,* 79–99.

Walters, V. (1991). Beyond medical and academic agendas: Lay perspectives and priorities. *Atlantis, 17,* 28–35.

Walters, V. (1992). Women's views of their main health problems. *Canadian Journal of Public Health, 83,* 371–374.

Walters, V. (1993). Stress, anxiety and depression: Women's accounts of their health problems. *Social Science and Medicine, 36,* 393–402.

Walters, V., Avotri, J.Y., & Charles, N. (1999). "Your heart is never free": Women in Wales and Ghana talking about distress. *Canadian Psychology, 40,* 129–142.

Walters, V., & Charles, N. (1997). "I just cope from day to day": Unpredictability and anxiety in the lives of women. *Social Science and Medicine, 45,* 1729–1739.

Walters, V., & Denton, M. (1997). Stress, depression and tiredness among women: The social production and social construction of health. *Canadian Review of Sociology and Anthropology, 34,* 53–69.

9

■ ■ ■ ■ ■ ■ ■ ■ ■

Conclusion

Linda M. McMullen and Janet M. Stoppard

WE HAVE HEARD the voices of many women in this book. We have heard from young women, older women, highly educated women, and less well-educated women. We have heard from white women, women of color, American, Canadian, Welsh, and Ghanaian women, from married, single, co-habiting, widowed, and divorced women, and from unemployed, working, and retired women. We've heard from students, women living in rural settings, women living in urban settings, mothers and women without children, lesbians and straight women, abused and not abused women, financially comfortable and impoverished women. From this diversity comes a picture of depression that goes well beyond the standard list of symptoms that are currently cited as its defining features.

Several authors in this book have provided understandings of depression that can stand as alternatives to the dominant presentation as a symptom-based mental illness. For example, Susan Hurst suggests that depression can be understood as demoralization that stems from profound betrayals by the most significant figures in a woman's life. Paula Nicolson proposes that postpartum depression can be conceived of as a normal response to the losses following childbirth, and Vivienne Walters, Joyce Avotri, and Nickie Charles conclude that depression might be more productively understood as socially based distress.

Through analyzing how women talk about their experiences of depression, other authors have brought into sharp focus how women's depression reflects a picture of gender. For example, Natasha Mauthner concludes that the cultural devaluation of motherhood can lead some women to feel that in order to have value they must live up to the image of the "perfect mother." Similarly, Linda McMullen shows how cultural definitions of what constitutes the limits of good mothering and successful (autonomous) adult functioning are implicated in how women make sense of their depressive experiences. Dana Jack reveals how forms of anger expression that do not facilitate dialogue and connection are, for women, associated with depression.

The link between depression and gender-based expectations about women's roles is also evident in discussions of how women coped with depression. Yvette Scattolon highlights how "going on" for the sake of others, doing what is required as a mother or wife, or otherwise continuing with one's life as usual, is paramount for many women who do not have access to treatment or other forms of assistance. Similarly, Janet Stoppard and Deanna Gammell reveal that women's choices to curtail paid employment and educational advancement as ways of responding to depression are outcomes of a medicalized approach to managing their depression.

In addition to the unique and particular claims of individual authors, several common themes emerge from these studies. We have learned that women's understandings of their experiences of depression are formed largely from the contexts of their everyday lives and are drawn from the shared meanings that are authorized by the cultures in which they live. These women understood their experiences of depression *in terms of* everyday difficulties such as financial insecurities, unemployment or underemployment, child-care responsibilities, abusive relationships with partners, interpersonal betrayals and disappointments, sexual and racial discrimination, and heavy workloads. We heard many accounts of the devastating impacts of impoverishment, of emotional, physical, and sexual abuse, of mistreatment and lack of support from family members and partners, of stress from child-care and employment responsibilities, and of discriminatory attitudes and practices. There can be no doubt that economic and social circumstances figured significantly in how the women made sense of their experiences of depression.

The consistency with which this diverse collection of women implicated economic and social circumstances in their accounts is both unsurprising and profound. It is unsurprising because a vast literature exists on the material and social conditions of women's lives. And this literature consistently shows that women earn less money than men, are confronted with barriers to employment or to advancement in employment, have the bulk of the responsibility for caring for children and other family members, do the majority of household duties, face discrimination on the basis of gender, age, class, ethnicity, and sexual orientation, and experience acts of violence from their partners.[1] That these conditions are connected to the form of distress that we label as depression is not surprising. What is surprising is that there is so very little discussion of the significance of these conditions in contemporary, Western theories of depression, in the diagnostic literature on depression, or in much of the literature on the treatment of depression.[2] There is a disjunction between the talk of professionals and that of many women who are described as depressed. Researchers and mental health service providers focus primarily on constructing ever more specific and precise descriptors of physical and psychological features to aid in diagnosing depression, on developing theories of depression that locate the source of distress in the characteristics of the person or, more typically, in the conjunction of personal characteristics and environmental stressors, and on the use of pharmacological or individually focused interventions. Women who are described as depressed talk primarily about the conditions of their lives.

However, the women's accounts, themselves, also revealed points of disjunction. On the one hand, many of the quoted excerpts consisted of detailed, evocative, poignant presentations of events or conditions that clearly communicated both the significance of these events and conditions for the women who had experienced them and how difficult their lives were. In actuality, these excerpts might be seen as quite extraordinary were it not for the fact that so many women living in such diverse circumstances relayed accounts that were variations on a recurring set of themes. On the other hand, the women often framed these events and conditions as "normal" life stressors, as features of their lives that were more or less severe at various times and were likely to be present to some degree in the future. There was a sense in the accounts of many of the women that economic or social difficulties were seen as taken-for-granted, pervasive aspects of their lives, as circumstances that were present and needed to be coped with. And they were to be coped with alone, with medication, or out of public view and behind closed doors—with a friend, support group, or therapist.

There was also a disjunction in how the women made use of cultural narratives to explain their "depression." On the one hand, they were able to identify that they had subscribed to these narratives. They described trying to live up to the standards of the "good wife" and the "good mother," believing that they should not express anger in certain ways, should be happy and fulfilled when they became mothers, should keep strong for the sake of others, should work from dawn to dusk, should take care of everything and strive to be perfect in all that they did, should be able to have children and work outside the home, and should be self-sufficient, self-reliant, and independent. They were able to identify the powerful effects of societal prescriptions and also to recognize that these standards were impossible. On the other hand, their resistance to these cultural narratives often took the form of chastising themselves for having fallen victim to these narratives, stating that it was their own responsibility to move beyond them, or seeking forms of treatment or intervention that were focused on individual change.

The strength and consistency with which the women made use of these narratives and of individual-based forms of resistance raises the question of the political functions that are served by such narratives. Why was the plight of women so often implicated in how these women made sense of their experiences and yet so infrequently used as a focus for change? The obvious answer, of course, is that focusing on changing one's self is seen as possible, whereas effecting change in discriminatory attitudes and expectations, violence toward and abuse of women, poverty, and inadequate employment opportunities is viewed either as improbable or as a very difficult and slow process. This belief is supported by the conviction that it is an individual woman's responsibility to take control of her life, by oft-cited examples in the media of persons who have exercised such responsibility, and by inadequate community and societal responses to the needs of women in distress. And so, women are left to believe that difficulties they understand to be largely economic and social in nature and which, in fact, are largely beyond their control, can be addressed only through individual means. Ironically, it is the acceptance of personal responsibility, itself, that may encourage women to blame themselves for the conditions of their lives, thereby fostering despondency and depression.[3]

Taking the economic and social conditions of women's lives as a starting point in addressing depression is also a serious challenge to the status quo. It would require that we re-think our deeply entrenched and still taken-for-granted beliefs about the gendered division of labor, about motherhood, about the value of girls and women, about the level of state support for children, about how employment is structured, and about how wealth is distributed nationally and internationally.

Recognizing that women understand depression primarily in terms of the economic and social circumstances of their lives requires that more attention be directed at economic and social solutions. In making this statement, we are not denying that some women will benefit from receiving antidepressant medications, and we are not saying that individual efforts to deal with depression are always ineffective or misplaced. What we are emphasizing is that educators, researchers, health professionals, politicians, and policy makers need to focus much more attention on the economic and social conditions of the lives of girls and women, and on strategies for reducing and eliminating gender-based inequalities.

To put the "costs" of not attending to these conditions into perspective, the contents of two recent reports on mental health are particularly revealing.[4] In an effort to estimate the toll on health and productivity of a variety of physical and mental health problems, the World Health Organization and the World Bank, together with researchers from the Harvard School of Public Health, attempted to quantify what they termed the "Global Burden of Disease." These researchers introduced an index referred to as the disability-adjusted life year (DALY), a measure that expresses the years of life lost to premature death and years lived with a disability of a specified severity and duration. In 2000, among the leading worldwide causes of lost years of healthy life, depression ranked second only to HIV/AIDS in the magnitude of its burden for women aged fifteen to forty-four years.[5]

Depression contributes to lost years of healthy life for women both directly and indirectly. It is associated with increased mortality from either suicide or physical illness (particularly heart disease), but, even more importantly, with chronic illness and disability, lost employment and reduced productivity, and incalculable suffering both for the woman who experiences depression and for her family. If we listen to what the women who participated in the collection of studies in this book have told us, then we must take the social and economic conditions of women's lives much more seriously if we are to reduce the enormous toll that depression is currently exacting.

Recognizing the role of structural conditions in women's experiences of depression is not a new idea. Like most problems that are considered to be mental disorders, depression is presently understood as typically being caused by the combination of a vulnerability or predisposition to develop a particular disorder (usually in the form of genetic, biological, and personality factors) and stressful life circumstances that overtax an individual's abilities to cope. This "individual + environment" understanding is clearly indicated in the U.S. Surgeon General's report on mental health and in the World Health Report on mental health. Both reports focus on the influence of biological factors (e.g., neurochemistry and genetics), psychological factors (e.g., personality), and social factors (e.g., socioeconomic status, racial, cultural, and religious background, gender, stressful life events, interpersonal relationships) in the development and maintenance of depression. While this biopsychosocial model has a great deal of currency among academics, mental health service providers, and policy makers, we suggest that this "even-handed" approach may actually focus attention away from the economic and social conditions of the lives of girls and women. It is easier to develop new pharmacological treatments and to offer individual psychotherapy than it is to alter discriminatory practices, provide adequate support for mothers and children, or ensure the availability of decent-paying jobs. Directing our efforts to ever-more precise ways of detecting and treating depression, while important, will not decrease the incidence of depression. Focusing squarely on the social and economic conditions of women's lives, however, actually has the potential to prevent depression.[6]

If we take, as our starting point, the understanding of depression that is presented in this book, then the challenge becomes how to focus the attention of educators, researchers, mental health professionals, policy makers, and politicians in ways that are really going to make a difference for women. For decades now, courses in women's studies have been available at postsecondary institutions in the Western world, research funding agencies have identified issues of particular relevance for women as targeted areas, interventions based on feminist principles have been developed for mental health practitioners, policies on gender harassment and employment equity have been in place in many institutions, and politicians have been sensitized to discriminatory practices and social inequities that have serious consequences for women. Although these efforts have not been in vain, they clearly have not led to massive changes. Still, we find that many women are understanding the distress that is labeled "depression" in terms of the social and economic conditions of their lives.

So, how can the conclusions we have come to have an impact? As a start, we need to ensure that accounts such as the ones contained in this book are widely circulated among students, academics, researchers, health service providers, policy makers, politicians, and the general public. We need to emphasize more strongly to all of these constituencies that when we attempt to understand depression from the standpoint of women, the importance of social and economic conditions becomes paramount. Specifically, we need to situate this understanding at the *core* of our future educational and research endeavors, of the design and provision of services, and of social policy.

In the educational domain, such a shift in focus entails placing this understanding in the foreground of existing theories of depression and explicitly recognizing that a theory of *women's* depression is a necessary addition. No longer can educators be content to teach nongendered accounts of depression. Students who are training to become mental health professionals (e.g., social workers, psychologists, psychiatric nurses, psychiatrists) must also be trained in methods of assessment and forms of intervention that address the social and economic conditions at the heart of women's depression. For example, gender-based assessments in which inquiries into the context of women's lives are given as much emphasis and credence as standard symptom-based psychiatric interviews should be an integral part of any training program. Similarly, considering the significant extent to which the accounts of this diverse collection of women map on to the assumptions and goals of feminist therapy, training in this form of intervention should be as common as instruction in cognitive-behavioral or psychodynamic therapies.

Knowledge of how the circumstances of women's lives are implicated in their experiences of depression is equally critical for those who are training to become family physicians, nurses, counselors, and members of the clergy. These professionals are often among the first consulted by women in distress, and having an understanding of how women make sense of their experiences might enable these practitioners either to intervene in a more effective manner or to make an appropriate referral.

Our conclusions also bolster the importance of system- and community-based interventions. For example, therapists who work with married women or mothers who are depressed might be encouraged to think, in the first instance, of marital or family rather than individual therapy. In addition, they might more readily promote the use of community resources, such as support, self-help, or advocacy groups, leisure or recreational programs, daycare or respite services. The need to develop and maintain community agencies and organizations that are focused on enabling women to further their education, obtain employment, or access much-needed financial assistance is also a crucial implication of our conclusions.

Taking the understanding of women's depression presented in this book as the core of a research agenda would entail less emphasis on describing and diagnosing women's depression or on determining the effects of various antidepressant medications and psychological treatments. Instead, a greater emphasis should be placed on research that is focused on developing, implementing, and evaluating community- and system-based interventions designed to address the social and economic circumstances of women's lives.

Changes in social policy that raise mental health from the bottom to the top of the health agenda would clearly assist the shift in focus being described here. Policy makers and politicians who know the extent to which depression is seriously compromising the physical and mental health of women and who understand the significant link between women's depression and the social and economic circumstances of their lives might conclude that not putting resources into addressing these circumstances is short-sighted. Similarly, making the conclusions in this book accessible and readily available to a wider audience has the potential to shift public opinion away from a view of women's depression as an individual weakness or type of mental disorder, and toward an alternative understanding—one in which women's depression is viewed as a statement of societal expectations and valuing of women. This impact would surely be welcomed by the women who shared their words with us.

Notes

1. See World Health Organization, *Women's mental health: An evidence-based review*.

2. Notable exceptions include G.W. Brown and T.O. Harris, *Social origins of depression: A study of psychiatric disorder in women*; J.M. Stoppard, *Understanding depression: Feminist social constructionist approaches*; and the World Health Organization report, *Women's mental health*.

3. See World Health Organization, *Women's mental health*, p. 7.

4. U.S. Department of Health and Human Services, *Mental health: A report of the Surgeon General*; World Health Organization, *The world health report 2001: Mental health: New understanding, new hope*.

5. See World Health Organization, *The world health report 2001: Mental health: New understanding, new hope*, fig. 2.2.

6. See World Health Organization, *Women's mental health*, p. 25.

References

Brown, G.W., & Harris, T.O. (1978). *Social origins of depression: A study of psychiatric disorder in women*. London: Tavistock Publications.

Stoppard, J.M. (2000). *Understanding depression: Feminist social constructionist approaches*. London: Routledge.

U.S. Department of Health and Human Services. (1999). *Mental health: A report of the Surgeon General*. Rockville, MD: U.S. Department of Health and Human Services, Substance Abuse and Mental Health Services Administration, Center for Mental Health Services, National Institutes of Health, National Institute of Mental Health.

World Health Organization. (2000). *Women's mental health: An evidence-based review*. Geneva: World Health Organization (unpublished working document WHO/GHW).

World Health Organization. (2001). *The world health report 2001: Mental health: New understanding, new hope*. Geneva: World Health Organization.

About the Contributors

■ ■ ■ ■ ■

Joyce Yaa Avotri completed her schooling and undergraduate degree in Ghana and then continued her studies in Canada. She graduated with a doctorate from McMaster University in 1997. In addition to her research on women's health, her interests include women and development and the experience of women of color in North America. She has published her work in *Social Science and Medicine* and *Canadian Psychology*.

Nickie Charles is Reader in Sociology at University of Wales Swansea, United Kingdom. Her main research interests lie in the field of gender and she is currently working on a project, with Vivienne Walters, looking at gender, health, and aging. She is also involved in research into the gender dimensions of job insecurity. Both these projects are funded by the Economic and Social Research Council (United Kingdom). She has recently published a book—*Feminism, the State and Social Policy*—published by Macmillan, and is working on another one titled *Gender in Modern Britain*, which will be published by Oxford University Press.

Deanna J. Gammell is a doctoral candidate in clinical psychology at the University of New Brunswick, Canada. Her research interests focus on the use of qualitative methods to investigate women's depression. Her dissertation research involves a qualitative study of adolescent girls' understandings of depression.

Susan A. Hurst received her doctorate in psychology from the University of Saskatchewan, Canada, in 1994. She has been working as a therapist since then at the University of Saskatchewan Student Counselling Services.

Dana Crowley Jack is a professor at Fairhaven College, an interdisciplinary college within Western Washington University, United States. She conducts research on depression and aggression, focusing on women. She holds her doctorate in human development from Harvard University. She presented a new model of women's depression in her book, *Silencing the Self: Women and Depression* (Harvard University Press, 1991, and Harper-Collins, 1992). She has also explored gender differences in lawyers' ethics in *Moral Vision and Professional Decisions: The Changing Values of Women and Men Lawyers* (New York: Cambridge University Press, 1989), co-authored with Rand Jack. Her book *Behind the Mask: Destruction and Creativity in Women's Aggression* (Harvard University Press, 1999) explores linkages of depression and aggression as well as presenting a phenomenology of women's aggression. Her major interests are in women's depression, anger, and aggression within varying social contexts. During 2001, she was a Fulbright Scholar in Nepal, where she conducted research on depression and taught at Tribhuvan University.

Natasha S. Mauthner is Senior Research Fellow at the Arkleton Centre for Rural Development Research, University of Aberdeen, Scotland. Her current research focuses on work and family life in rural areas, and on the impact of economic restructuring on children and families. Her research interests also include postnatal depression, and methodological and epistemological issues in qualitative research. She received her first degree in psychology from the University of Cambridge, where she stayed on to do research on postnatal depression for her doctorate. She continued with her research on motherhood and postnatal depression on a postdoctoral fellowship at Harvard University. Her book, *The Darkest Days of My Life: Stories of Postpartum Depression*, was published by Harvard University Press in 2002.

Linda M. McMullen received her doctorate from the University of Saskatchewan in Canada. She was trained as a clinical psychologist, with a specialization in adult psychotherapy. She has been a faculty member in the Department of Psychology, University of Saskatchewan since 1980, where she currently is Professor. Her areas of research have included dyadic verbal interaction (including investigations of how features such as status, acquaintance, and gender influence conversation) and the use of metaphor and narrative by clients and therapists in psychotherapy. At present, she is studying the discourse of interrelatedness in Canadian culture. She presently serves on the editorial boards of *Canadian Psychology/Psychologie canadienne*, *Metaphor and Symbol*, and *Psychotherapy Research*.

Paula Nicolson is Professor of Health Psychology at the University of Sheffield, United Kingdom, in the School for Health and Related Research. Her areas of research expertise are women's reproductive and mental health and gender issues in organizations. Along with her colleague, Jennifer Burr, she has developed a series of distance learning packages for qualitative researchers for health and social care professionals and academics. She has written numerous journal articles and book chapters in these areas. Her recent books include: *Gender, Power and Organisation: A Psychological Perspective* (Routledge, 1996); *Postnatal Depression: Psychology, Science and the Transition to Motherhood* (Routledge, 1998); *Postnatal Depression: Facing the Paradox of Loss, Happiness and Motherhood* (Wiley, 2001); and *Having It All? Choices for Today's Superwoman*, which will be published by Wiley in September 2002. She is editor of *Psychology, Evolution and Gender*, a journal published by Bruner-Routledge which is now into its fourth volume.

Yvette Scattolon completed her doctorate in clinical psychology in 1999 at the University of New Brunswick in Canada. Currently, she works as a clinical psychologist in Halifax, Nova Scotia, dividing her time between the Nova Scotia Rehabilitation Centre, the Eating Disorders Clinic at the Queen Elizabeth II Health Sciences Centre, and private practice. Her research and clinical interests include women's issues, depression, eating disorders, and health psychology.

Janet M. Stoppard completed her undergraduate training in psychology in England and did postgraduate work in clinical psychology in Belfast, Northern Ireland. After emigrating to Canada, she completed a doctorate in psychology at Queen's University in Kingston, Ontario, followed by a postdoctoral year as a clinical fellow at the University of British Columbia. She is currently Professor of Psychology at the University of New Brunswick in Canada. Her book, *Understanding Depression: Feminist Social Constructionist Approaches*, was published in 2000 (Routledge). She also co-edited (with Baukje Miedema and Vivienne Anderson) *Women's*

Bodies/Women's Lives: Health, Well-being and Body Image (Sumach Press, Toronto, 2000).

Vivienne Walters is Professor of Sociology at McMaster University and Honorary Research Fellow at University of Wales Swansea. She has a long-standing interest in the social production of illness with particular emphasis on women's health. Her research has been published in several journals, including *Social Science and Medicine, Sociology of Health and Illness, Gender, Work and Organization, International Journal of Health Services, Atlantis, Canadian Psychology,* and *Canadian Review of Sociology and Anthropology.* Her current research focuses on the health concerns of women in their fifties and sixties (in Canada) and the effects of social aging and gender on the health of women and men (in Wales).

Permissions

■   ■   ■   ■

We gratefully acknowledge the Canadian Psychological Association for granting permission to reprint revised versions of the following articles originally published in *Canadian Psychology/Psychologie canadienne*, Vol 40, No. 2, 1999:

"Metaphors in the Talk of 'Depressed' Women in Psychotherapy," Linda M. McMullen (chapter 1). Copyright 1999. Canadian Psychological Association. Reprinted with permission.

"Women's Experiences of Treatment of Depression: Medicalization or Empowerment?" Deanna J. Gammell and Janet M. Stoppard (chapter 2). Copyright 1999. Canadian Psychological Association. Reprinted with permission.

"Ways of Listening to Depressed Women in Qualitative Research: Interview Techniques and Analyses," Dana Crowley Jack (chapter 3). Copyright 1999. Canadian Psychological Association. Reprinted with permission.

"'Feeling Low and Feeling Really Bad about Feeling Low:' Women's Experiences of Motherhood and Postpartum Depression," Natasha S. Mauthner (chapter 4). Copyright 1999. Canadian Psychological Association. Reprinted with permission.

"Loss, Happiness, and Postpartum Depression: The Ultimate Paradox," Paula Nicolson (chapter 5). Copyright 1999. Canadian Psychological Association. Reprinted with permission.

"Legacy of Betrayal: A Grounded Theory of Becoming Demoralized from the Perspective of Women Who Have Been Depressed," Susan A. Hurst (chapter 6). Copyright 1999. Canadian Psychological Association. Reprinted with permission.

"'Getting on with Life:' Women's Experiences and Ways of Coping with Depression," Yvette Scattolon (chapter 7). Copyright 1999. Canadian Psychological Association. Reprinted with permission.

"'Your Heart Is Never Free:' Women in Wales and Ghana Talking about Distress," Vivienne Walters, Joyce Yaa Avotri, and Nickie Charles (chapter 8). Copyright 1999. Canadian Psychological Association. Reprinted with permission.

Index

abandonment, 7, 151–152, 196
abuse, 69, 74, 142, 144, 147–148, 157, 208, 210. *See also* violence
Adler, Z., 86
Alder, E., 137
Ali, A., 86
American Psychiatric Association, 14, 37, 160
Andrews, B., 86
anger, 27, 29, 156, 208, 210; aggressive expression of, 74–76; and consequences for health, 83–84; of despair, 68–69, 84; displaced, 63, 80–81; expressed outside the relationship, 73–74, 79–82; of hope, 68–69, 84; indirect expression of, 76–79, 80; positive and direct expression of, 71–73, 80, 81, 83, 84; reaction of others to, 70–71, 82; and relationships, 83; silenced, 63–64, 71, 76, 80; turned against the self, 63, 69, 81–82
Angier, N., 205

Anyinam, C. A., 205
Appleby, L., 137
Ardayfio-Schandorf, E., 205
assertiveness, 91
Attra, S. L., 86
autonomy, 33, 91, 109, 208
Avotri, J., 6, 8, 205, 206, 207

Backett-Milburn, K., 111
Baldwin, M., 86
Banister, P., 14
Bassett, M. E., 86
Benditt, R., 86
betrayal, 7, 142–144, 146, 147–151, 153, 155–157, 158, 207, 208
biopsychosocial model, 212
Bland, R., 15
Blaxter, M., 60
Boath, E., 137
Bonge, D., 87
Bordo, S., 14, 182
Bowlby, J., 86
Boyatzis, R. E., 14

Brandt, J., 60
Bridge, L., 86
Brodsky, A. M., 60
Brown, G. W., 14, 86, 137, 215
Brown, L. M., 14, 110
Brown, L. S., 60
Bruce, M. L., 182
Brydon-Miller, M., 15
Budman, S. H., 160
Burman, E., 14

Canino, G. J., 15
Caplan, P. J., 37, 60
caregiving, 52, 53,167–169, 170, 208,
    209, 210. *See also* mothering
Charles, N., 6, 8, 205, 206, 207
Collins, L., 86
control, 33, 34; lack of, 52, 55, 142,
    144–145, 156; over life, 40, 122,
    210; over self and other, 75. *See
    also* self-control
Conway, J. B., 38
Cooper, P. J., 137
coping: difficulty in, 45, 172; with
    stress, 46, 49, 53; ways of, 41, 47,
    48, 56, 57, 80, 104, 122,
    173–178, 180–181, 208, 210
Corbin, J., 15, 160, 161
Cox, J. L., 137
cultural rules and standards, 65, 81,
    91–92, 94, 156–157, 210, 211.
    See also "good
    woman/wife/mother"
cultural values, 19–20, 32–33, 208,
    211

Dalton, K., 137
demoralization, 142, 146, 149,
    153–154, 155–157, 159–160, 207
Denton, M., 206
dependency, 27–28, 91, 145; financial,
    148–149
depression: causes/understandings of,
6–7, 18, 19, 32, 45–46, 51, 52, 66,
    69, 81, 146, 154–155, 160,
    169–171, 171–173, 183, 202,
    207–214; definition of, 2–3; diag-
    nostic criteria for, 3; as distress, 17,
    41, 53, 56, 168, 179, 184,
    187–189, 201, 207, 209, 213; and
    existential losses, 151, 156; feminist
    understandings of, 39–41, 156; fre-
    quency of, 1, 211; historical con-
    ceptions of, 18; interpersonal per-
    spective of, 66; medicalized under-
    standing of, 39–41, 42, 50–52,
    55–58, 59, 208; medication for, 1,
    3, 7, 39–41, 46, 47, 51, 102, 202,
    209, 210, 211, 212; metaphors for,
    19–20, 89; narratives of, 6–7, 64,
    94; and obsessiveness, 93; and
    physical appearance, 167; and phys-
    ical illness, 211; as physical illness,
    2–3, 7, 39, 43, 51; risks for, 6;
    symptoms of, 2–3, 41, 81,
    187–189; theories of, 209, 212
Dill, D., 87
disability, 156
disconnection, 35, 66, 71, 74, 77, 82,
    91–92
discourse analysis, 8, 9–10, 18, 164
discourses of femininity, 7, 24,
    168–169, 179. *See also* "good
    woman/wife/mother"
discrimination, 73, 84, 149, 150, 153,
    156, 208, 209, 210
disrespect, 148–150
Doucet, A., 14, 111
Doyal, L., 205
Duarte, L. M., 86
DuBois, B., 160

education, 49, 53–54, 56–57, 201,
    208, 214
Ehrenreich, B., 61
Elliot, S. A., 110, 137

employment, 48–49, 53–54, 56–57, 202, 208, 209, 210, 211, 214. *See also* motherhood, and paid work; postpartum depression, and loss of occupational identity
empowerment, 40–41, 42, 52–55, 56–58, 73, 158
Endler, N. S., 14
English, D., 61
Eshleman, S., 14
ethnicity. *See* race/ethnicity

fear of rejection, 100–101, 107
Fehr, B., 86
feminist therapy, 40, 58, 213
financial hardship, 162, 169–170, 174, 183, 189, 190–193, 201, 208
Findlay, D. A., 61
Fine, M., 14
Frank, J. D., 160
Freud, S., 63, 110

Gaines, C., 138
Galvin, S. L., 87
Gammell, D. J., 7, 8, 61, 208
Gavron, H., 137
gender, 10, 142, 147, 150, 198, 208, 209; and anger, 66, 67, 84; and depression, 5, 41, 92, 115; and qualitative research, 9; roles and relations, 98, 149, 156–157, 162, 183–184, 193–196, 201
gendered division of labor, 94, 127, 194–196, 201, 211
Genest, M., 61
Gibbons, M., 161
Gilligan, C., 14, 86, 110, 112
Glaser, B. G., 14, 160
"good woman/wife/mother," 7, 64–65, 92, 95, 97, 106, 166–167, 168–169,172, 173, 179–180, 208, 210
Graham, H., 61, 205

Gratch, L. V., 86
Graveline, M. J., 182
Green, J. M., 137
Greenspan, M., 61
grieving, 132–133, 134
grounded theory, 8, 9, 140, 141–142, 157, 164–165
guilt, 67, 76, 127, 129
Guptill, A. M., 15
Gurman, A. S., 160

Hall-McCorquodale, I., 37
Hamberger, L. K., 87
Hamilton, J. A., 14
Harris, B., 137
Harris, C. C., 205, 206
Harris, T. O., 14, 86, 137, 215
Hays, S., 110
Henry, W. P., 37
Henwood, K. L., 182
Holmes, T. M., 137
hopelessness, 67–70, 74, 145–147
Hughes, M., 14
Hurst, S. A., 7, 8, 9, 11, 61, 160, 207

implications: for educators, 212–213; for health professionals, 58, 104, 105, 107, 108, 134–135, 180–181, 202–203, 212–214; for policy makers, 202–203, 212–214; for politicians, 202–203, 212, 214; for researchers, 212, 214
inadequacy, 20, 64, 75, 106, 107, 180
individualism, 33, 34
inductive analysis, 9
isolation, 35, 88, 103, 107, 115, 152–153, 156, 162, 164–166, 177–178, 180, 190, 195, 201, 210

Jack, D. C., 7, 8, 9, 14, 86, 87, 93–94, 111, 160, 182, 208
Jackson, S. W., 37
Jelabi, C., 137

Jensvold, M. F., 14
Johnson, M., 38
Jones, C., 111
Jordan, J. V., 111

Kaplan, A. G., 111
Karp, D. A., 37, 160
Keita, G. P., 61, 87
Kendler, K. S., 14
Kessler, R. C., 14
Kidder, L., 14
Kitayama, S., 38
Krieger, N., 87
Kroger, R. O., 15

Lafrance, M. N., 15
Laidlaw, T. A., 61
Lakoff, G., 38
language: analysis of, 8, 9, 50; figura-
    tive, 18; use in psychotherapy, 18
Leaf, P. J., 182
Lee, C., 138
Leverton, T. J., 110
Lewis, S. E., 138
Lohr, J. M., 87
loneliness. See isolation

Malmo, C., 61
Manuh, T., 205–206
Marecek, J., 14, 61
Markus, H. R., 38
Marris, P., 138
Marshall, H., 111
material deprivation. See financial hard-
    ship
Mauthner, N. S., 6, 8, 9, 14, 111, 208
Mays, J. B., 15
McGonagle, K. A., 14
McGrath, E., 61, 87
McKears, J., 111
McMahon, M., 38
McMullen, L. M., 6, 8, 9, 11, 38, 208
melancholia, 18, 63, 93

Miller, J. B., 87, 111, 112
Miller, L. J., 61
Morris, J. B., 111
Morris, L., 206
mother blame, 32
motherhood, 32, 89–91, 94–97,
    104–108, 120–121, 123, 131,
    198–201, 208, 210, 211; and loss,
    132–135; and paid work, 95–97,
    105–106, 109, 148, 180, 190–193,
    210
mothering, 21–25, 35, 94–95, 174,
    194–196, 208
Murray, L., 137
Murray-Parkes, C., 138

narratives, 9, 158
Nelson, C. B., 14
Nettleton, S., 206
Nicolson, P., 6, 8, 111, 138, 207
Nolen-Hoeksema, S., 38

Oakley, A., 111, 138
O'Hara, M. W., 138
"Over-eye," 65, 93–94

Page, J. R., 87
Parker, I., 14
Parker, R., 138
Parry, O., 111
Patterson, S., 86
Paykel, E. S., 87
Payne, S., 138
Penfold, P. S., 61
Perkins, R., 61
personal responsibility, 30–31, 33, 34,
    121, 202, 210
Phillips, J. R., 161
Phoenix, A., 111–112
Pitt, B., 112
Popay, J., 61
postpartum depression, 93, 108, 109,
    171–172; frequency of, 89, 114;

and loss of appearance, 119–120, 123–124; and loss of autonomy and time, 118–119, 121–123; and loss of femininity and sexuality, 124–126; and loss of occupational identity, 119, 126–129; and psychological reintegration, 129–133; risks of, 115; thematic approach to, 118; understandings of, 114–115, 132, 135
Potter, J., 15
poverty, 6, 83, 149, 156–157, 191–193, 202, 208, 210
power, 5, 9, 32, 109, 148, 156–157
powerlessness, 68, 77, 81, 144–145, 201
Pryce, A. J., 137
psychotherapy: experience of, 103; implications for, 11, 34–35, 58, 159, 214; as treatment for depression, 11, 47–48, 51, 58, 209, 212; varieties of, 35

qualitative research: data collection methods in, 7–8; description of, 7–8; ethical issues in, 10–11; focus of analysis in, 8–10; interviewer's role in, 186; materials used in, 8; reflexivity in, 20, 35–36, 164, 178–179; versus conventional approaches, 4–6, 11. See also discourse analysis; grounded theory; thematic approaches; voice-centered approach
Quartaro, G. K., 161
Quinn, N., 38

race/ethnicity, 9, 10, 64, 73, 84, 153, 156
Rahe, R. H., 137
Raskin, V. D., 138
Rees, T., 206
relational psychology, 91–92

relationships: and anger, 66–67, 69–70, 71–84; and betrayal, 147–152; as contributing to depression, 45; and isolation, 152–153; with men, 29, 83, 107, 125, 148–150, 193–198; and postpartum depression, 91–92, 106–108, 127–128
Remer, P., 61
Rennie, D. L., 161
responsibilities, work and family, 45, 53, 119, 126, 129, 132, 134, 166, 167–169, 170–171, 180, 208
Rich, A., 138
Richardson, J. T. E., 15
Richman, J. A., 138
Romito, P., 112
Ross, C. E., 87
Rosser, C., 206
rural communities, 162, 177–178, 180, 181
Russell, D., 61
Russo, N. F., 61, 87

safety, 48, 76, 78, 104, 105, 148, 156–157
Sampson, E. E., 38
Sanjack, M., 110
Scattolon, Y., 6, 7, 8, 9, 182, 208
Schacht, T. E., 37
Schiesari, J., 18, 38
Schreiber, R. S., 15, 161
self as deficient/flawed, 17–18, 20, 33, 42, 70, 75, 81, 89, 93, 146, 156, 159
self blame, 33, 35, 92, 158–159, 173
self-control, 28–29; loss of, 77–78
self criticism, 31, 63, 93
self-esteem, 63, 65, 67, 69, 72, 76
self harm, 81
services, 40, 104, 162, 180–181, 213, 214
shame, 43, 44, 45, 67, 75, 76, 88–89

silencing the self, 64–65, 86
social class, 9, 10, 95, 170
social inequalities, 5, 66, 83, 213
social support, 108, 113, 115, 127,
    153, 154, 175–177, 194, 201,
    208. *See also* support groups
Solomon, A., 15
Spelman, E., 87
Spitzer, R. L., 161
Steiner-Adair, C., 112
Stern, P. N., 15
Stevens, H. B., 87
stigma, 43, 57, 162, 177–178
Stiver, I. P., 111, 112
Stoppard, J. M., 7, 8, 15, 38, 61, 138,
    182, 206, 208, 215
Strauss, A., 14, 15, 160, 161
stress, 45–46, 48, 52–53, 57,
    169–171, 171–173, 208, 212; nor-
    malizing, 41, 169–174, 179–180,
    209, 210
Strickland, B. R., 61, 87
Strupp, H. H., 37
Sturdivant, S., 61
Styron, W., 15
submissiveness, 26–27, 150, 154
suicide, 83–84, 211
Sullivan, A., 112
support groups, 103–105, 176–177,
    180, 213
Surry, J. L., 111, 112

Taylor, J. M., 112
Taylor, M., 14
thematic approaches, 8, 118, 164
Thomas, S. P., 87
Thompson, J. M., 86, 87
Thurtle, V., 138

Tindall, C., 14
Tolman, D. L., 15
Toner, B., 86
trust, 25–26, 101

unworthy, 142–144
U. S. Department of Health and
    Human Services, 215
Ussher, J. M., 15, 61, 138, 182

Van Willigen, M., 87
violence, 83, 197, 209, 210
voice-centered approach, 8, 9

Walker, G. A., 61
Walters, V., 6, 8, 61, 205, 206,
    207
weak, 18, 43, 44, 45, 46, 48, 107,
    214
Weissman, M. M., 15, 87
Welburn, V., 138
Wetherell, M., 15
Whiffen, V., 138
Wilkinson, S., 112
Willard, A., 112
Williams, J. B. W., 161
Willig, C., 15
Wittchen, H. U., 14
Wood, L. A., 15
Woollett, A., 111–112
Worell, J., 61
workload, 40, 193–196, 198, 201,
    208, 209, 210
World Health Organization, 15–16,
    138, 215

Zelizer, V. A., 38
Zhao, S., 14